"Inspiring and brave, *A River Could Be a Tree* defines what we all need in some way—the freedom to discover our own unique path in life and the courage to choose it. Throughout Angela's journey of self-discovery and spiritual awakening, we recognize beauty in the uncertainty of life. Her ability to illuminate this is a true gift to her readers, and her story serves as a powerful reminder that we don't have to settle for what is expected of us. We can all find pieces of ourselves reflected in this delightful memoir."

—RUTH WARINER,
author of The New York Times bestseller, *The Sound of Gravel: A Memoir*

"In *A River Could Be a Tree*, Angela Himsel falls in love with Judaism, and we fall in love with her. Her passion, humor, and curiosity shine through as she discovers it isn't the answers that give life meaning, but the quest for answers and the people met along the way."

—CHARLOTTE ROGAN,
author of *The Lifeboat*

"Angela Himsel's memoir *A River Could Be a Tree* is one woman's incredible journey down the proverbial road to Damascus, except that Angela's conversion was more process than presto. This coming-of-age memoir takes the reader from the faith of a childhood immersed in the Worldwide Church of God, to Orthodox Jewish New York, by way of Israel and Germany. Angela traces her genealogical and theological roots in a search for identity and connection, and gives her readers stories of heartbreak, humor, longing, and love."

—LUCIA GREENHOUSE,
author of *fathermothergod: My Journey Out of Christian Science*

"Adherents to any faith know well that religion can be both constricting and fulfilling at the same time. And at the core of everyone's spiritual journey is a belief that we are all seekers, searching for something deeper beyond ourselves. Himsel eloquently embodies this notion in her compelling new memoir. In often raw and engaging fashion, she takes her readers along for the ride—through love, loss, and religious rearrangement—to a conclusion that is both satisfying and enlightening."

—BENYAMIN COHEN,
author of *My Jesus Year: A Rabbi's Son Wanders*
the Bible Belt in Search of His Own Faith

"A River Could Be a Tree is an odyssey of love and faith, told in a voice mixed with pathos and humor. Angela Himsel shows us how intricate, layered, and painful are the bounds of family, and finally how it is possible to honor both the ties we are born with and the ones we choose to create on our own."

—GABRIELLE SELZ,
author of *Unstill Life: A Daughter's Memoir of Art*
and Love in the Age of Abstraction

"Honest, yet humane, Himsel masterfully describes her spiritual walk along life's long and narrow bridge from an impoverished childhood in rural Indiana with parents fiercely devoted to an apocalyptic cult, and ending in the embracing warmth of the Jewish community of the Upper West Side. Her journey is a testament to the importance of having no fear. In this regard, Himsel is not just a force of nature; she's the Mary Karr (author of *The Liar's Club* and *Lit*) of Indiana."

—MORT ZACHTER,
author of *Dough: A Memoir,* winner of the AWP Award

A RIVER
COULD BE
A TREE

A RIVER COULD BE A TREE

A Memoir

ANGELA HIMSEL

FOREWORD BY SHULEM DEEN

FIG TREE
BOOKS

Published in the United States by Fig Tree Books LLC,
Bedford, New York

www.FigTreeBooks.net

Jacket design by Jennifer Carrow Design
Interior design by Neuwirth & Associates, Inc.

Library of Congress Cataloging-in-Publication Data Available Upon Request

ISBN 978-1-941493-24-3

Printed in the United States

Distributed by Publishers Group West

First edition

10 9 8 7 6 5 4 3 2 1

For my parents, with gratitude and love

AUTHOR'S NOTE

In writing this memoir, I relied not only on my own memory of events, but also interviewed my parents, cousins, aunts, siblings, and others to fill in gaps and to confirm (or dispute) my own recollection. If, despite my very best efforts, I got something wrong, I apologize.

The following names are pseudonyms: Mr. and Mrs. Davis; Aziz, Eve, Laila, and Suleiman.

FOREWORD

by Shulem Deen

As a child, little held my imagination as did the mystery of the Sambatyon River.

Like every Hasidic child in our insular enclave in Brooklyn, I was raised on the stories of the Bible and Talmud. From an early age, I learned of the Israelites who'd been driven away by Sennacherib the king of Assyria, who conquered the northern kingdom of Israel and scattered our brethren tribes to places unknown. That left only us, the Judeans—the tribes of Judah and Benjamin—as the known remnants of the ancient people of Israel. The others became known as the ten lost tribes.

Lost—except we knew one thing: they lived beyond the Sambatyon River, which we could not cross. For one thing, according to Talmudic tradition, the Sambatyon prevents passage by tossing boulders in the air six days a week, resting only on the Sabbath when crossing a river is forbidden. More importantly, the Sambatyon's very location remains a mystery. And so the ten lost tribes remain apart from us until the Messiah will come and lead us to them, at which time the Sambatyon will rest forever.

I remember, at around age ten, studying a world atlas and wondering how it was that we could not find the Sambatyon. The remotest islands in the Pacific, the forbidding peaks of the Himalayas, the enormous Amazon River snaking its way through thousands of miles of dense jungle, all were fully charted. Only the Sambatyon they could not find?

How could the lost tribes have gotten so lost?

Turns out, they were just living in Indiana.

Or so believed Angela Himsel, who, in her memoir *A River Could Be a Tree*, tells us about her upbringing in Jasper, Indiana, within the Worldwide Church of God, an apocalyptic, doomsday Christian sect led by Herbert Armstrong, a former Ku Klux Klan member who preached a version of British Israelism, a doctrine that claims the ten lost tribes ended up in Great Britain. Armstrong himself claimed to be descended from those lost tribes, and so his followers, too, at least spiritually, were identified with them.

Angela Himsel was similarly raised on stories. To a young Angela, seventh of eleven children, the biblical figures of Adam, Noah, and Joseph were as real as her shotgun-toting Catholic grandfather and her Lutheran German-speaking grandmother. "I was a literal-minded child," she writes. "I imagined God hanging out in the neighborhood, popping up on the street unexpectedly. I wished God would do that still, show up at the courthouse square in Jasper or maybe just appear in the backyard while we were playing Red Rover."

It is not only the literal-mindedness of the stories that would come to guide Himsel's life, but also a yearning for that divine encounter, that of bumping into God in the backyard. Specifically, what she yearned for was an encounter with Jesus and the Holy Spirit, who would be her path to salvation, to the afterlife, to the rapturing of the faithful to the city of Petra, Jordan—Armstrong's very specific apocalyptic fantasy—where Jesus was to greet them in a great fatherly embrace.

Which brings us indeed to Jesus—embodying Christian charity and goodness and love and eternal salvation to some, apostasy and persecution and pogroms to others. To Angela though, Jesus was no abstract notion, no theological symbol cloaked in a metaphor of God made flesh, but the central figure in a cosmic drama so real that every smallest deed affected her role within it.

"Life . . . requires life-supporting illusions," wrote Joseph Campbell, the great scholar of mythology. "Where these have been dispelled, there is nothing secure to hold on to." As the myth of the Sambatyon and the lost tribes was to me, so the myth of Petra, the place of safety to which the faithful would be raptured, where Jesus himself awaited, was to Himsel. The "life-supporting illusions" of our respective faiths were the stories that gave our everyday life meaning.

What happens, however, when the myths are dispelled?

When the myths are dispelled, the stories lose their power, and as often as not, the edifices built upon them first shake then crumble. Not without a showdown, though, body wrestling with soul, our infant selves yearning for stories with literal meaning and our evolved minds forced to a painful reckoning with truth. "Truth"—life's certainties previously handed to us in tales of literal, material reality—we now learn, is barely within human grasp, and where does that leave us and our wondrous illusions?

For Himsel, that reckoning arrived slowly, as it did for me, as it does to all of us with imaginations so fierce, so protective of our need for story, that our souls scream in protest for our illusions to remain intact. Illusions, though, have ways of dissolving, and when they do, they leave us fallen, stricken, to contend with a sterile reality.

A chance encounter with a photo-covered brochure of the land of Israel was the gateway to Himsel's own forced reckoning. A student at Indiana University, she discovered an opportunity to study abroad—specifically, at The Hebrew University in Israel. This was not, to her, Israel the modern state, but Israel, ancient homeland of the Israelites and all the other biblical figures. "I imagined John the Baptist fasting in the desert and David fighting Goliath. . . . Israel was the place that God had chosen for Abraham's descendants, the place where Jesus had walked and preached." The tantalizing fantasy of myth actualized. "Modern Israel was just a conduit to the distant past, which was where I hoped I would find the Holy Spirit."

It was in Israel that Himsel discovered that her mythology required a serious reorientation. These were "not Jews who rode on camels, but people like me who complained it was too hot or too rainy, who told jokes and swore and had their own opinions." First in her biblical studies classes at The Hebrew University, and then on an archaeological dig, Himsel found the historical basis of her cherished Bible stories in doubt, and so, too, their truth.

"God created Man in His Image," one of her professors joked, "and man, being a gentleman, returned the favor."

Therein lies a truth not only about God but all our beliefs and values, as well as our stories. All of it made by man in his own image.

Civilizations are built on stories, written in different times in different places repurposed by different populations for different reasons, until they come to tell us something far beyond their literal meanings. We still do that today, as we visit movie theaters or get lost in novels, seeking symbols in stories. They speak to our desires, fears, joys, and so they guide us toward meaning. Our stories, Joseph Campbell wrote, speak "not of outside events but of themes of the imagination."

This more evolved understanding of the function of stories, however, is new to us. It is a relative blip in time from when we considered the historic and the mythic to be one and the same. Christopher Columbus, a sophisticate for his time, who believed in a spherical rather than a flat earth, was also convinced that the Orinoco River, the mouth of which he encountered as he passed between the island of Trinidad and the northern coast of South America, was in fact the biblical Gihon River, flowing directly from the Garden of Eden through the Mountain of Purgatory of Dante Allighieri fame.

To Columbus, Eden was no mere symbolic truth, but material reality. In "History, Prophecy, and the Stars," Laura Ackerman Smoller writes that Columbus, in addition to having been an enlightened adventurer (as well as an opportunistic plunderer), was "also stirred by a curious blend of astrological prognostications and apocalyptic fervor." From his journals and letters, we learn that Columbus believed the world had less than 200 years to go before the end times, thus seeing it his mission to convert the natives of the New World to Christianity before Jesus's return.

A century or so later, in the city of Prague, Johannes Kepler worked out the laws of planetary motion, grounded in mathematics and the empirical evidence of his day, even as he maintained a side gig as an astrologer. As James A. Connor writes in a biography of Kepler: in medieval times, astrology, even to men of science, contained "the story of God's relationship with the human race."

In Prague, around that same time, was also a Jew, the great mystic Rabbi Judah Loew, known as the Maharal, advisor to Emperor Rudolf II on the teachings of the Kabbalah. Also: creator of the famed Golem of Prague, a man made of clay, created by Loew using a magical Kabbalistic formula and who was to protect the Jews of Prague from anti-Semitic persecution.

Like the Sambatyon, the golem's existence was, in my own childhood, as true and as real as any historical fact. The Sambatyon was as real as New York's East River, and the golem as real as Prague itself, which was, to me, as real as Brooklyn—why would it not be? The Maharal and the magical powers of the Kabbalah required no more corroboration than the existence of the moon and the stars beyond. That the golem's creation defied nature was a marvel, but so was the airplane and the rocketship and the submarine. So was the electronic calculator on my teacher's desk. I understood none of it, and so all of it was real.

I remember when I first encountered the notion that the golem's existence might have been fictitious. I was well into adulthood, around age 24, a father of three, when a friend of mine who had left our insular Hasidic enclave to study at institutions with more modern orientations, where Hasidic lore was ridiculed and all mysticism was suspect, returned with a storehouse of ideas that cast doubt on much that I knew to be true.

"You thought the golem was real?!" I remember him asking once, and the incredulity in his voice made me feel at once foolish and angry. Foolish for my own gullibility. Angry at him for spoiling the myth.

The myths would be spoiled further, over and over again, as I would come to see that some of our stories were truer than others. It wouldn't be long until much of the narrative that upheld my life and my universe, my "life-supporting illusions," fell to the demands of historical evidence, including much of what I had once believed about the stories of the Bible and the Talmud; the world atlas, upon which I tried in vain to find the Sambatyon, would serve forever as a sad reminder of a shattered illusion.

The ecstasy of discovering material truth in a mythic story is matched only by the devastation that follows on discovering that material truth to be utterly implausible if not demonstrably false. And so we understand Himsel's desperate desire to find her stories not only in books, but in the very ground she digs in, in the archaeological work she takes part in as part of her university studies. She seeks not merely to discover but to confirm the myth she already holds. When she finds just the opposite, we are hurtled with her into the psychic mess that follows.

Is there a bridge from historic truth to metaphoric truth? Is there a way through the initial cognitive dissonance to an embrace of multiple truths, to the view, put forward by science writer Stephen Jay Gould, of "non-overlapping magisteria," that the "truths" of science and religion, existing at first blush in unresolvable contradiction, are not, in fact, in conflict?

With this we must all grapple—believer or heathen. Our stories are shaped in the image of our beliefs, and when what once was history becomes myth, the stories and their meanings, our beliefs and values, remain. What to do with the stories is the question. For the believer: How do we maintain the myth when history rejects its literal truth? For the non-believer: where do we find our life-supporting illusions when our scientific instruments interrupt our imaginations?

For Himsel, the answer comes slowly, agonizingly, as she attempts a vertiginous balancing act between her critical reading of the old tales, and her desperate desire to cling to the stories so deeply embedded within her they cannot be excised, only reoriented. Jesus takes on an even more fully human figure: a Semitic man, a Jew, living in the Galilee. Through that understanding, she grows enamored with Israel's Jews and their story. Still, she struggles with what appears to be Jewish indifference to Jesus, blending the Jesus of history, the Jew from Galilee, with Jesus the mythic figure in the great apocalyptic drama to come, her own yearning for that great encounter still beating. In a friend's sukkah during the Sukkot holiday, she finds herself agonizing over this:

I looked up at the Jerusalem sky. . . . Without believing in Jesus, I thought, Jews were missing out on a big part of the meaning of the Feast. It didn't just recall Moses wandering in the desert for 40 years. It also represented

the second resurrection. If I remained in the church, I would be there
when the last trumpet was blown and the dead were resurrected from
the ground. I wanted to be there.

Where we thought she had let go of Jesus, we find she has not.
She herself, over and over, thinks Jesus gone, only to find that he has
returned. And with that, somehow, the myth lives.

Back in the states, after moving to New York City, she encounters
Jews once again. This time, she must reconcile the seeming contradiction of Jews who maintain the centrality of their own story, even
as many choose to ignore the faith built upon it. Her boyfriend Selig,
son of an Orthodox rabbi but himself not observant, confounds her
most, with his ease in finding the synthesis that so eludes her. Most
of all, she struggles with the inexpressible burdens of the mythology
within her. "The power of Jesus's blood, and my stubborn refusal to
completely let go of the church," she tells us, "was not easy to explain."

Again and again, there he is, Jesus, appearing and reappearing, just
as she thinks she's moved on. "Like an old boyfriend I still had feelings
for, but to whom I couldn't quite commit. If I actively rejected Jesus
whose blood had been sacrificed to give me eternal life . . . the door to
the Next World would be forever shut to me. I would never see those
I've loved and lost and who resided there."

Not Jesus of history, not Jesus the Jew, not even the Jesus of the
theologian, mere doctrinal symbol, but Jesus and his crimson, metallic
blood, as true and as real as the blood of her own finger when pricked.
Jesus who might show up in front of the courthouse in Jasper. Jesus,
to whose bosom she yearns to be close. Jesus, whose blood sacrifice is
to give her eternal life.

Himsel ends with: "You always return for blood." Indeed, blood is
a recurring theme in Himsel's story. The blood of her own German
ancestry. The blood binding her to her family, even as she embraces the
story of another tribe. The blood of her menses, which she discovers
the Jewish faith fears obsessively. The blood of Jesus, sacrificed for her
sins. Most of all, the blood of Jesus.

What, however, is blood about?

"For the life of every creature is its blood," the Bible tells us in Leviticus, and if blood itself has a life force within it, it is story. It is history. It is myth.

As Himsel clung to her own stories, I, too, find myself clinging to mine. The atlas will never show the Sambatyon, but its force still has power over me, the legend of the lost tribes still exciting my imagination. The Maharal and the golem, too, are forever true to me; they will never be otherwise, even as the historic truth says otherwise.

When the myth is dispelled, there is nothing secure to hold onto. When the myths lose their power, the edifices built upon them shake, crumble, and with them, we fear, goes life itself. And so the task then is to keep the story alive. To retain the myth. The myth that gives us life. The story within the blood.

On a warm, slipping-into-autumn, New York City morning in September 1988, just before my twenty-seventh birthday, I realized my period was a day late. Or maybe even two days late. I wasn't rigorous about keeping track of it. My period was like my bank account—if it was within my mental ballpark, I didn't worry. But then it was three days late, and five days, and finally my younger sister Sarah said, "You know, you might be pregnant."

"I don't think so."

Denial was one of my trademark characteristics. But in this case, I had reason not to be too concerned. My boyfriend, Selig, was fourteen years older than me and had been married before. A doctor had told him and his then wife that he was infertile.

When I met Selig, I was twenty-two and had just moved to New York City from my hometown in southern Indiana. I was ambivalent about marriage, kids, or commitments of any kind, the residue of growing up the seventh of eleven children in the Worldwide Church of God, a small, apocalyptic, doomsday faith whose ministers shouted, "Brethren, Satan roams society like a lion seeking to devour you! God has raised up this Church to warn the world that the End Times are coming!"

Who would choose to bring kids into a world that was coming to an end very soon?

So once, just once, Selig and I were careless about birth control.

"Take a pregnancy test," Sarah urged.

The blood never came.

CHAPTER 1

My mostly German ancestral blood determined my physical characteristics: tall, very light-skinned, blue eyes, and blonde hair. And while blood doesn't determine one's spiritual beliefs, it certainly has an influence.

Until the year 1500, both my mother's and my father's German ancestors in Pettendorf and Hummeltal, Hamburg, Berge, Prignitz, and Mistelgau were Roman Catholic. Maybe they were devout. Maybe not. Maybe they resented that the Catholic Church demanded taxes and church fees. Common practice in Catholicism at the time was that if they couldn't pay, they were threatened with excommunication or denied the sacraments they needed to save their souls. Whatever they may have privately felt about the Roman Catholic Church, they wouldn't dare speak out. But then, a German monk named Martin Luther challenged the papal practice of selling indulgences. Luther believed that forgiveness was for God to decide, and buying an indulgence would not absolve people from punishment or ensure their salvation.

Martin Luther became synonymous with the Protestant Reformation—the protesters against Catholicism. Protestants stripped Christianity down to its essentials. The Bible, not the pope, reigned supreme. All who believed in Christ were "priests." Clergy could even marry. At age forty-one, Martin Luther himself married a nun, a woman he had helped smuggle out of a convent in a herring barrel. While irrelevant to Luther's religious beliefs, a nun in a herring barrel is always worth mentioning.

The religious schism in the seventeenth century between Catholics and Lutherans culminated in the Thirty Years' War, a war that splattered the blood of one-fifth of all Germans—millions of souls—into the soil. Until World War II, it was one of the longest and worst catastrophes in European history.

Ultimately, my mother's German ancestors remained Catholic, while my father's sided with Evangelical Lutheranism. It wasn't either family's decision. Each village was obliged to accept whatever religion the local lord chose. Some villages went back and forth between Catholicism and Lutheranism for centuries.

In the 1840s, both my mother's Catholic family and my father's Lutheran one uprooted themselves and pressed westward across the ocean to America, escaping internal revolts, high taxes, and crop failures in their farming villages.

They replanted themselves in the wooded, rolling hills of southern Indiana, where their seeds of every kind took root. Though transplants, they never forgot their homeland, nor did they leave behind their traditions, their mother tongue, or their prejudices. In the Midwest of the 1950s, when my mother, a Catholic, fell in love with my father, a Lutheran, it was practically considered a mixed marriage.

My mother, Viola, was born into a staunchly Catholic family, the eldest of seven children. She grew up on the family farm on Schnellville Road in Jasper, Indiana. She was raised on chicken dumplings, lard sandwiches, sauerkraut, turnip kraut and sausages, frog legs and turtle soup. My mother hunted squirrels, set rabbit traps, and caught frogs that she skinned and butchered and then fried in flour, salt, and pepper for supper. She wore dresses that her mother sewed out of feed sacks. When manufacturers realized their sacks were being used for clothing, they deliberately designed them with flowers and pretty colors. Like everyone else in the county, my mother went to first grade in 1939 speaking German and very little English. She finished eighth grade, but after that, there was no school bus to pick her up on her country road. For high school, she rode into town with her dad at six in the morning when he went to work and stayed with her aunt Victoria for an hour and a half until it was time to walk another half hour to school. My grandfather picked her up after school, but more often than not he stopped at the Sunset Tavern to drink. She'd either have to wait in the car until he was finished or go into the bar to get him.

After a few months of this schedule, she quit school and cleaned houses for five dollars a day. She also worked in a cannery peeling tomatoes for a nickel a bucket. The highlight of those days was piling into a car with one of the boys from the cannery and going out for a Coke, equal in cost to one bucket of tomatoes. In the summer, she picked strawberries for five cents a quart.

At one point, she considered becoming a nun: for a girl with no possibility of getting a higher education, the nunnery represented security. "It would have been an easier life," she said. "No babysitting or housekeeping or working in the field."

Despite the threatening letters that many of their neighbors received during World War I, and the understandably negative public opinion about Germany after both world wars, my family and the entire county was German and proud of it. Whether it was sentimentality or nostalgia for a lost world that they'd idealized, or pure, sheer stubbornness, the people of Dubois County held on to their German language, not to mention their German work ethic, thriftiness, stoicism, and tendency to sweep everything under the carpet. For over fifty years they ignored the sexual abuse of young boys by a revered priest, Monsignor Othmar Schroeder, the founding pastor of the Holy Family parish in Jasper, who served from 1947 until 1975. The scandal was exposed nationally in *The New York Times* in 2007. My mother said that had any of the boys told their parents, they would have been beaten for saying such a thing about a priest. At the same time, these German-Americans cherished their deeply rooted suspicion-bordering-on-hatred of anyone not white, Christian, and heterosexual.

Years later, my mother recalled her uncle Lawrence getting very drunk and going outside at night and shouting up at the sky, "Hi-ho, Hitler!"

"You mean 'Heil Hitler'?" I suggested.

"Maybe it was." She suddenly realized what she hadn't understood as a child. Her fun-loving uncle was a Nazi sympathizer.

On my father's side, after World War I ended and my paternal grandfather Ed had finished his army service, he met my grandmother Helene in Hamburg. They could not have been more different. My grandfather had only been able to attend school through sixth grade before leaving to work on the farm, while my grandmother finished high school in Hamburg, regularly attended the opera, and her sister Margaret was a ballerina touring Europe. Ultimately, my grandmother decided that whatever life in the United States offered, it had to be better than remaining in postwar Germany, where hyperinflation rendered millions of marks worthless. By the end of 1923, a loaf of bread in the Weimar Republic cost, literally, a billion marks.

In March 1924, after getting married in Germany, these grandparents arrived in Haysville, Indiana, to dirt roads without streetlamps and men who spat chewing tobacco toward a bucket in the kitchen but often missed. There, just a few miles north of my hometown of Jasper, my father was born in a three-room log cabin that had belonged to his great-grandfather, Johann Conrad Himsel.

When World War II broke out, my great-aunt Margaret fled Germany with her Jewish husband, Walter. The Nazis had come to their apartment building to take Walter, and they escaped to the roof. My grandparents put up the farm as collateral and sponsored them to come to the United States. They lived on the farm for almost a year before relocating to Boston. Walter died before I was born, and my father recalled him fondly as a good man. Because I never knew him, I didn't give him much thought until years later when I began to understand what the Holocaust had been, and how people like Walter were considered "other."

At eighteen, my father was drafted to serve in World War II. He was in an engineering unit, building bridges for the Allies and blowing up enemy bridges from Belgium to Luxembourg to France to Germany. In a small box, my grandmother kept the letters he wrote home. Throughout the summer and fall of 1944, while he was in basic training in Texas, he followed the hunting and planting season from a distance.

He wrote:

How does the corn look by now? . . . So Robert and dad went fishing and didn't even get a bite. I think they started fishing too late. They should have fished in June already. . . . Have you got a good clover stand in the wheat field? . . . I guess squirrel season closes today. It won't be long and the rabbit season will open again. . . . I suppose by now it should be pretty cold up in Indiana and I guess old cottontail rabbit is getting hell about now.

On November 6, 1944, he wrote:

Here in England as you know everything is black out and you have to feel your way around. If censorship would not prevent us from writing certain things, then I could write you a plenty, but as it is now we cannot write it so we might as well forget it. I guess by now you're done husking the corn and busy rabbit hunting and cutting firewood. Well, I certainly hope that there are lots of rabbits around.

And in 1945:

Well today I'm starting my second year of army life. . . . By the time this letter reaches you I know that you'll probably be planting corn, picking cherries, etc. I hope that you had plenty of mushrooms this year, and I hope that I'll soon be able to help you hunt them again soon. I suppose by now the woods are so green that you can't see through them anymore. Well here spring is a little later than at home, and you remember those flowers I always liked at the old house well they are just beginning to come out here. I can still remember what a nice day it was last year at this time when I was inducted but it doesn't do me any good to look back.

Then, on VE-Day:

We just got back from the brewery about an hour ago where we got six cases of beer, and that's the way we're celebrating the end of the war. . . . I imagine by now there are very few men left at home, and it may very well be a hard year at home for the threshing season. Well, now we are allowed to tell of our past experiences in the E.T.O. but at the present time we cannot talk much about Germany. . . . All of us think we're going to the Pacific, of course no one knows for sure.

President Truman dropped the bomb, and instead of boarding the boat in the harbor in Marseille that would take them to the Pacific, my father returned to the United States. Like many veterans, he spoke little of his specific experiences during the war. In later years, he recalled the Battle of St. Vith in Belgium, and how after, "People crawled out of their basements like rats. Everything was gone."

Now and then he referenced the concentration camps that all of the American troops in Europe were required to see, to bear witness. He said that when he told the local people in the county what he'd seen in the concentration camps, they hadn't believed him. "They didn't believe Germans could do that, so they didn't believe me. But I seen it with my own eyes, we were forced to go in there for that very reason, so nobody could say that it didn't happen, but you can't tell these hardheaded people around here nothing!"

When he returned, he found a job in Peoria, Illinois, and moved there. In 1946, he came home for Christmas, having just turned twenty-one.

Walking to church on Christmas Eve, my grandfather was struck and killed by a young drunk driver who, like many others, had spent the evening at the bar. My father and his younger brother Robert found my grandfather in a ditch, his bloodstained cap still on his head.

In the trial after my grandfather was killed, a priest who'd been seen helping wash the blood from the accused's vehicle took the stand and swore that the man, a Catholic, had been in church. The Catholic judge and jury acquitted the man who'd killed my grandfather. The word of a priest was sacred, undisputed. Never mind other eyewitness accounts and forensic evidence that proved his guilt.

Those centuries of barely slumbering hatred for Catholics and their presumed willingness to do anything, forgive anything, just for a contribution to the church, were roused, and my father vowed to kill the man. My grandmother talked him out of it. In a second trial, the family was granted a small sum of money in recompense for my grandfather's life and blood. "He could have at least said he was sorry," my grandmother said.

The young man died not long after, in a car accident. My grandmother said to his mother, "You see, God is getting even."

His teenage sister, who had been in the car with him and had asked, "Did we hit that man?" became a nun.

Throughout his lifetime, my father was fairly certain that the Catholic Church was the Antichrist, a sentiment that had been passed down through the ages starting 500 years before with Martin Luther, the priest-turned-founder of Lutheranism, but was validated for him when a Catholic priest protected a murderer.

He'd hoped to travel and to continue doing engineering or mechanical work. But then he became responsible for the family's 140-acre farm and nursery business, and so he remained and made certain his thirteen-year-old sister, also named Viola, went to high school.

Several years later, at a local dance, this dutiful Lutheran man met my mother, a Catholic woman who once considered becoming a nun. We were all aware of the irony of her going on to give birth to eleven children.

My parents were caught between my shotgun-toting, get-the-goddamned-hell-off-my-property, devoutly Catholic maternal grandfather, and the foot-stamping fury of my paternal grandmother, who often repeated the story of Martin Luther crawling on his knees to the Vatican. To hear Grandma tell it, you would think she'd been there.

At first, my parents devised their own Catholic/Lutheran compromise. Wanda, the oldest of my ten siblings, was baptized in the Catholic Church and had Catholic godparents. But my mother became more and more disenchanted with Catholicism, and the next three children—Jim, Ed, and Mary—were baptized Lutheran.

My mother grew up in an age when mass was still said in Latin, and Catholic doctrine taught that after death, the dead person remained in purgatory until thirty masses were said on his or her behalf. Those masses needed to be paid for by the family, and if a family was too poor, purgatory lasted longer, no matter the deceased's spiritual merit. This offended my mother.

Seeking answers to age-old questions such as "Who was God?" and "What did God want from us?" my mother set out on a quest to find the one, true path to God. Since both my mother and my father felt like outsiders in many respects they were drawn to non-mainstream Christianity: preachers who simultaneously told them that they were special and had been chosen but reminded them that they were sinners and worms. No religious movement was too fringe for them to consider. My older siblings recalled attending a Baptist church for a while, going to tent revivals farther afield, and studying with a small group of local Jehovah's Witnesses.

My mother gave birth to ten children within eleven years. As she was stuck at home, she listened to the radio while she warmed baby bottles on the stove, rolled out homemade dumplings on the kitchen table, canned tomatoes and beets, and pushed clothes through the wringer washer then hung them on the wash line. The radio evangelists provided her with adult company during the day and reassured her that God was out there, and He had a plan for her.

Radio evangelists were charismatic preachers who encouraged people to leave their ancestral denominations and follow them to salvation. In the late 1950s, both of my parents felt an affinity for the radio evangelist Herbert Armstrong, the founder of the Worldwide Church of God. Armstrong offered explanations for why bad things happened, why mankind existed, as well as provided an overall master plan and purpose of life that entailed God's chosen people—the church members.

As a young man, Herbert Armstrong had belonged to the Ku Klux Klan. He'd studied *Mein Kampf* as well as L. Ron Hubbard's *Dianetics*, the basis of Scientology. When Armstrong's wife became involved with the Seventh-Day Adventists, he began reexamining the Bible and was later ordained as a minister in that church. He was eventually kicked out, though he maintained he left of his own volition, and created the Radio Church of God, which later became the Worldwide Church of God.

Armstrong claimed that he could trace his own genealogy back to Edward I of England, and through the British royal genealogy, back to King Heremon of Ireland, who had married Queen Teia Tephi, daughter of Zedekiah. Though Armstrong's bloodline to Zedekiah was never substantiated, we unquestioningly accepted the church's version of history. British Israelism was a cornerstone of the church and cemented our sense of being God's chosen. I strongly identified with those lost tribes, in exile, at least spiritually, in Indiana. I didn't realize at the time, nor for a long time, that the ancient Israelites were alive and well and spread throughout the world. They were called Jews.

Armstrong's radio program, *The World Tomorrow*, named after the theme of the 1939 World's Fair held in New York, was devoted to analyzing "today's news with the prophecies of the WORLD TOMORROW!" In other words, End Times prophecies. My parents tuned in and listened to Armstrong's bombastic broadcasts like this one from the 1950s:

You and your family are seated around the dining table. Your RADIO is tuned in to your regular entertainment program. Suddenly a great Voice thunders forth from your radio, 'This is GOD SPEAKING! I interrupt your program to bring you a STARTLING DECLARATION OF WORLD-SHAKING MAGNITUDE! I come to announce the imminent arrival of a TERRIBLY DESTRUCTIVE WORLD-WIDE UPHEAVAL of nature! OF EARTH! OF SKY! Yes, even of the WATERS! It is TIME YOU WAKE UP to the fact that you and your nation, the nations of the world and their leaders have sinned!

Having lived through the Depression and witnessed World War II and the first atomic bomb, the end of the world seemed entirely plausible, even imminent, to many Americans, including my parents.

Herbert Armstrong culled doctrine from his former church, the Seventh-day Adventists, the Jehovah's Witnesses, the British Israelism Movement, as well as the Mormons. These were all religious groups that stemmed from nineteenth-century America and were led by charismatic men with a vision of a more "authentic" Christianity. Free magazines and pamphlets were given out explaining the Worldwide Church of God's doctrine. This appealed to my mother, who was wholly incapable of turning down anything she didn't have to pay for and never left a restaurant without pocketing condiment packets, straws, and a fistful of half-and-half containers.

"*Should Christians Celebrate BIRTHDAYS?*" (No.) "*Is it a SIN to Have INSURANCE?*" (No insurance can replace faith.) These were just a couple of the topics covered in the freebies, liberally punctuated with exclamation marks and capital letters to convey urgency. Eventually, my parents mailed away for the church's Ambassador College Bible Correspondence Courses and, when we were all in bed, they sat in the kitchen and studied together.

They created a new bond over the material they were learning, a bond that overcame the gulf that separated them as Catholic and Lutheran. The correspondence course was practically like higher education, which neither had had access to before. It required them to read and think and study. "Why Study the Bible?" was one of the courses, as well as "Here's the Good News . . . MESSAGE sent from Heaven." By the time I was born, my parents were well on their way to being baptized in this new faith.

The church's booklet *Pagan Holidays—or God's Holy Days—Which?*, and others like *The Plain Truth about Christmas* and *The Plain Truth about Easter*, explained that all true Christians should eschew Christmas, Easter, and Valentine's Day, as they were steeped in paganism. Instead, like Christians had done until the fourth century, we celebrated all of the Holy Days mentioned in the Old Testament, the Hebrew Bible, such as Passover, the Feast of Unleavened Bread; Yom Kippur, the Day of Atonement; Rosh Hashanah, the Feast of Trumpets; Sukkot, the Feast of Tabernacles; and Shavuot, or Pentecost. We also observed the Sabbath on Saturday, not Sunday.

We were the only family in the ocean of Catholics and Lutherans in our county who belonged to the Worldwide Church of God, believing that we had found the authentic, first-century Jesus.

In 1965, when I was four years old, my younger sister Sarah—the tenth of ten at that time—was born with what appeared to be a life-threatening abnormality. Her esophagus led into her lungs instead of her stomach, and from the X-rays the doctors determined that an operation offered her a fifty-fifty chance for survival.

My mother remained in the hospital recovering from a Caesarean section, and my Catholic grandmother came over to our house. "Let's pray for Mommy and the baby," she said to us. We knelt by the couch. My grandmother bent her head low. With fingers interlaced, she prayed with her rosary beads hanging from one of her hands. I had no idea exactly what it meant to pray, but I knelt too, and bowed my head, keeping an eye on my grandmother so I knew when we were finished.

While we prayed, my father and my mother's sister, my aunt Shirley, drove the baby an hour and a half to a bigger hospital in Evansville. The new set of doctors took X-rays and declared that there was nothing wrong and the baby could be taken home. My parents believed that not only had God performed a miracle on our behalf, it was their faith in this new religion that was responsible for it. The prayers of my Lutheran and Catholic relatives were completely discounted.

A few months later, I suffered a near-fatal bout of double pneumonia. It felt like a hot air balloon was pressing against my chest, preventing me from breathing. My mother put cold washrags on my forehead and a mustard compress on my chest. It was winter, and a well-meaning friend of my parents brought us a Christmas tree, unaware that we didn't celebrate Christmas. Because I was sleeping in my parents' bed, I overheard my father say to my mother, "We can't keep this thing, we got a sick girl in the house!" as if the Christmas tree carried the plague and might kill me. In the middle of the night, my father hauled off the Christmas tree.

I awoke to a minister from the Worldwide Church of God placing his hands on my forehead. There was a jumble of "Our Heavenly Father . . . in Jesus's name, Amen," then a dry, white prayer cloth was pressed against my forehead. That night, I fell deeply asleep. The hot air balloon pulled me up into the air and out of bed, and I drifted above the room, looking down at the bundle of blankets on the bed and at my parents huddled nearby. Then, with a thump, the hot air balloon collapsed. I landed hard in my bed. Though it was still a struggle to breathe, I could get air into me. I'd turned a corner.

My father attributed my recovery both to the minister's prayers and to the fact that he hadn't allowed the pagan Christmas tree to remain in our home.

God, through the ministers of the church, had performed two miracles in quick succession. Thus, my parents realized they had found the right religion, the Worldwide Church of God. They were baptized shortly thereafter and viewed it as a rebirth, the beginning of a new relationship with God, the beginning of traveling the path to God. Eschewing the spiritual soil in which they were raised, while remaining firmly planted in the physical soil of their youth, they had crossed spiritual boundaries heeding God's call, similar to the biblical Abraham who had left his idols behind to follow God's call to the Promised Land.

CHAPTER 2

Five hundred years after Martin Luther split with the Catholic Church, the descendants of both the Lutherans and Catholics whose blood ran through my veins agreed on one thing: this new church was crazy.

What kind of Christian didn't celebrate Christmas or Easter? Or eat pork or shellfish? For the past 2,000 years, Jesus's death on the cross effectively nullified all of the Hebrew Bible's laws, including its holidays. Christians believed that the New Testament was a new covenant. You received salvation by belief in Jesus as your Savior, not by fasting on the Day of Atonement or observing Saturday as the Sabbath.

Despite their disapproval, we didn't shun our parents' families, as the church told us we should. None of my grandparents were cozy and warm, and I didn't recall them ever kissing any of their grandchildren except as babies. But they were family, and the blood bond was deep and heartfelt, even if it was not expressed outwardly.

Every Sunday we visited my grandma Himsel, who lived in a white clapboard farmhouse a few hundred yards from the old log cabin, which my father and his parents and two siblings had moved into when he was seven.

Uncle Robert was typically in the kitchen listening to either *The Lutheran Hour* or Billy Graham on the radio. He greeted us with "Hey, you little squirts!" in an almost affectionate manner. Robert spent each weekend feeding his dogs bologna sandwiches, chopping wood for the black, wood-burning kitchen stove (used both for cooking and to heat the downstairs), and wiping down the kitchen table with rubbing alcohol. If he wasn't armed with Lysol, attempting to single-handedly rid the world of germs, Robert was gargling with Listerine or gripping a container of Dristan or pushing a long iodine-saturated Q-tip up his nose, pulling it out, then looking at whatever it had caught, a scene by which I was for some reason transfixed. Never married and living with Grandma, Robert had loved to draw as a child but was teased for it. Only sissies did art. Or girls. He gave it up and worked at the power plant.

Robert wasn't quite certain what to do with the tribe of boisterous children who clamored to gather eggs, feed the chickens, pump the well water into the tin coffee can on the wooden fence, and investigate the log cabin, with its patches of faded, floral wallpaper from the Depression. During the hot summer months, my father, his parents, and his siblings had slept on the porch. "We'd fall asleep to the music of the crickets and cicadas," he once said, his voice nostalgic. The log home was a reminder of the two different eras that my father witnessed. He was born into a horse-and-buggy world in which peddlers came around to sell knives, thread, and pots and pans, gypsies were accused of stealing children, and neighbors made moonshine during Prohibition. He went on to witness atomic bombs and space shuttles and the possibility of obtaining any commodity in the world simply by punching keys on a computer. He liked to recall the past—the father he lost too young and the world he grew up in that had changed so very much.

My father once told me about a little wren that had made its home in a wooden shoe worn by one of his ancestors. His grandmother had sternly admonished him to leave the wren alone, but not because she felt an emotional attachment to it. Rather, wrens killed the bugs on the crops. My father, however, did feel emotionally attached to the birds. And to the old log cabin. To all of his old cars. And most of all, to the way things once were, and the way they still should be. He didn't view it as inconsistent that he'd broken with his past and his traditions when he took on a new faith. He believed he'd found the truth, an objective truth, and everyone else should likewise believe it.

On Sunday mornings, Grandma returned home from her Evangelical Lutheran church often still singing "Come, Holy Spirit, God and Lord"—or the German version of it: "Komm, Heiliger Geist, Herre Gott"—in her clear, beautiful soprano voice while she was working in the kitchen or the garden. She sang with such joy and sincerity, the notes floating in the quiet of the farm, that I couldn't imagine that God didn't hear her just because she was Lutheran. But should such a perplexing thought cross my mind, I quickly chased it away. I didn't want to be one of those people in the church who had doubts.

One day when Grandma was bending over the hoe in the garden, humming and singing German words I didn't understand, her long dress rode up in the back. I saw that Grandma's legs were a map of her life's journey. Above the knees, her legs were sophisticated, big city, white and pale where the sun didn't hit them, remnants of her life in Hamburg where she'd never planted so much as a flower. Everything she'd left behind. Below her knees, her skin was brown and leathery from constant exposure to her new life on the farm, plowing, baling hay, and sowing beans. Grandma, in many respects, was a transplant who didn't quite take to the new soil she'd been stuck in.

Invariably, Grandma had a pork roast on Sunday that she wanted to feed us and which we stalwartly, with great principle and moral fiber, refused. My father would say, "Now, Mom, you know we don't eat that stuff."

"You used to. I don't understand you, James. Vat's the matter vith some pork?"

Within minutes, the two of them would be in the midst of a fierce argument, breaking into heated German, and ending with my father throwing up his hands and yelling, "I don't know what the HECK is the matter with you, Mom! You think up is down and down is up. I'm so mad, I could bite the head off a tenpenny nail!" and he would stomp out the door. My father was a yeller and screamer.

Grandma offered us long diatribes on what a good man Martin Luther had been and what a bad man that Armstrong was. About Luther, she said, "Zat poor man, he valked on his knees up ze steps of ze Vatican!" Grandma didn't understand how her son had given up Martin Luther for "Zat nasty man! I don't know vhy you give your money, vhich you vork very hard for, to zat nasty man." This short, white-haired, rotund dervish would sometimes confront her tall, broad, strong son as if he were a small child. "Ja, he iss nasty, I tell you!" and Grandma would stomp her foot (my father and grandma were both enthusiastic stompers) and let loose a barrage of German, enraged that my parents gave so much of their money to the church. I snuck out the door when they fought. The last thing I wanted was confrontation.

I hated to agree with Grandma, but even though I knew that we had to suffer the sacrifice of the material for the spiritual before Jesus returned and saved us, it would have been nice to have had new shoes instead of hand-me-downs. Or to have curtains cover the living room windows so that people couldn't see straight in when they drove past. I wanted Baggies for our lunch sandwiches instead of reused brown paper bags. I wanted new clothes, not skirts and shirts that had been handed down from twenty years ago and had to be safety-pinned to fit. And yes, it would have been wonderful to have a car without rust running down the fender, seats with foam rubber emerging from big gashes, and a loud, clanging muffler.

I was acutely aware that belonging to the church placed me firmly on the periphery of the community. Having so many siblings, living out on a country road, using food stamps, and not having money for new clothes just added to the whole weird package. Once, when my younger sister Liz and I were driving with our father, I half-ducked my head so no one would see it was me. Liz kept her head up and laughed at me. She refused to be intimidated by anyone who dared judge her for driving through town in a pink Caddy that died at stop signs and groaned going up hills. The sacrifices of the material for the spiritual were just part of the necessary trials and tribulations.

My father had had to quit school after eighth grade to help his dad on the farm, and without a high school diploma, he could only find jobs that necessitated physical, not mental, ability. He worked in construction to support his ever-growing family, leaving early in the morning, dressed in gray or navy-blue work pants and shirt and heavy boots. My mother packed him beef bologna sandwiches on whole-wheat bread for lunch, and he returned by five or six, hungry and weary. He belonged to the laborers' union and was sent out to build a reservoir in the county, work at a power plant, lay concrete on I-64, and do various other jobs requiring his formidable strength and endurance.

However, he was also an avid reader and picked up books at antiquarian book fairs, including *Plutarch's Lives* and *The Decline and Fall of the Roman Empire*. One of his favorite books, which he attempted to get all of us to read, was *The Two Babylons: Or, The Papal Worship Proved to Be the Worship of Nimrod and His Wife*. He was fond of quoting this book, published in the mid-1800s by a Protestant minister named Alexander Hislop, which claimed that the Catholic Church was a continuation of the pagan religion of Babylon and was nothing less than the Whore of Babylon referred to in the book of Revelation.

I read parts of the book several times, and given the extensive footnotes, it seemed to be a reliable and even scholarly work. Yet, I could never read much of it without putting it down. Not only was the language dense and bombastic, essentially an attack against the Catholic Church as "a synagogue of Satan," but I was disturbed by something else in the pages, something that I couldn't articulate even to myself. The book put forth many of the same arguments as our church—that the Catholic Church was the Antichrist, which had to be vanquished before Jesus could return—but it was overly self-righteous and lacking respect for another faith, even if I was taught that that faith was wrong.

Several times, in a fine fury, Grandma shouted that the Worldwide Church of God was a cult. This really incensed my father, and he would decide we couldn't go to the farm anymore if Grandma was going to be so contrary and foolish and perhaps even influenced by Satan. Herbert Armstrong preached that anyone who disagreed with church doctrine likely had the devil working on him or her.

Poor Grandma, I thought at the time. She was doomed.

———

After leaving Grandma Himsel on Sunday afternoon, we drove past open fields, farmhouses, and barns and silos, through Jasper and across the Patoka River to my mother's parents. We turned onto Schnellville Road and crested Pete's Hill, where my grandparents' farm came into view: the white farmhouse, the summer kitchen, and the still-in-use outhouse that my grandmother referred to as "a damn-filthy, stinking shithouse."

Tumbling out of the car, we'd often find my grandfather and uncles in the middle of butchering a pig, conversation between them limited to how much they should freeze, how much to keep. My brothers usually ran off with some of the other male cousins to fish down at the pond or maybe shoot at sparrows or go turtling at the creek.

The five youngest at the time—Abby, me, Liz, John, and Sarah—immediately asked our grandmother if we could hunt eggs. She gave us little plastic buckets and reminded us, "If the egg is marked with an 'x,' don't you take it! That's a nest egg, and if you don't leave it, the hen won't have her egg to hatch." So we scooped up eggs from the smokehouse, the tractor seat, the combine, the hayloft, and behind the barn, placing them gently in our buckets. We were as careful to leave the nest eggs as my father had been not to disturb the wren's nest.

We brought the eggs back to the kitchen, where the aunts reigned, peeling potatoes, opening jars of homemade turnip kraut, and making Jell-O salad and ribley soup (from the German *Riebelesuppe*), which consisted of eggs and flour beat together then crumbled into hot chicken broth. Should a barn cat venture into the kitchen, my grandmother would mutter, "You little shitass," and kick it out. I delighted in hearing my grandmother say such forbidden words in her dismissive way. She not only called the cats shitasses but also her husband and grandchildren.

We then returned to the barnyard, maybe checked out the baby kittens in the hayloft, or sat in the corncrib, where corn covered our bodies up to our waist, or we asked my grandfather if we could help slop the pigs. I liked the word "slopped." There was something in it of sun-spattered mud puddles and late-night giggles. When my grandparents said "slop," though, they pronounced it "*schlop*," and the word became an earthy, sensual thing—the sound of pigs squealing and snorting, swallowing and salivating.

In his bib overalls, heavy work boots, and the John Deere cap that covered his half-bald head, my grandfather was a lonely figure. Tagging along at his side, we helped slop the pigs and pluck the chickens. Cigarette dangling from his lower lip, ax in one hand and chicken in the other, he lowered the ax, and the chicken's head was a small bloody mess next to the concrete block while the body flew and hopped and jumped around until it came to a sudden flopping stop.

Then he dipped the chicken into a pot of boiling water, swirled it around, and after it had cooled, he handed it to us to pluck. We sat in comfortable silence on wooden crates, ripped off the feathers, and brought the bare chickens into the kitchen, where we rested them on the table covered in newspaper. My mother and aunts made quick work of gutting them, saving the liver and gizzard and heart, and tossing everything else away.

My father often said that our mother was just like her dad. "They are both stubborn as all get out," he declared. "Hardheaded, them two stick up for each other. They're thick as thieves." He meant many things by this, but one of the things he was referring to was my grandfather's excessive consumption of Falls City Beer and my mother's refusal to either criticize him or listen to anyone else's criticism of him.

We usually didn't leave until night fell, when big clusters of stars crowded the black sky. Then we made our way sleepily to the car, and all around us the farm was quiet save the chirping of crickets.

I grew up with these hardworking, beer-drinking, potbellied, red-faced, old-time, bib-overalled men and gray-haired, Dutch-talking, coarse-handed, strict, and reserved women. I went to Strassenfests, or street fairs, and at parties I sang, "*What's that smell comin' from over the sea? Must be the smell of old Germany. Singin' glorious! One keg of beer for the four of us! Glory be to God that there ain't no more of us, 'cause one of us can drink it all up. Damn quick!*"

If the world didn't end before I became an adult, I would take my place among them, continuing the traditions that had been passed on for more than a century, from the barn-raising and butchering days of old, to the Sundays of the 1960s.

I couldn't imagine that in just over a decade, the wren would give up the wooden shoe and leave the nest, exchanging ribley soup for matzah ball, the Midwest for the Mideast.

CHAPTER 3

If Sunday belonged to family, then Saturday, the seventh day of the week, belonged to God.

The Sabbath began at sunset Friday night and ended at sunset Saturday night. On any Friday night, as the sun set behind the red barn and after we'd eaten the usual fried chicken and mashed potatoes and gravy for supper, we then-ten children gathered in the living room for Friday night prayer and Bible study. We took turns reading aloud from the church's children's Bible stories.

The gray, soft-backed books retold biblical events and were illustrated with black-and-white drawings: innocent Job, covered in boils, though he was sinless; Lot's wife looking back over her shoulder, though warned not to, her eyes wide and frightened, before being turned into a pillar of salt, God's punishment for her disobedience; Joseph, full of himself in the multicolored coat that got him into so much trouble.

I loved the stories, loved thinking about them and trying to figure them out. Joseph was thrown into a pit by his jealous brothers and then ransomed into slavery in Egypt. God destroyed the world in the flood, and only Noah and his family survived. Cain killed Abel, his own brother. They were harsh stories, and within them, God walked and talked and communicated with people. I was a literal-minded child, and I imagined God hanging out in their neighborhood, popping up on the street unexpectedly. I wished God would do that still, show up at the courthouse square in Jasper or maybe just appear in the backyard while we were playing red rover.

Friday evening ended with us kneeling at the couch and chairs, heads bowed, and our father led the prayer. "We thank you great God for your Sabbath, and for all of the spiritual blessings you've given us, and we pray that you will continue to bless us and open our minds to your Truth, in Jesus's name we pray, Amen."

I added my own private prayer: that my parents would get along; that my extended family would join our church so we could all be saved; that I would get into the Kingdom; and that I would receive God's Holy Spirit.

On Saturday mornings, my father roused us with "Boys, girls, get up! You got to make hay while the sun shines!" We exited our rooms—there were two or three or four siblings per room, depending on the year, and we fought over access to the one bathroom. My brothers had it easy— they could go outside and pee behind the garage.

Then we ate a quick breakfast of oatmeal or Cream of Wheat. My mother was a devotee of anything natural and unprocessed and authentic. Wheat germ and blackstrap molasses were mainstays. We looked suspiciously on Cap'n Crunch.

My four brothers, scrubbed and pink-cheeked, ears jutting out below the almost military-style haircuts the church demanded, wore ill-fitting hand-me-down suits. My five sisters and I wore dresses that came to the middle of our kneecaps, in accordance with church doctrine. Just as Saturday was set apart from the rest of the week, I felt distinctly set apart from, and indeed superior to, our neighbors on the Sabbath. But still I longed to belong. I learned early to squelch personal desires like exchanging Valentine's Day cards with my classmates, giving and receiving Christmas presents, eating turtle soup at my grandparents' house. Anything that didn't fit in with the life I was supposed to live. Anything that prevented me from getting closer to God.

Usually running late, which my father blamed on my mother, we piled into one of the rotating, fixer-upper, ancient Cadillacs and drove past weathered barns and billboards that urged us to "Chew Mail Pouch Tobacco." Stacked on top of one another in the car, we grumbled and complained. We were bored. Jim took up too much room; Ed was deliberately bumping his legs up and down, causing Liz, who was seated on his lap, to lunge forward almost into the front seat. Wanda wanted the window rolled up because her AquaNet-ed hair was getting messed up, and Paul was sure that I had deliberately elbowed him. Within minutes my father yelled, "Would you kids PIPE IT DOWN!"

It was an hour and a half drive to Evansville, where we attended church services at a seedy gray building that the church rented from the Order of Owls, a fraternal society founded in South Bend, Indiana, in 1904 open to white men only. The church had no connection to the Owls, except to rent "The Owl's Home" on Saturday afternoon. The church did not build or own houses of worship. This would have cost money and deprived it of money needed to preach the gospel to the world. Instead, rented movie theaters, Masonic lodges, auditoriums, and various other public spaces served as our "church" for Saturday services.

During the long ride, my father railed against the evils of drugs, miniskirts, evolutionists, and women's libbers, all of which seemed to have overtaken America like a scourge in the late 1960s and early 1970s. It was the time of Woodstock, the Summer of Love, the long-haired Beatles, and women burning their bras.

Incensed that women no longer knew "their place," Dad made his case: "God created a role for everything in the universe. Just think what would happen if a river thought it could be a tree! God is not the author of confusion, it says that in the Bible, and women are confusing the way God intended them to be. They're so mixed up these days that they're mixing everybody else up. A wife is supposed to submit herself to her husband, for he is her head even as Christ is the head of the Church."

The ministers often quoted this verse from the book of Ephesians, the apostle Paul's letter to the church at Ephesus, to justify why wives should neither make decisions on their own nor work outside the home if their husbands didn't want them to. In all things, one's husband had final say.

"And Mama," my father continued, "you should know that. It won't work, with you pullin' gee, and me pullin' haw." I imagined my father hitched to the plow, calling, "Haw!" while my mother shook her head and pulled in a different direction, "Gee!" He often accused her of deliberately undermining him. Which she did: covering for my older teenage siblings when they went out on Friday nights, the Sabbath, and turning a blind eye to my older sisters rolling up the waistband of their skirts to shorten them when they left for school.

I tuned out my father's loud, tiresome, and contentious diatribes that made my heart jump and immersed myself in a word search puzzle or reading Trixie Belden. With books, I learned the useful art of tuning out things I didn't want to hear.

When I was in my teens and the 1970s women's movement—*Ms.* magazine; *Roe v. Wade*; Helen Reddy's feminist anthem song "I Am Woman"—was in full swing, I challenged my father on this sexist and patriarchal attitude that I thought all religions should have long abandoned. While I still believed the Bible was God's sacred word and contained laws that regulated how we should live, I thought the Bible could be interpreted in more than one way. I questioned why things had to remain the same.

I argued, "Daddy, I don't believe that God created men and women unequal, or that one of us is supposed to serve the other. We're all the same in the eyes of God."

"Tater Doll," my father literally threw up his hands and said, "you're so stubborn, a team of twenty mules ain't gonna change your mind. You would argue with the devil if you thought you were right!"

I took that as a compliment.

When we arrived at church, a deacon—maybe Mr. Davis or Mr. Cooper—stood at the door and greeted us with a big smile and outstretched hand. "Mr. Himsel, Mrs. Himsel." Close to 200 people attended services with us every Saturday. They came from the tristate area: southern Indiana, southern Illinois, and northwest Kentucky.

Until the mid-1970s, they were all white. Growing up, I was oblivious to the lack of racial diversity in the church. Though why would any black person wish to join a church that stated dogmatically that blacks were intended by God to be slaves because their ancestor, Noah's son Ham, was cursed to be "a servant of servants unto his brethren"?

My mother greeted other women warmly by their first names, while my father offered a formal handshake and addressed everyone by "Mr." and "Mrs." We walked down the aisle to claim a row of hard metal chairs, where we would sit for the next two hours. Wanda, eight years older than me, and Mary, four years older, often sat with friends they'd made. My older brothers, Jim, Ed, and Paul, sat with us. Sarah, the youngest, sat between my parents and occupied herself with her coloring books. Abby, Liz, John, and I—all of us a little over a year apart in age—were clumped together, and we shared a hymnal, passed notes, and poked each other if someone was yawning loudly or if a whisper had become too loud.

In the back was a soda vending machine. The deacons had placed a piece of paper over the coin slot so we could not buy soda on the Sabbath, as we were forbidden to shop or spend money. While we were, of course, not allowed to work on the Sabbath, the church shifted its position on what exactly constituted "work" whenever "new truths" were revealed to Mr. Armstrong. At one point, we were not even allowed to buy gas for the car to drive to services; later, a new truth emerged to allow us to buy gas if it was an emergency. It was difficult to keep track of the ever-changing rules, and just as I'd figured something out, it was altered. It felt like walking on spiritual quicksand.

I liked to turn around in my chair and look at all of the other church members. I had yet to learn that staring was rude. There was a pale, emaciated woman with jet black hair. She fascinated me because she looked so different than everyone else. Only many years later did it occur to me that she was anorexic. Her best friend was one of the heaviest women in the church, a nice lady who would host us in her home when we needed to stay close by to attend church socials on Saturday night or church softball games on Sunday.

I remember being mesmerized by a woman scratching her elbow back and forth in an almost hypnotic way. White flakes fell from her elbow onto her black dress, like stars against a night sky.

Another couple, who had two sons, sat with each other during services, but didn't live together. Though married, they had been forced to separate because she was previously divorced. According to church doctrine, anyone who got divorced and then remarried must leave his or her current spouse and either return to the one they'd divorced or remain unmarried.

I never knew how the family felt about the rule. If anyone disagreed with church doctrine, they didn't dare verbalize it. Otherwise, the minister would show up at the house unexpectedly and give them a talking-to. He would remind them that Herbert Armstrong was God's appointed one. If we wanted to grumble and complain like the Israelites had in the desert to Moses, then, just as the Israelites didn't make it into the Promised Land, we wouldn't make it into the World Tomorrow when Jesus returned. Church members lived in fear of those surprise visits.

The ministers had dropped by our house unexpectedly a few times. I never knew exactly why. My oldest sister, Wanda, who was more keenly aware of what was going on, thought it was because they wanted to remind us that they were in control. Or they wanted to make sure our parents were accurately tithing. Wanda surmised that the minister had told my parents not to have more kids, or maybe he was concerned about the spankings my father meted out, mostly to my older brothers, whom he deemed "rebellious."

The spankings were, in fact, more like beatings. "Spare the rod, spoil the child," was my father's definition of parenting, at least of the older ones. Corporal punishment was encouraged, and when you went into the bathroom during church services, you would often hear the sharp slapslapslapslapslap of a mother's hand against a child's bare bottom. Not until the child stopped crying would she exit the stall, toddler in hand, the three-year-old's face blotchy with crying. The mother felt no shame. In fact, she had done her parental duty.

I was completely unaware of the personal lives of any of the members. I found out that a man we all thought was upstanding actually liked young girls. One of the regular door greeters drank three martinis during Spokesman Club and got looped at restaurants. Several of the men spanked their wives to discipline them. And children were beaten regularly for any infraction.

When everyone was seated, the music director went to the front and said, "Please rise for the opening hymn." Old and young voices joined together to sing songs from *The Bible Hymnal*, most written by Herbert Armstrong's brother Dwight. The first song, "Blest and Happy Is the Man," taken from Psalms 1, was a crowd favorite:

> *Blest and happy is the man Who doth never walk astray,*
> *Nor with the ungodly men Stands in sinner's way.*
> *All he does prospers well,*
> *But the wicked are not so;*
> *They are chaff before the wind,*
> *Driven to and fro.*

I imagined myself, a fluff of chaff, being tossed about in the wind, never coming to a rest. I feared being wicked.

Next, another deacon offered the opening prayer. Heads bowed, eyes closed, hands clasped either in front or behind us, we listened. "Our merciful Father in Heaven, we thank you great God for bringing us here together on your Sabbath Day, and Lord, we pray that we will take the spiritual nourishment we need today. We pray that your work be done here on earth, and that you just strengthen and lift up your apostle, Herbert Armstrong, to witness to the nations and spread the gospel. In Jesus's most holy name we pray, Amen." The deacon's prayer filled the creaky old room, and it was as if the entire congregation was one soul, praying to God, who bent His ear toward us, taking note of what was being asked.

Depending on the deacon, the prayer could go on for quite some time and incorporate asking God to help us remain strong in the face of persecution ("persecution" was code for one's extended family or community opposing the church) and thanking God that we knew the Truth, and praying for those in our families who had not yet come to the Truth. Then we sat, placed our Bibles and notebooks in our laps, and listened to the sermonette, followed by the sermon.

Whether the topic of the sermon on any particular Saturday was "What Is Spiritual Sin?" or "Why Were You Born?," it invariably became a shouting exhortation to remain steadfast in the church because these were the End Times. "You can be alive in Christ or dead in Adam!" the minister would scream. "You must love correction, and diligently seek the sin in yourself. Satan roams society like a lion seeking to devour you! God has raised up this church to witness for the End Times!

"God's Holy Work must be done so Jesus can return," the minister would remind us. "God needs YOU! God has called us—the weak and the poor—to confound the wise. Many are called, but few are chosen. This church and God's chosen prophet, Herbert Armstrong, need your prayers, your loyalty, and your money to do the End Times work."

My parents tithed ten percent of their income and gave it to the church; another ten percent they set aside to spend at the Feast of Tabernacles, plus there was a third tithe in the third and sixth years of a seven-year cycle that went to the poor, as well as the various "free will" offerings and pleas for money from Mr. Armstrong. My parents believed that our relatives, who disapproved of the money we gave the church, failed to understand that we'd been chosen for an important purpose: so Jesus could return. I was proud to be a part of God's work on earth, even in a small way. As God's soldier, I was heralding Jesus's return to the earth. Nothing could be more important than that. I was proud that my family was chosen but also worried that too much pride was a sin. It was hard to calibrate how much pride was acceptable and how much would get me in trouble.

If Jesus didn't return, it was the church's fault. It meant that we were sinning, or not giving enough money to the church's coffers so that Mr. Armstrong and the evangelists could spread the gospel worldwide. You could never pray enough, never give enough. God, who we were taught was good and merciful, was also insatiable in His demands. God was as inconsistent as the church, as my parents.

The screaming, dire certainty with which the minister announced that we were in danger of losing our eternal life—*"If you are lukewarm in your love for God, if you are a spiritual DRONE, then your ETERNAL LIFE is at stake! You will NOT make it into the Kingdom!"*—the fear of the End Times, the threats of the looming Lake of Fire where sinners would be tossed, and the incessant accusations that, as sinners, we needed to do more, be more, and give more, terrified me as a child. With their every exhortation, a sense of panic and doom squelched my childish optimism, my faith that tomorrow would come. We had to obey every command. Do it God's way. Our lives, our salvation, were in jeopardy. The stakes were very high.

CHAPTER 4

For years, the question nagged at me: If my parents had to choose one of us ten kids to eat, who would it be?

It was a Saturday in 1968, and I was seven, sitting in church in a long row with my family listening to another sermon. *"In the End Times, the time of the Great Tribulation,"* the minister shouted from the pulpit, *"there will be mass murder, corpses will litter the streets, and the world will reek of the stench of dead bodies!"*

This was the fate of those who, in the End Times, had been left behind at Jesus's Second Coming, and hadn't made it to the Place of Safety.

"Jesus will return, like a thief in the night. Do not slumber, do not sleep, do not let your love wax cold! The great God is going to spank this world, and he is going to spank hard! Worldwide droughts. Starvation. Parents will eat their children!"

Alarmed, and with a terrible sense of foreboding, I wondered which of us our parents would devour first. A girl and skinny, I was hardly worth killing. Mary, four years older than me, was the nicest, always helping others finish their chores. They wouldn't eat her. Wanda was the oldest and bossy. My parents wouldn't dare eat her. Probably one of my older brothers. They were always in trouble. Jim did not close his eyes during opening and closing prayers, and Ed made blasphemous jokes about prayer cloths.

These small, white flannel cloths came from church headquarters in California. Someone there—an evangelist, or perhaps Mr. Armstrong himself—prayed on the cloth, thus making it a "prayer cloth," then sent it to ailing members, including me when I had pneumonia. One woman believed that it could also repair her car and asked the minister for a prayer cloth so it would stop stalling. After hearing about this, whenever our car rattled or steam rose from the radiator, Ed would mutter an irreverent "prayer cloth."

I worried that if I were slumbering when Jesus returned, the rest of the brethren would be lifted into the sky and transported on "wings of eagles" to a Place of Safety, according to the book of Revelation. Herbert Armstrong had identified that place as Petra in Jordan. According to the church's booklet *This is PETRA!*, the ancient Jordanian city locked in by mountains and carved almost entirely of stone was the Place of Safety. Some members of the church were actively looking forward to living in caves.

According to the church's booklet *1975 in Prophecy*, the world would end in 1975. A German-dominated Europe would:

> *. . . blast our [US] cities and industrial centers with hydrogen bombs . . . and so now God is about to punish! . . . It's later than you think! You have been warned! . . . and I say to you on authority of God Almighty that it is absolutely sure!*

The words were accompanied by illustrations that resembled horror movies or science fiction: a barren landscape with a hand sticking up from the ground; people fleeing a city where a hydrogen bomb flamed against the backdrop of the buildings; skeletal figures whose eyes popped out of their sockets; and frightened faces cowering against giant hailstones crashing from the skies.

I later learned that many of the horrors the church described were based on the atrocities committed during the Holocaust. The church itself was fashioned with a Nazi-like structure. The administrative offices in Pasadena, California, were referred to as "Headquarters," and its hierarchy paralleled that of the military. Herbert Armstrong, the "apostle," was akin to a general; and the counterparts to the church's evangelists, preaching elders, local regional elders, local church elders, deacons, and members were colonels, captains, first and second lieutenants, sergeants, and privates.

This structure even extended to families. At one point, the church required children to address their parents as "Sir" and "Ma'am," not Mom and Dad. Five-year-old children sharply and obediently said, "Yes, sir! No, ma'am!" as if they were speaking to a sergeant in boot camp. And just like in the military, you didn't dare question authority. "Rebellion is as the sin of witchcraft," said the ministers, quoting the biblical verse. God who loved us was also a totalitarian dictator.

My father tried to maintain order in our chaotic household by insisting that we say "Yes, sir," or "No, sir," "Yes, ma'am," or "No, ma'am." My mother took to calling my father "sir" as well, and we all knew that it was a taunt of sorts, much the same as the way she snuck bits of beef tongue into the potato hash without my tongue-hating father knowing it.

As terrible as the horrors of the Great Tribulation, Jesus's Kingdom was a fat, juicy, delicious carrot dangled in front of us. Once the Tribulation was over, as described in Matthew 24, *"Then shall be great tribulation, such as was not since the beginning of the world to this time, no, nor ever shall be,"* then Satan would be bound for 1,000 years, unable to make mischief in the world, while Jesus ruled His Kingdom.

I prayed fervently that I would manage to get into the Kingdom. I prayed to have a converted mind, prayed for God's Holy Spirit. I desperately feared being left behind when Jesus returned. Even though I went to church every week, even though I knelt each night at my bed and prayed, even though I tried not to be rebellious, there was no guarantee that I would get into the Kingdom.

The Kingdom, God's harvest of souls, was exemplified in the annual harvest holiday of the Hebrew Bible, the Feast of Tabernacles, or Sukkot. It represented the Second Resurrection, the time when those who had died without knowing the Truth would have a chance to be saved. I did not know then or for a very long time that our holidays were Jewish holidays, and that modern-day Jews continued to celebrate them. I assumed God had created them just for the church.

My parents took us out of school to celebrate the eight-day holiday of Sukkot. My mother woke up her ten kids before dawn and bundled us into the car to drive to one of the church's Feast sites. When we pulled onto the empty road, the stars were not yet absorbed into the still-gray sky, and I imagined that only God and my family were awake.

One year we drove to the church's Feast site in Texas, another to Georgia, and once to the Poconos, but mostly we went closer to home, to the Lake of the Ozarks in Missouri, staying at church-arranged hotel rentals and cabins. Just as the Israelites had not lived in permanent homes during those forty years in the desert after they escaped slavery in Egypt, we'd left our physical homes behind to remind us that they were temporal, but God's Kingdom was forever.

In what almost amounted to a caravan, church members from around the country flooded the Feast sites with our beat-up cars. Every morning, clad in our Sabbath dresses and suits, we left our motel and drove off to attend services in the immense, aluminum-sided, unheated "tabernacle building," where we sat from oldest to youngest on the typical hard, metal folding chairs.

Throughout the eight days of the Feast of Tabernacles, we heard sermons and sermonettes, morning and afternoon, from ministers and preaching elders and evangelists from around the country. At the top of the page of our notebooks we wrote the dates—October 8, 1968; October 17, 1970; October 15, 1973—and the titles of the sermons: "The Coming Armageddon," or "The Plan of God," and the name of the minister, preaching elder, or evangelist such as Mr. Waterhouse, whose legendary rambling, four-hour sermons filled me with dread.

Mr. Waterhouse had a genial southern accent, made self-deprecating jokes about his golf game, but leapt from topic to topic in a way that was difficult to follow. At the end of services, the various deacons passed around an offering basket. Down each aisle it went, and we all put in our money, some sealing it in envelopes, others laying the bills in a pile. We were incredibly proud when they tallied the money and told us the next day that we had exceeded last year's offering.

It would be over thirty years until I discovered what Mr. Armstrong was doing with that money. The tithe that was intended to go to the needy instead went to his Rolls Royce cars, his private airplane, Swiss bank accounts, gold mines in Africa, extensive real estate, gold, silver, and much, much more.

At that time, though, it did not seem wrong to me that Mr. Armstrong was running around the world on his private jet while church members subsisted on food stamps and welfare. My own family replaced broken windows with squares of cardboard, just so we could continue to send our tithes to the church.

During those eight days of Sukkot, in the company only of other church members, I felt like I was one of the Israelites who'd left Egypt: special. To imagine that I was like the biblical Hebrews, part of a select group that God Himself had chosen, was intoxicating.

In 1969, when I was eight years old, in preparation for the world ending, my parents sold our big house on Main Street in Huntingburg. My older siblings were in high school and had friends. The last thing they wanted was to move out to a farmhouse in the boonies of Jasper. I was starting third grade and had no clear idea how my life would change, nor did I know why we were moving. What I did know was that worldly goods were unnecessary because Jesus was soon to arrive.

Our new home was a dilapidated two-story farmhouse. Cornfields flanked the house, and behind us were woods where we played in the creek. On summer afternoons, Abby, Liz, John, Sarah, and I packed peanut-butter-and-honey sandwiches on whole-wheat bread and trudged down the path, past the mulberry tree, across the swampy bottom, and into the woods, where we stayed for the day. We dug in the smelly sand alongside the creek, and made dungeons and castles and moats, placing sticks in the castles for flags and flat pieces of bark in the sides for windows. If the water was warm enough, we ran through the shallow creek, splashing and yelling and screaming, "Clear the wa-aay!"

My older brothers liked to hunt and trap, and set up traps for mink and muskrat, though the occasional raccoon was caught in them as well. Ed ignored when deer season began and ended and hunted as he wished. He even liked to tease the younger siblings by chasing us around with the skinned carcasses. The game warden was tipped off, came to the house, and found the carcasses of deer that had been hunted out of season. Ed spent several weekends in jail as a result. He was definitely the one my parents would eat.

In the basement, a wood and coal furnace provided heat. For a long while, we had no washing machine, so we relied on a wringer washer to do our laundry. Each piece of clothing had to be fed between the rollers individually to squeeze out the excess water. I loved to feel the rollers pull a sock or a pair of underpants from my hands and watch it squish and suck the water out of it so it resembled a flattened cartoon character.

An indoor wash line was strung across the back of the basement so we could dry our clothes downstairs during winter. In the corner, a small, dark, spider-webby room dubbed the "root cellar" contained shelves full of peanut butter and jars of olives. Nobody liked them, but they were free, army-surplus food. The same room housed my mother's homemade goods: jars of blackberry and grape and elderberry jelly, as well as canned apple butter, tomatoes, beets, pickles, and other assorted vegetables.

Wooden barrels held my father's various homemade wines—elderberry, blackberry, strawberry, and grape from the grapes we picked at my father's aunt Almeda's and which we delighted in crushing with our hands. The church would kick a member out for smoking cigarettes, but drinking alcohol was fine as long as it was in moderation. Apparently Jesus drank wine but didn't smoke.

With three bedrooms upstairs, two down, and one bathroom, we played musical beds. In Huntingburg, I'd slept with Abby and Mary and Liz. In Jasper, it was mix and match. Sometimes I shared a room with Wanda and Mary, but two years after we moved in, Wanda had graduated from high school and moved out. Then it was Liz and Sarah, while Mary and Abby were together.

The two floors of the house were filled with stuff, lots of stuff, both because twelve people lived there, and also because my mother compulsively collected and kept items from Goodwill, yard sales, and relatives. Broken furniture, bags full of huge granny underwear, musty-smelling books—if it was free or practically free, my Depression-era mother took it. I often thought how deprived my mother must have felt as a child that she couldn't let go of anything.

Once, my father saw a laundry basket filled with jeans to be patched and shouted, "Mama, what's this? What if Jesus Christ appeared right now, would this be any way for a Christian to live? Junk stacked to high heaven? Let me tell you, Satan and his demons have got their feet in this door, and we have got to get our house in order!"

My mother argued in her defense, "It's my stuff, and you have a bunch of junk cars outside. Why don't you do something about them?"

My father said, "Mama, you don't know what the heck you're talking about. You're talking out of your rear end again. I think you got a demon in you, I really do." Said with complete seriousness. I looked at my mother anew and wondered if the demon would manifest itself somehow. I couldn't imagine how a demon might affect my even-tempered, kind mother. Later, my mother muttered, "He's got the demon."

What remained consistent was my mother's free-floating parenting style versus my father's attempt to keep everything under control. He was the head of the household, and on his shoulders had been placed a particular burden—to keep his kids in church, to make certain we did the right thing, and to ensure that we all made it into the Kingdom.

To my father's dismay, our house was a teeming, frothing cauldron of meanness. We stomped, slammed doors, kicked, screamed, punched, wrestled, chased, and threatened one another on a daily basis. We locked each other out of the house, chased each other up trees, called each other ugly, stupid, dumb shit, asshole, and pig. We teased and tortured, threw hairbrushes and baseballs at one another. We pulled chairs out from under each other, laughing hysterically when someone fell onto the floor. We made off with the peanut-butter sandwich that a sibling (John) had painstakingly prepared for himself. We were territorial over our own things, but ignored our siblings' boundaries. We fought over the one telephone (a party line shared with our neighbors down the road) and, especially, the one bathroom.

"Get out, you've been in there over five minutes."

"Are you reading comic books or did you fall in?"

Then, when the bathroom hog exited, there was a mad rush for the hotspot.

"I was here first."

"No, I was."

"You lost your place in line when you got the phone."

"Sarah saved my place."

"No fair saving someone else's place."

"That's not true, the rule is you can save someone else's place if they're only gone for five minutes."

We never said excuse me, please, or I'm sorry. We threatened to beat each other to a pulp, to whup the other, to choke, disfigure, or maim the other. Yet, despite how vigorously and aggressively we teased and taunted one another, we knew that we were in this together. Only we could ever truly understand what it was to be a member of this specific clan bound by blood and history. So we settled in to wait on Portersville Road for Jesus to return and rapture us to Petra. Soon. It would happen soon, but only if we continued to support God's work. My mother and my father were consistent about one thing: the world was coming to an end, and only through the church could they make it to salvation.

CHAPTER 5

One summer evening in 1969, after running around with our cousins all Sunday at our grandparents' farm, my sister Abby's face suddenly became bright red. Her heart beat erratically, and she developed a strange twitch on one side of her body. Sixteen months older than me, Abby was nine years old.

At Grandma Himsel's insistence, my parents took her to a doctor, which was against church doctrine. Because of Abby's twitches, she was first diagnosed with chorea. Then they said it was rheumatic fever, which could, in rare cases, lead to chorea. Finally, my mother explained that Abby had a hole in her heart that made her tired. No medical treatment was available, or so we were told, so she swallowed fistfuls of vitamins every day. The church and my mother remained convinced that anything natural was from God and was thus better than any medicine, which was man-made.

Abby weakened quickly and missed a whole year of school. On bad days, she could barely walk to the bathroom. Once my best friend, the one I played jacks with on the floor, the one who was invariably on my team for hide-and-seek, her illness created a distance that I was too young to understand, too young to surmount. She was on a different side now. And I could only look at her from across an emotional chasm.

Abby's face lost all color, and her stomach swelled up, filled with fluid her heart couldn't pump out. It became harder and harder to look at her. This wasn't my fearless older sister who jumped out of the swing when it was at its highest and, when she fell to the ground, picked herself up and laughed.

The minister came over many times to anoint Abby. He smudged olive oil on her forehead and, holding her head between his hands, asked God to heal her. Every other week my parents requested a new prayer cloth from church headquarters. My mother held it against Abby's forehead, much like the ministers anointed her with oil, and silently offered a prayer.

Abby and I had taken bubble baths together, patting the bubbles onto each other's faces to form moustaches and beards, which, I privately feared, made us look like that pagan Santa Claus. We'd caught lightning bugs on summer evenings and stuck them on the end of sticks, brandishing them about like flashlights. We'd held hands, leaned back, and turned around and around and around in the living room, delighting in getting dizzier and dizzier until we fell down. Abby and I had slept in the same bed listening to our father read us bedtime stories until he said goodnight, sleep tight, and tucked us in, leaving the bathroom light on for Abby.

Now, because of her heart condition, Abby could no longer race me around the house or chase me during a game of frozen tapper. She was not the sturdy child with rosy cheeks, shiny reddish-brown hair, hazel eyes, and a big sparkly smile. She was lethargic, and because she couldn't play outside with us, my mother bought her paint-by-number oil paintings of dogs and rural scenes to work on so she wouldn't get bored.

The four little ones—me, Liz, John, and Sarah—trudged down to the creek and played in the sand and built our castles without Abby. Sometimes I told them I didn't want to go, and I would stay at home, spread a blanket on the floor underneath Abby's hospital bed that she periodically used. While she very seriously and quietly painted the two collies, filling in first all the tan of their fur, then the blue sky, I entertained myself with a book or with my Barbies. I flew them through the air and took them on adventures in distant lands.

My parents also relaxed the no-television rule and purchased a black-and-white television with rabbit ears and spotty reception so Abby could watch television during the day. We sat on the couch and watched *Gilligan's Island*, and I very pragmatically wondered how it was that the castaways kept blowing the chances they had to get rescued. When *Perry Mason* was on, I slid closer to John and grabbed his hand when the scary music began. It took very little to frighten me, just a few bars of "bu-dum-dum-dum."

We watched *The Brady Bunch*, noting that Florence Henderson grew up in nearby Dale, Indiana. She and Abe Lincoln, whose formative years were spent in Little Pigeon Creek, less than sixty miles south of us, were Hoosiers that we were proud of.

The Waltons premiered on television in 1972. A family drama set during the Depression, it chronicled the lives of seven children, their parents, and their grandparents in the Blue Ridge Mountains. While the family fought, they always made up and discussed things rationally. It was a wonderful, feel-good show, but even more far-fetched than *I Dream of Jeannie*, which we watched furtively when my father wasn't around. Anything with supernatural elements was obviously off-limits, according to the church. Demons.

When my father came home, he invariably sat down in his easy chair for the *CBS Evening News with Walter Cronkite*. Whether it was the casualties in the Vietnam War, the 1969 moon landing, Martin Luther King's death in 1968, or the antiwar riots in Chicago, Cronkite signed off with his trademark "And that's the way it is, Monday, September 11, 1972," or whatever the date. My father's inevitable comment was, "Well, this old world can't last much longer, that's for sure."

We attended church services less and less often, because Abby couldn't go. My older brothers and sisters quietly did whatever they wanted on the Sabbath. They had after-school jobs and made their own money, so they had cars and went to basketball and football games on Friday nights. My brother Jim was on the wrestling team, and he competed on Friday nights and Saturdays. Ed was on the high school basketball team, and Paul played for the middle school team. Sometimes my mother attended both the wrestling matches and the basketball games on the Sabbath. I worried about her salvation. Was she breaking the Sabbath, just by being in attendance?

Wanda wore makeup and went to the Calumet, the local dance hall that featured rock 'n' roll bands and where you could buy beer without showing ID. She went to the drive-in with boyfriends.

As the only ones in the county who belonged to the Worldwide Church of God, it wasn't at all easy to have a social life while practicing the church's doctrines.

My father sporadically yelled at my older siblings for their transgressions, while my mother insisted, "They're just going to a get-together at a friend's house." No one was fooled, least of all my father, who was most preoccupied with making a living for his family, while worrying about Abby, but those little lies enabled us to live with one another.

The rest of us—the younger ones—continued to observe the Sabbath, and we didn't shop or participate in events on Friday night through Saturday. Nor did we eat pork or unclean meat or fish. In our own way, we remained in the church, even if we rarely attended services. And, of course, my parents tithed. Not tithing kept you out of the Kingdom.

From the moment that Abby got sick, we prayed for her, ending our Friday night Bible studies kneeling at the couch and chairs in the living room and, hands folded and heads bowed, we prayed to God that His will be done, that she would be healed, in Jesus's name we prayed, Amen.

We had faith that God would heal her, just as we had faith that this world was coming to an end and a better world was around the corner.

CHAPTER 6

Once a month, the bookmobile visited Boone Township School, the three-room brick schoolhouse I attended from third to fifth grades from 1969 to 1972 after we moved to Jasper. Surrounded by fields, a blacktop road wound past the school, and our isolation was broken now and then by a tractor's hum or a pickup truck rattling along. Although any vehicles were cause for celebration, the green-and-white bookmobile conjured the free-spirited adventurer I dreamed of becoming. On the days the bookmobile came, I was on the edge of my seat waiting for our teacher to say, "The bookmobile is here now. Remember, walk, don't run!" The row of first-graders, then the row of second-graders, and finally the kids in my third-grade class took turns entering the bookmobile to choose our allotted four books.

It was dim inside and smelled like old paper. Being inside was like actually entering a well-loved, dog-eared book. One of my favorites was a thick book with a picture of a mother and five children on the cover. Back in my classroom, I lifted the wooden desktop and placed the book inside. Then, while my teacher taught the story of King Midas, I quietly raised the desktop and immersed myself in the 1880s and *The Five Little Peppers and How They Grew*. Undisturbed by the sounds of the teacher and the other children, I spent the afternoon with widowed Mamsie and her brood, who said peculiar things like, "My whockety!"

I made my way through all of Louisa May Alcott's *Little Men* and *Little Women* books, as well as Laura Ingalls Wilder and her *Little House in the Big Woods* series. In nineteenth-century domestic dramas about families who prevailed despite hardship and loss, the authors drew on their own lives to write their novels and thus were more intimate and honest than the Trixie Belden and Boxcar Children books I'd favored.

In fifth grade, I migrated to the back of the bookmobile, where I discovered the Hardy Boys and Nancy Drew mysteries, and a whole section devoted to the doctor/nurse romances of Cherry Ames and Clara Barton, as well as Donna Parker, special agent. Although I identified with the Peppers because they were poor and their lives were filled with adversity, the romances suggested something completely new: that a girl didn't have to choose between a career and a boyfriend. She could have both, a notion the church vehemently decried as impossible, even heretical and anti-God's plan.

For three years, I moved with the same nine classmates from one room to another, from one wooden desk to another. But when I opened a book, I could visit Heidi in Switzerland, share the adventures of the Boxcar Children, or time-travel to nineteenth-century America's frontier. I was far removed from my sick sister and also from the world that was about to end. I imagined exotic places filled with drama, different in every sense from my taciturn, proud, stubborn, stolid German community who never asked forgiveness and never forgave. They were as uncompromising as the language they still considered their own. In German, the verb was always second in a sentence, there was no way around it, and never try to bend the rules or change them. Obey.

I have often thought that the bookmobile contributed not only to my love of reading and passion to write, but also to my belief that the written word equaled possibilities. Civilization. I was a dreamy ten-year-old, impatient to grow up and board a plane whose wings would lift me far, far away. But for the moment, books would have to do.

When I looked out the school window, I imagined a nebulous future that lay somewhere beyond the fields. I fantasized about being either a librarian or a gypsy on the open road. With my platinum blonde hair, pale skin, and blue eyes, I couldn't pass for a gypsy, which seemed truly unfair. Yet my gypsy soul might be nurtured by becoming a librarian. I was enamored with the town librarian who, contrary to stereotype, wore short, short skirts and sported poufy, brittle bleached-blonde hair, had talon-like, blood-red fingernails, and whose eyes, lips, and cheeks bore the unmistakable stain of forbidden, harlot-ish makeup. The librarian clearly hadn't been called by God. At this point, the church's position on makeup was set forth in another booklet, *Truth About Makeup:*

> . . . *the act of painting the face (whether eyes, cheeks, or lips) is falsifying, intended to DECEIVE, an expression of VANITY which is the very basis of all sin, and therefore it becomes, with a plain THUS SAITH THE LORD, a SIN!*

What I would be when I grew up and where I would live was, however, probably a moot point. The world was going to end in just a few years, in 1975, and I would not have time to get married, have children, travel, or become an adult. Live a life.

From 1969 to 1972, Abby was homeschooled. She had lain in a hospital bed in the living room much of the time, and my father often had to carry her to the bathroom. She looped her stark, skinny arms around his sun-weathered, strong neck, and he set her down gently in the bathroom, returning to carry her back to bed when she'd finished.

I missed the person she had been, my playmate. Seeing Abby so weak, so ill, was unbearably sad. I often wanted to turn away from her. Looking at her, I felt the same constriction in my chest as when the ministers screamed and shouted about the End Times.

She had to use a wheelchair, and I pushed her around the house, as if I were pushing a small child on a swing. There were more prayer cloths, more anointings, and then, a few months later, she seemed better. Abby was out of the wheelchair, and we baked oatmeal cookies together. Sometimes she ventured outside, a white wraith, and though she was not allowed to run, she sort of chased me, and I ran slowly and let her catch me.

Social workers came over to check on her, and my mother warned us not to answer questions. The social workers asked my mother if Abby had seen a doctor lately, and she said yes, she had, though I didn't recall Abby having seen a doctor in the past few years. In fact, the talk at home was all about God healing her.

The church's publication *Does God Heal Today?* claimed that the medical profession was pagan in origin. Armstrong preached that "Poison plus poison equals poison." If you had faith and adhered to church doctrine, you would be healed. If you weren't healed, it indicated a lack of faith or having done something that displeased God and made God vengeful enough to choose not to answer your prayers. Armstrong's son Richard had died after an automobile accident in the 1950s because he hadn't received medical care. His wife, too, died because she refused to go to a doctor when she suffered from an obstructed bowel. No one mentioned that faith had not healed either Armstrong's son or his wife.

––––––––

In 1972, it appeared as if our prayers had been answered. Abby was well enough to attend sixth grade with me. Boone Township School had ceased operating, and we transferred to the middle school in Ireland, a few miles away.

In the spring of 1973, Abby joined us mushroom hunting in the woods behind our house. In May, around Abby's thirteenth birthday, she walked along with us behind the barn and down the path to the mulberry tree, then back into the woods to the creek where we'd built our intricate sand castles, and we checked our brothers' raccoon and mink traps. Next to me, I could see that Abby was happy, even if she was breathing hard. There was a trace of healthy red in her pale cheeks, and just for a moment, I had a brief glimpse of the girl who'd sat companionably with me, coloring our Disney workbooks.

At my brother Jim's high school graduation party in June, even our grandparents, looking at Abby, had to admit that a miracle had occurred. Our faith had been rewarded. She'd been healed. This would be the third time God had intervened on our behalf—after Sarah's birth, and when I'd had pneumonia.

On the morning of July 2, 1973, our mother took us to town. Mary was attending a drivers' training class, and Liz, John, Sarah, and I were enrolled in a summer arts and crafts program. Abby was tired. She didn't want to ride along. She'd been more tired than usual the past few weeks. The heat, we figured. My mother said, "Sugarplum, are you sure you'll be okay here by yourself?" She muttered yes. My brother Ed, who was sixteen at that time, would be home later in the morning, my mother reassured Abby.

I went into the room Abby now shared with Mary, to borrow her sandals. On their walls were David Cassidy and Bobby Sherman posters that they had pulled out of the centerfold of *16* magazine; a Lee Majors poster hung on the door—every night, Mary and Abby kissed the Six-Million-Dollar Man goodnight. "I'm taking your sandals, okay?" I grabbed them. Abby simply looked at me from the hospital bed. Didn't respond. Grouchy, I figured.

The summer program was for poor kids, and we played games sometimes, but this particular day, we were learning about the food pyramid and how to cook healthy foods. Popcorn didn't need to be slathered in butter, and we should have something green on our plate each meal. I felt like the teacher was talking down to us, as if we were not only poor but stupid.

When we returned home in the early afternoon, I bounded into the house after Mary to tell Abby a joke I'd heard at the summer program: "What's green and red and goes sixty miles an hour?" Answer: "A frog in a blender."

Mary went in first, put her books on the dresser, then screamed, "Mother! Mother!" Our mother, Liz, John, Sarah, and I rushed into their bedroom. Abby sat in her chair, her head tilted back. Her eyes were wide, the irises rolled up. Her mouth was slightly open. Her hands lay limply on the armrests.

Our mother went straight to the chair, felt for Abby's pulse, her heartbeat, pressed her hand against Abby's forehead, and said, "She's dead."

"She's not dead!" Mary kept saying. "Do something, you have to do something!"

"There's nothing we can do."

I turned away and went out the door and into the kitchen, such a normal kitchen, dirty plates from breakfast in the sink, towel hanging over a chair, wastebasket half full, wall calendar scribbled with my father's notes about how much it had rained and the daily temperature. Tupperware container of food scraps for the compost pile. Everything was the way we'd left it, the way it should be. And the clock was ticking. I was mesmerized by the second hand. It was a little after one. It was now seventeen minutes since we'd found Abby, and the second hand simply went 'round and 'round, as if nothing had happened. A normal kitchen, and Abby lay dead in the next room.

My mother called our father at work and, since we shared the same party line with several families on the Portersville Road who, if they picked up their phone quietly, could listen in on whoever was using the phone, pretty soon all of the neighbors had heard the news. My mother called her parents, Grandma Himsel, and the aunts and uncles, and in that same calm voice delivered the news. Sarah, John, and Liz sat together on the couch, sometimes crying, then silent. Ed came home—he'd been back for lunch before going to the woods to set his traps, and had checked on Abby then. "She was okay when I left, I gave her some Sprite. She seemed okay," he repeated. "What happened?"

"We don't know these things," our mother said. "God doesn't always tell us." This had long been my mother's standard answer for anything we didn't understand, from where the angels lived to why people die. Of course, even I knew that God didn't need to inform us of His plans, but I thought Abby had been healed. I thought it was cruel of God to trick us into believing.

It all seemed removed from me as if I had stepped into some strange world in which I knew the characters and heard and understood exactly what they were saying, but in which I was not at all a part. I felt like we were stumbling around, trying to figure out this new, senseless landscape, which couldn't possibly be.

I went upstairs, lay across the bed, opened a book, and read. The sun streamed in through the curtainless windows. The heat felt harsh yet comforting against my face and bare legs. I was not going back downstairs. I would stay in bed, alone and quiet with my book, until it was all over.

Books had long had the power to transport me, connect me to the past, to others, and enable me to travel freely across the boundaries of time and space. Books both opened a window into other worlds beyond the cornfields and allowed me to retreat within myself and block out the world: Abby, in a wheelchair or lying in her hospital bed, a frail, pale shadow of the girl who had sat with me in the backyard and wove necklaces and bracelets of clover with me. Who had pretended to be Batman, a white cloth diaper safety-pinned around her neck, jumping fearlessly from the top step of the porch. And now, Abby, downstairs. Dead. And I read.

An hour later, I heard my father's broken, "Oh, no! Oh, no!"

The sun waned. The commotion below quieted. I decided to go back downstairs. Weeping, my father held Abby's thin body in his arms on the couch. His sobs shook her so that her arms dropped and dangled. The ambulance arrived. The sober-faced young medic tried to get my father to release Abby to him. He couldn't let go. Then the funeral director himself sat on the couch with my father and spoke to him quietly in German, his mother tongue, the tongue of his ancestors, of his home and his childhood. It calmed him. Reached him. Finally, and painfully, as if he were giving up a part of himself, my father allowed them to take Abby from his arms.

In Abby's room, her jewelry box remained on the dresser. The game of Parcheesi that we loved to play was still on the closet shelf, along with the Dating Game and the creepy-crawly bugs kit and the Easy-Bake Oven. On her chair lay *Little Women*. It was as if she'd walked out the door, leaving her things behind, never to return, as if Jesus had picked her up in the middle of the day and carted her off. And we'd been left behind.

———————

At the funeral home, we sat in a long row, much as we had before Abby had gotten sick and we'd attended church weekly. Except Abby wasn't sitting with us. She was in the coffin. Alone. Friends and neighbors and family walked past her, paying their respects. It seemed obscene that everyone was allowed to look at her when she was dead. The coffin reminded me of the wooden lost-and-found box at church, in which one might find ChapStick, a lone glove, a worn Bible or notebook, a few Matchbox cars. Lost, separated from the one to whom they belonged.

The minister read from the books of Ecclesiastes and Revelation. A time to live and a time to die. God's will. Ways of man, not the ways of God. Ashes to ashes, dust to dust. Our Father's house has many rooms, and death is much like passing from one room into another, but you are still in the same house. I saw myself pounding on a shut door, a door I feared I'd never be able to open.

In the church, you weren't baptized until you were an adult, when you could recognize that your way of life was wrong, repent of your sins, and consciously choose to accept Jesus Christ as your Savior. Because Abby had died without being baptized, she would be in the Second Resurrection in the Second Millennium, depicted in the autumn harvest festival, the Feast of Tabernacles, when the dead were harvested from the earth and would rise and get to know Christ. Were I baptized in the Worldwide Church of God, and remained in it, I would be in the First Resurrection (the First Millennium), and I would be there to meet Abby when she was resurrected a thousand years later. If I didn't get baptized and left the church, I would be thrown into the Lake of Fire in the Third Millennium and be separated from my family forever.

Abby's arms were sticks. She looked chicken-like, pasty and cold. It didn't seem as if she were really my sister, more like a wax figure or some mannequin dressed up to look like her.

Was Abby's death God's fault? Or had we not had enough faith, not prayed hard enough, I wondered? Our father had said that it was his fault—he hadn't kept the Sabbath a few times, he'd worked on Saturday, and God was punishing him for that. Or had the demons simply been stronger than our efforts? So focused on watching for Jesus's return, I'd had no idea that someone in my own family was soon to depart from the earth.

I stood over her and stared. I would imprint her features on my memory, my heart, never to forget. Across her nose was a sprinkling of light brown freckles. She had silky brown hair and a narrow face. A little blush on her cheeks. Blush, as if she were going to a party? Blush, for a thirteen-year-old girl whose church denounced makeup as harlot-ish? Her light brown eyebrows arched delicately over her closed eyes. When no one was watching, I opened one of her eyelids. I just saw the whites. She was not looking at me.

I'd been numb, but then the tears came. They poured from my eyes. I could not control them, could hardly see, and the pain in my chest exploded into sobs. I went back to my seat, then back up to the coffin, then to the bathroom to blow my nose and try to pull myself together.

We were somber, polite, and shook hands when neighbors and family came through the line: "You have my sympathy, you have my sympathy . . . sympathy . . . sympathy . . . ," they said. There was Abby's teacher, Mrs. Danhafer, and some of our classmates, the science teacher, the bus kids, the neighbors from down Portersville Road, some church families, my grandparents and aunts and uncles, all gathered together like we would gather on Sunday evenings at the farm for supper.

The minister offered the final prayer, the coffin was closed, and we followed the hearse to Haysville. The procession of cars moved slowly, reluctantly, lights flashing, behind the hearse. The oncoming cars, the Fords and Chevys and Buicks with strangers inside, silently and respectfully pulled to the side of the road when they caught sight of the hearse and the blinking lights, as was the custom when a funeral snaked its way through town. They were acknowledging our loss without words, but with their actions, and would let us go on our way, unimpeded. It was the first time I really understood the kindness of the gesture and the decency of strangers toward other strangers whose family had been ripped asunder and who needed metaphorical space to breathe.

It hit me then, like it had not hit me before: Abby wasn't coming back. I'd had faith for so long that Abby would one day be the girl she used to be—the girl I'd had staring contests with; the girl who'd chased me through trails we'd made in the snow. Like each other's shadows we had run, blood hot and coursing through our veins, noses dripping and red-cheeked against the white snow. Under the pale blue sky, we'd run, and life then was cold snow and frozen feet and fingers thawing under the hot tap water.

On that hot, hot July day, I realized that it was all over. There was no hope. Abby was put into the earth close to my grandfather, resting with generations of Himsels. We returned home to a different home. The world I'd known until then had ended.

CHAPTER 7

"Here's how I'm going to decorate my house in Paris," my new church friend Alise revealed. It was 1973, and I was eleven, Alise thirteen. My parents were attending church every Saturday again. My father believed, and would remain convinced throughout his lifetime, that it was his lack of rigorously observing the Sabbath that had killed his daughter.

Alise lived in Princeton, about an hour from Jasper, and years later she confessed that her interest in being my new friend was because "You had a sister who'd just died, so I was morbidly fascinated."

On that first visit to her house, Alise impressed me by showing me her Parisian house, which she had constructed from a cardboard box. She'd divided it into rooms, and in each room she had placed scraps of fabric for rugs and curtains. She'd cut pictures from magazines and placed them in folders, and the chandeliers, gold-plated faucets, Persian carpets, ornate furniture, and heavy drapes served as the model for her future home. "The bathrooms," she explained, "will all have gold faucets and gold bathtubs, and the walls will be purple. What about your house, Angela? What's it going to look like?"

When I imagined myself as an adult, where I lived and what I put on my walls were not on my fantasy radar. Rather, I dreamed of something far more intangible and seductive than plush carpets, something that I barely could formulate even to myself: freedom. Freedom to read all night. To travel beyond Indiana. To meet people who looked different from me, who spoke other languages. To see other landscapes besides cornfields and woods. To explore externally what had thus far been a vague, internal vision of other places, like those I read about in books. To hear language as foreign as the "My whockety!" in *The Five Little Peppers and How They Grew*. I didn't expect to be able to have any of that, of course, since the world was soon to end. But privately, I entertained all sorts of outrageous dreams.

"What are you going to be when you're older?" Alise persisted. "I'm going to be like Barbara Walters. A television newscaster. And live in Paris."

Alise's willingness to admit to wanting something more just for herself, something more in this world, Satan's world, was decidedly odd to me. The meek, not the brash, would inherit the earth. If I were to ask someone if she wanted a Coke, the correct response was, "It doesn't matter." Saying, "Yes, I do want a Coke," was being forward. "It doesn't matter," meant yes, I do, without actually stating it out loud. For Midwestern, German-American Christians, desires were private matters, never exposed to anyone else lest they accuse you of being greedy.

While I had absolutely no expectation that any of my dreams would become reality, Alise's daring was intoxicating and encouraging. I decided to take the plunge and confess my own, until then barely formulated, ambition: "I'm going to be a writer." I lived my life in a landscape inside my head, in my imagination. My heroes, my role models, were people like Louisa May Alcott and Laura Ingalls Wilder, women who'd defied their societal roles and had had the courage to write their world. To tell stories just for pleasure, unlike the Bible, whose curious stories captivated me, but were intended to teach and to warn.

I wanted to write about distant places and foreign people. Anything but the drudgery and ordinariness of my day-to-day, peel-potatoes-for-supper, go-to-church-on-Saturday, visit-grandparents-on-Sunday life.

Alise said she wanted to write a memoir. The oldest of five, Alise came from a colorful family, and I found her story fascinating. The church had "disfellowshipped" her family—forbidden them from attending services—for six months because of her mother's drinking problem. Her fun-loving mother, Alice, screamed and shouted, drank and cursed, and then, in the next moment, laughed and hugged. I found Alice riveting, as she was a direct contrast to my calm, even-tempered, capable mother. Alise's parents had never married, and I never met her father. Alise rarely saw him, which she said was fine by her.

Alise often entertained me by imitating her grandma, who also attended the church and who, on the surface, was soft-spoken and well-mannered. Her grandma kept an ever-present smile on her face, and her hand was extended in an eternal handshake. Alise would stick her right hand out and give me a sickening, sweet, toothy smile—"the grandma smile."

Her grandma often babysat her five grandchildren for days at a time, during which she woke them up at three in the morning to weed the garden under floodlights. Or, they rose at three to go fishing, with no food or water. "She has no tolerance for talking while working," Alise told me. "We have to do all of our chores—gardening, taking care of the chickens, goats, and geese, bringing in water and the laundry and all of that—in complete silence. If you break the silence, you get a whipping. If she gives you instructions to do something and you forget what they were or whatever, you get a whipping. She tells me all the time, 'You're too stupid to follow directions.'"

Once, as teenagers, when Alise spent the week with me in Jasper, we decided to venture into Satan's den: St. Joseph's Church. Imposing, brown, and Gothic-looking, its spire dominated the skyline. I'd only been there a time or two for family weddings. We thought of St. Joe's practically as a brothel, completely off-limits to those of us in the church, for whom Catholics and the Antichrist were one and the same.

Alise and I walked over the threshold, fearing that our hair would catch on fire, feeling incredibly wicked, and wondering if God or one of His hovering angels was waiting in the doorway to strike us down. I ducked my head as we went through it. Nobody hit me, and I took a quick look at the stained-glass windows and the altar with Jesus hanging from the cross, then Alise and I, giggling nervously, high-tailed it out of the pagan sanctuary.

Late at night on one of my many sleepovers at Alise's house, we lay in her canopy bed, a complete and utter black silence around us. Alise regaled me breathlessly with stories of vampires, adamant that not only did they exist, but they had been sighted in southern Indiana.

"So what can we do?" I asked, fearful, doubtful, excited.

"Put garlic around the windowsill. Vampires hate that," she said with the same certainty she'd announced her career and the color of her walls.

I had assumed that vampires were made-up entities, but if they existed, they surely belonged to the demonic realm, which was deliciously forbidden and wonderful. However, it was possible that vampires had been created by the devil. Just as a demon might slip into one's house, so might vampires. I decided you could never be too careful, not with vampires or demons. I insisted that Alise go downstairs, get garlic, and drape it around the windowsill. Despite my doubts, I was transfixed by stories and had a hard time distinguishing between truth and fiction.

After listening to Alise's big plans for her life, I acknowledged to myself that I wanted more. Not that I deserved more, but that I wanted more. Not more money. It was harder after all for a rich man to get into heaven than it was for a camel to go through the eye of a needle. But more. I wanted to know more, understand more, meet more people from other countries, perhaps even Hindus who worshipped cows. And that was the dilemma: how to live in the pagan, demon-infested world without giving up God and the church. I was standing on a precipice, with Satan and the Lake of Fire on one side, salvation and the Place of Safety on the other. Petra-fied.

Many times, the ministers announced that there would be a "special" sermon from Mr. Armstrong. On a movie screen in the Owl's Home, Mr. Armstrong, who bore an uncanny resemblance to Grandma—same white hair and blue eyes and pale skin; same ability to work himself up into a froth—loomed large. I imagined that the special message would be late-breaking news: "We have discovered the Antichrist," or "The world will come to an end at precisely 2 p.m. on October 13, 1977." But no.

Instead, Mr. Armstrong pounded his fist and screamed in his signature gravelly voice filled with anger and reprimand, "All of these material goods, brethren, are worthless! And I am deeply disappointed that YOU HAVE NOT GIVEN THEM UP! I CANNOT CALL YOU COWORKERS IN CHRIST UNLESS YOU ARE WILLING TO SUPPORT HIS WORK!" The congregation remained respectfully silent as Mr. Armstrong berated us from afar, screaming, pleading, his voice trembling and wavering.

He also sent out monthly "coworker" letters to members. In them, he pleaded for money, asking members to borrow from banks and empty their own bank accounts for the church. Many did.

In 1974, Herbert Armstrong convened a doctrinal committee, which concluded that while the Bible appeared to forbid divorce, it could and should be read differently. In one of his monthly coworker letters, Armstrong explained why he was changing the divorce and remarriage doctrine: "This church has always confessed and corrected error."

After that, the married church couple who'd been forced to separate were allowed to live together with their children.

The doctrinal committee also changed the day that Pentecost should be observed. Instead of counting fifty days after the start of Passover, they started the count on the Saturday after Passover, so Pentecost always landed seven weeks and a day later, which was a Sunday. That upset my father greatly. In principle, he was opposed to any holy day landing on Sunday, the "so-called Christian" Sabbath. Only people in the Worldwide Church of God were real Christians. All others were "so-called Christians." And Sunday represented everything he hated about so-called Christianity and its pagan, Roman roots.

In addition, interracial marriage was tacitly accepted, men were allowed to have long hair and grow sideburns, and women could wear dresses above their knees. The makeup prohibition was lifted just in time for my teenage years, and out I ran to Ben Franklin, the local five-and-dime. Within weeks I had stockpiled a stash of mascara, an eyelash curler, eye shadows ranging from shimmery blue to deeper purple, both bubblegum and watermelon Bonne Bell lip gloss, Cover Girl foundation and blush.

My mother inexplicably came home with little white tester tubes of Avon lipsticks. These free samples went in the bathroom closet, and every day, I traced the waxy, hot-pink lipstick across my girlish lips and it transformed me into, if not a woman, then at least someone less mousy. Being an Avon lady was, I thought, something to aspire to, even if it still seemed a little sinful. To carry around that makeup all day, to be able at any moment, just on a whim, to smudge on the gray or the blue eye shadow. Or to rim my eyes in black liner, to draw the line out ever so slightly and create the illusion of cat eyes . . . Could life be any more blissful than to be able, with the flick of a wand, to transform myself into someone else? Exactly. It could not.

The church also changed the ruling on seeking medical attention. If you lacked faith, it was allowed. No one ever brought up whether Abby might have survived had she received medical care. In fact, it was not until many, many years later, long after I had left the church, that it even occurred to me to wonder whether Abby's death had been preventable. It's impossible to know, though when I told a doctor friend about Abby's symptoms, she said, "She probably had a seizure, and she'd had strep. Without antibiotics, it got into her heart valves."

My parents preferred to believe that it was their lack of Sabbath observance that had caused their daughter's death, instead of not providing adequate medical care because of their religious beliefs. If they'd acknowledged that, then the church and its teachings, the choices they'd made, would all be up for grabs. And so they doubled down.

––––––––

The year 1975 came and went, and the world did not end. Gerald Ford, a nice guy from the Midwest, was president and attempting to heal the country of the wounds caused by Nixon's resignation and the Vietnam War. Neither of my parents had voted. The church taught that it was not for us to determine the world's leadership, but for God. Another of Armstrong's hundreds of free publications posited the question: *Election '76—Does It Make Any Difference Who Wins?* The answer to which was an obvious no. God alone should rule, not man. That mentality was also responsible for many good Christians not concerning themselves with the ills of the world: environmental disasters caused by human beings; child labor and poverty; war; famine or disease. When Jesus returned, he would take care of all of that. While my parents didn't vote, they believed that God would put in power men (always men) who would make certain that abortion was illegal and that homosexuals had no rights.

With great disappointment, my father accepted that the oldest five had "gone the way of the world." My sister Wanda, eight years older than me, had recently married a Catholic man. My older brothers, long defiant, had refused to go to church after Abby got sick. They'd been much older when my parents were baptized and, unlike me, recalled a time before the church. It shocked me that they had been able to walk away from the Kingdom, and undoubtedly toward Satan and his demons. Leaving the church was like turning one's back on Moses holding the tablets at the foot of Mount Sinai: "No, thanks, I'd rather be thrown in the Lake of Fire."

Since they were no longer attending church, I worried that they were in the devil's grip. But I turned my attention to more pressing things: my babysitting jobs, which provided enough money for me to buy makeup and white jeans at Ben Franklin; getting a perm from my aunt Lindy so my hair would be fluffy and wavy instead of straight and fine; and spending time at the public library, investigating Keats and Yeats, heavy stuff for a teenager in southern Indiana.

At the same time, my mother decided to get her GED, her high school equivalency diploma, and then she became certified as an EMT. She started working in a nursing home, utilizing her extraordinary ability to listen, empathize, and never scold, and ensure that those in her care felt secure and safe and comfortable. My father fought against her working, but my mother prevailed. "We need the money," she said. We certainly needed the money, but more than that, my mother was happy. Her mouth was no longer set in a thin, grim line. She laughed. She played baseball outside with us. She was once again the young girl who'd jumped into the car with the boys and drove off for nickel Cokes.

In the summer of 1975, I was thirteen years old, lying in the barnyard in a bikini with baby oil slathered all over my white skin in my hopeless pursuit for a shade that was gleaming brown, gypsy-like. I was listening to *Best of My Love* and *Have You Ever Been Mellow* on the radio which, through a series of cords—a fifty-foot electrician's cord, a brown cord that liked to get tangled, and a frayed white cord—I'd managed to plug into the kitchen wall and snake out through the window into the barnyard.

My older sister Mary came out to join me on the blanket I'd spread on the spiky grass. "Did you notice anything new about Mother?" she asked me.

"No," I answered. "Like what?"

"Like, she's getting kind of fat."

"So?" Our mother had never been exactly skinny, so it was hard to tell if she'd gained five or ten pounds.

"And she's been throwing up," Mary continued.

"So?" I was increasingly puzzled and somewhat alarmed. She'd never been sick, to my knowledge. She wouldn't dare.

"I think she's pregnant." Mary finally came out with it. Mary was seventeen years old and usually the most rational, dependable of people, but I suspected she was a little sex-obsessed. My parents had ordered the church's booklet *The Missing Dimension in Sex*, which I'd read looking for something juicy. I was greatly disappointed. The "missing dimension" wasn't some kinky sexual move. It was God.

"That's disgusting! She's not pregnant."

"I think she is," Mary insisted.

"She's too old," I pointed out.

"No, she's not."

"Yes, she is." I felt I was being quite reasonable in the face of Mary's ludicrous theory. Putting aside the absurd possibility that my mother was still having sex at her age, I didn't mention that the world might still be ending this year, even as I increasingly hoped it wasn't true.

"She's forty-two," Mary addressed my point.

"Exactly. She's too old."

We argued back and forth and finally came up with a plan to settle the issue: we would ask her. But how? We were not the kind of family to inquire about somebody else's private business. In this case, it was tantamount to asking our mother if she'd had sex recently, the answer to which we did not want to know.

This was a job for Sarah. Four years younger than me, Sarah was the youngest, the cutest, and ever since her miraculous birth, the favorite. She had a sweet, quiet voice, dirty-blonde hair, and big hazel eyes with dark eyelashes, which I coveted. We had often used Sarah to persuade our father to stop at McDonald's or Kentucky Fried Chicken after church, or to stay longer at our grandparents' farm on Sunday evenings. Sarah would do anything we told her to do because she badly wanted Mary, Liz, and me to include her. Now and then, we did.

We hunted Sarah down in the house and made it sound like a very important and exciting job that only she could do. We had written the question on a piece of paper: "Mother, are you pregnant? Check one: Yes, No, Maybe, None of your business." Sarah obediently took the paper and ran in to our mother, who was lying in bed in the middle of the afternoon, which was unheard of and made me suspicious. Within seconds, we heard her laugh. I assumed she was laughing because we were so off base, and it was such an outrageous question. Sarah raced back and importantly handed us the note. She'd checked: "Yes."

Mary said, "See, I told you!"

Once I got over the initial shock, it seemed absolutely right that a baby should join our home.

Two and a half years after Abby died, Rachael was born. My parents began to laugh again. To heal from the gaping, bleeding wound that Abby had left inside their hearts. To create their home anew.

CHAPTER 8

My life had long been compartmentalized between the secular school world I lived in Monday through Friday and the church world on the weekend. In high school, both because I was older and because high school brought together five middle schools resulting in a freshman class of 300 students—1,200 total for the high school—those worlds became even more polarized. On weekends, I attended Sabbath services on Saturdays (now held at a movie theater instead of the Owl's Home), and there was all the "End of the World," "Woman was made for man, not man for woman" rhetoric I'd heard for years. On Sundays, with Alise and my sisters, there were church hayrides, softball games, car-wash fund-raisers, and swimming at Kentucky Lake.

My older siblings, Wanda, Jim, Ed, and Mary, had graduated from high school, no longer attended church, and were in the local workforce. Paul was three grades above me and came to church with us now and then.

There was a social hierarchy in high school. It wasn't racial, since there were only white, Christian kids in the county, but rather country kids versus city kids. It wasn't overt, nor was it even unkind. It just was. The city kids had lived close enough to one another growing up that they went back and forth between each other's houses. They socialized with each other. Went to the same church. Some belonged to the country club. And they did things I didn't even know existed. They played tennis and piano and took ballet lessons. The country kids, like me and all the kids who'd ridden my bus to Boone Township and then to the Ireland Middle School, dropping off and picking up at farms along the way, tended to be more shy, less sure of ourselves and without the means to do any of these things.

Still, we mixed and matched, and city kids and country kids became friends, even if there remained a certain loyalty to the kids who'd traded their fish sandwiches for Jell-O during lunch at the Boone Township School.

It was 1976, America's bicentennial year. Vietnam and Watergate had hit America's morale and sense of self-righteousness hard. Against this backdrop, I began my all-white, all-Christian, all-American high school, where I became friends with city kids and Catholics and Lutherans. The bus continued to pick us up on the Portersville Road at 7:30 in the morning, and after an hour we arrived at the high school. It was only ten minutes to the school if you were to drive, but my mother worked, so we took the bus.

I decided to take German. Though both of my parents' first language was German, the dark shadow of World War I hovered, and in 1919, Indiana had banned German-language instruction in schools. Teaching German, "the Hun language," was punishable by fine and six months in jail. One publication reminded Americans that the reason the colonies had fought against George III was because, as a German, he was autocratic.

The attempt to purge German culture of any kind from America extended to all things: Beethoven and Wagner were not played in concert halls; German books were burned; sauerkraut was referred to as "liberty cabbage"; German measles were "liberty measles"; and even German shepherds and dachshunds were vilified. There were only twenty-six registered dachshunds in the United States in 1923, after World War I.

So I began to learn the language of my parents and ancestors and to resurrect it on my own tongue.

I was smart, I liked people, I made up stories in my head, and I wrote insightful book reports on *Tom Sawyer* and *Great Expectations*. I remained curious about everyone and everything. I also inherited my grandmother's ability to get worked up over anything, or maybe I learned it from all the Sundays I spent at the farm watching Grandma in a froth over Martin Luther or a bad crop of peppers.

I turned that passion toward the theater and starred in high school and local plays. My first production was *The King and I*. My hair was sprayed black, and I wore thick, brown pancake makeup. I remember thinking that when I was on my own, I would really dye my hair black, changing my external self to reflect my internal image.

The plays were performed on Friday and Saturday nights, and though my father would make a comment about breaking the Sabbath and how he was the one responsible to answer to God on Judgment Day for his family, he didn't prevent me from participating. However, he felt compelled to remind me, "You can't serve two Gods. You can't serve both man and God."

"I don't want to serve anyone," I replied with customary defiance.

I became co-editor of the newspaper, *The Comet*, for which I also wrote a mostly satirical column that even won a few awards. And I joined the speech and debate team and could convince my opponents of anything. My penchant for arguing with the devil served me well. With the church's new, relaxed rules and my parents consumed with my baby sister Rachael, it was easier to participate in speech meets on Saturdays. Instead of sitting in church in Evansville and passively listening to sermons that mentioned, at least once, that women should learn in silence, I was instead standing in the front of the room expressing my very own thoughts and ideas and interpretations, competing against other kids in an oratory contest—and very often winning.

Then there was another world entirely, not visible to anyone, not one I shared with the church, with my family, or with my community, though sometimes with Alise. It was a world of longing, of wanting something I couldn't name, didn't know where to find, but knew it existed somewhere outside southern Indiana. Later, I might identify it as intellectual freedom, or the freedom to simply be who I was, without the various labels attached at birth. It was a world of curiosity, which had been awakened in me by the books I'd read and the new world of high school. That world beckoned, but I couldn't find a path through that wouldn't include walking hand-in-hand with the devil.

I was bending over the water fountain getting a drink of water, and when I straightened, Mr. Lythegoe, the English Literature teacher, rocked back on his heels and proclaimed, "Propinquity!"

"What?" I asked.

And he repeated, "Propinquity! That's what life is all about! Propinquity determines whom you will marry, where you will live, and what kind of a job you will have. Propinquity means being close. And research says that most people live within a few miles of where they grew up, and they marry someone in the same town, and they will take a job also within a few miles' radius. Propinquity!" he proclaimed once more, and he bent over to drink from the water fountain.

I left, and I thought about Mr. Lythegoe's proclamation then and for many years after. Propinquity had held true of my ancestors and probably most of the world. Still, I really didn't think that I would live a life of propinquity.

One by one, my older friends in the church were getting baptized. I, however, felt more and more alienated from church teachings, even as I struggled not to let my love wax cold. If the world was only 6,000 years old, as the church preached, how could we explain dinosaurs? Had Satan placed their bones in the earth to trip us up? Were the scientists, who worshipped reason and not God, being influenced by demons? Did God only talk to us? When the Catholics claimed that God had healed one of them, were they lying or was it, again, one of those demons, so sneaky they could actually do good to confuse you?

The thing that made me seethe, though, was the church's attitude toward women. Why were men inherently superior to women? The ministers incessantly reminded the congregation that it was Eve who had tempted Adam, Eve who had disobeyed, Eve who was responsible for the world's ills. The church railed against the proposed Equal Rights Amendment as being an assault against the family. Women had their role, but in their role they could *never* rule over a man. It was unnatural, ungodly, un-Christian.

Even more dangerous and insidious than those doubts was a bigger issue, something potentially more threatening to my salvation. I would randomly think, "If there is both God and Jesus, then isn't that two Gods?" It was a frightening notion because without belief in Jesus, there was no possibility of salvation. In the book of Mark, Jesus made it clear, "He who believes and is baptized will be saved, but he who believeth not shall be damned."

The church explained that God and Jesus, though Father and Son, were a family, and a family unit was one entity. In various portions of the Hebrew Bible, the church said, it was Jesus speaking, not God, and in fact, it may have been Jesus appearing to Abraham in the guise of an angel. So wasn't that *two*, I privately wondered?

Despite my rebellious nature, my inability to reconcile church doctrine with scientific evidence, and my desire to straddle Satan's world and the church, I still expected that one day I would get baptized and make it into the Kingdom. I had to if I wanted to see my sister again.

My personal, internal upheavals corresponded with rumors of wrongdoing within the church, which was, of course, the work of the devil and, as such, to be ignored. Herbert Armstrong's son Garner Ted Armstrong was a charismatic, handsome man who had guest-starred on the popular television variety show *Hee Haw* in the 1970s and drew large audiences for his radio and television broadcasts of *The World Tomorrow*. Church members confidently assumed that Herbert and Garner Ted would be the two witnesses mentioned in the book of Acts who would behold Christ's resurrection.

Herbert Armstrong had kicked his son out of the church in 1972 for being "in the bonds of Satan"—code for sexual impropriety. Garner Ted had repented and returned and was thereafter named Herbert Armstrong's "anointed heir." In 1978 Garner Ted was disfellowshipped for the last time following more rumors of gambling, drinking, and sexual immorality, after which he formed his own church—the Church of God International.

In 1977, at the age of eighty-five, Herbert Armstrong married his thirty-nine-year-old secretary, Ramona. No one dared overtly object to Mr. Armstrong's marriage. Not only was Ramona divorced, but also her father had been a member of the Cherokee Indian tribe. While intermarriage would no longer get you disfellowshipped, it was certainly still frowned upon. Some believed the rule had deliberately been lifted to enable Armstrong to marry Ramona.

It was difficult to reconcile Herbert Armstrong and the church of the 1950s and 1960s with its changed tenets of the 1970s. I personally didn't care who married whom, old or young or of a different race, but I did think for more than a few seconds that Armstrong was hypocritical. If anyone other than he had done this, the ministers would have set up a meeting to "counsel" them. That Herbert Armstrong wanted to have sex with such a young woman (or that she wanted to have sex with him), was too crazy to contemplate.

The following year, in 1978, when I was seventeen years old, the church went into receivership. Six disfellowshipped former members had filed a class action lawsuit against the church, and the attorney general of California appointed a judge as receiver. The State of California froze the church's bank accounts while the IRS investigated its finances. Church members were told to send their tithes and offerings to Arizona, where Herbert Armstrong was living. Armstrong said, "The people of God have always been willing to suffer whatever they have to do for the living God! If we have to begin to suffer the persecution of being thrown in prison, I will be the first to go. God is fighting this battle for us, and God is stronger than man!"

Our local minister forbade us to listen to any of the lies or read the Satan-inspired press that was appearing in major national newspapers and magazines about the church. Satan was using the receivership to get at the church and thus at Jesus. In coworker letters to church members, Herbert Armstrong wrote, "No wonder Satan moved in his subtle, deceptive and diabolical way to influence a few of those who have been God's MINISTERS. They began by 'Questioning' this, that and the other doctrine . . . SATAN is the real author of this rebellion against God's Work . . . these deceived ministers [are] allowing Satan to use them." The church was the battlefield over which God and Satan were duking it out.

My parents obeyed the church's stricture not to read or investigate what the receivership was all about. And so neither they nor any of us ever knew that the State of California had discovered unsavory information about Armstrong's personal life as well as the church's expenditures. I didn't find this out until well after the advent of the Internet, when this information was available with a click of a button for those who were willing to face the truth.

Church literature, like the monthly *The Plain Truth* magazine, featured photographs of Mr. Armstrong meeting with dignitaries and heads of state around the world. Over the years, he would be photographed with Mao Tse-Tung, King Hussein, Prince Mikasa of Japan, the younger brother of Emperor Hirohito, and countless other ambassadors and government officials. Without the knowledge of church members, Armstrong gave them Steuben crystal and donated millions of our tithe dollars to various projects in these countries, especially Jordan so that, when the time came to flee to Petra, the Jordanian government would allow us access.

When we saw the photographs of Armstrong with Prince Charles—heir to the British throne and a descendant of Ephraim, one of the other lost tribes—it seemed to legitimize our funding of the church and the gospel that Armstrong was preaching. How were we to know that Prince Charles simply took a check for one of his favorite causes, the Royal Opera House, and in return shook Armstrong's hand? Or that it was our tithes that paid for a meeting with Prime Minister Margaret Thatcher? The truth was not plain, nor was it true.

The negative secular press, as well as a publication called *The Ambassador Report*, written by former church members that detailed the corruption and immorality within the church, persuaded quite a few members to leave under a cloud of bitterness and anger. Over 3,000 members and pastors worldwide had been disfellowshipped—kicked out, not allowed to return—and almost 2,000 church members had left on their own. Given the fact that in 1973 there were 53,000 members worldwide, 5,000 people constituted a mass exodus. While my family knew people were leaving, we didn't know why. We didn't have access to the information then, and while others in the church did, we avoided them like the plague. Or like they were demons.

It wasn't until thirty years later when my sister Liz called me and said, "Ang, we were raised in a cult," that I discovered what had been actually happening. Despite my initial denial, Liz sent me a letter dating from 1981 addressed to the Board of Directors and Council of Elders of the Worldwide Church of God. Someone on the board had released it anonymously. These many years later, it was being circulated on a website called thepainfultruth.org. In the letter, Herbert Armstrong's incestuous relationship with his daughter for the first ten years of his ministry as well as other "sexual perversity" was mentioned but not denounced. "He is a man motivated by strong passions, and is perhaps one of the most naturally selfish men to have walked the earth, ever."

The words hit me hard. While I'd personally had misgivings and disagreed with many of the church's doctrines, I had always assumed that Mr. Armstrong's personal behavior was above reproach.

The real thrust of the letter, however, was the church's financial wrongdoings. Someone embezzled a quarter of a million dollars. The church was involved in a $50,000 kickback scheme to a Mexican bank. And:

> . . . the use of church coffers as a sort of personal piggy bank for instant credit (always interest-free) or outright appropriation had grown to outrageous proportions through constant circumvention of the system by Mr. Armstrong and his family.

The letter went on to inform the Board that Armstrong took $10,000 in cash with him on his trips, which was unaccounted for, and the church paid for a $30,000 yacht rental in Monte Carlo.

When I investigated further on thepainfultruth.org, the years of corruption and immorality was laid bare: cruises, sex spas in Romania, a $6,000 crystal chandelier, hundreds of thousands of dollars in bonuses, and much more. Mr. Armstrong had flown off on his private jet—paid for with members' tithes—to all corners of the world, ostensibly to preach the Work. He was especially fond of Thailand and the beautiful Thai prostitutes. While church members died of ruptured appendixes, Armstrong used doctors routinely. Throughout the 1970s, Armstrong flew around the world for up to 200 days a year on his jet, nicknamed "The Flying Whorehouse."

We didn't know in 1977 about any of these allegations. Instead, as church members departed, my father concluded, "The Almighty is sifting them out. He's not going to make spirit beings of somebody he can't trust."

The church relied on people like my parents—people they could trust not to rock the boat. To keep on paying. To turn a blind eye. They would suspend their disbelief, ignore their questions and concerns, deny what was right in front of them—anything to get into the next world.

One Saturday in 1979, right after we sang our hymns and concluded the opening prayer, the minister announced from the pulpit that no one was to have any contact with Mrs. Davis, the deacon's wife. She'd been "marked." Contact with her could jeopardize our faith in God's work and thus our salvation.

Mr. and Mrs. Davis had hosted us teens at their home on many occasions. She'd seemed to be a committed, model member of the church. Before I could process what this might mean, Mrs. Davis—a small, pretty woman with brown, wavy hair, a smile for everyone, and a quiet demeanor—charged up the aisle. Standing in front of the minister, she threw her shoulders back, clenched her fists at her side, and practically shouted, "You can't do this to me. I want you to tell these people the truth. You are lying to them!"

Shocked quiet. A few gasps. It was as if she had a gun and was threatening all of us. Listening to her shouting at the minister, who was God's representative here on earth, it was obvious to me that she'd come unhinged. Demons. It was scary (but a little thrilling) to see the demons at work, having been on the lookout for them for so long.

"Deacons, please escort Mrs. Davis out. Mr. Davis, please take your wife," the minister said with confidence and authority. And two somber-suited deacons, both of whom were good friends with the Davis family, came forward, looking as if they were pallbearers carrying out a coffin. They, along with her husband, took her by the arms and walked her out even as she continued shouting, "Don't listen to them! Don't you see what they're doing to you? You have to know what—"

Then it was over. I felt as if I'd been holding my breath, but then she was gone. We listened to the sermon, prayed another prayer, and soberly fellowshipped with one another when services ended. This incident proved my worst fear: you could be possessed by a demon and not even know it. Mrs. Davis had been drinking from the poisonous well of lies that were being spread about the church. But she was actually trying to convince us to leave the church.

No one brought it up again, at least not in front of me. Later I wondered if it had been a man that had gone up there, would he have been listened to? Was it just a woman who was considered crazy?

A few months later, the State of California dropped its case against the church. The legislature passed a law barring the attorney general from investigating religious organizations. Jesus was still on our side. The devil was vanquished.

At that time, in 1979, the church claimed 100,000 members, had $80 million in assets, and an annual income of nearly $70 million. *The New York Times* reported:

> . . . *(the church) has been in turmoil for several years resulting from allegations of sexual misconduct by the founder's son in 1972, the defection of some of its members in a doctrinal dispute in 1979, the public*

denunciation of the church by its most famous convert, Bobby Fischer, the
chess master, in 1977, and the excommunication of the heir apparent,
Garner Ted Armstrong, last summer in a power struggle.

I didn't read *The New York Times* article, nor any of the other media information on the church, for over thirty years after the events had transpired. Burying my head in the sand, not facing what was evident to everyone else, was what I did to survive.

CHAPTER 9

My high school guidance counselor called me to her office one day. I couldn't imagine what I'd done wrong.

She sat at her desk, a file folder in front of her. "You've scored in the top ninety-ninth percentile on all of your standardized tests," she said to me, and it sounded like an accusation.

"Yes?" I already knew that.

"And you're very involved in extracurricular activities, and you've won speech contests and debates and so on," she said.

"Yes?"

"Have you thought about applying for college?"

It was my junior year. I had not thought about college. The church didn't forbid anyone from going to college, but it did actively discourage it in sermons that warned that worldly colleges contained demonic influences. God had not inspired those professors. The church scorned "so-called intellectuals," much as they scorned "so-called Christians."

The church's college in California, Ambassador College, taught women how to be Christian wives and mothers. A family friend of Alise's had paid for her to go, her ticket out of southern Indiana. She was in her first year and was dating a nice church boy named Tim.

My family could not afford Ambassador College.

"No, I hadn't really thought about college," I admitted. My brother Jim had gone for one year, then dropped out, and was now a construction worker. My brother Paul had just started at Indiana State University. My father told Paul he didn't need any education because Jesus was going to return, and he shouldn't waste his time or money. Despite Jesus's not returning in 1975, we still heard every week that it was going to happen soon.

"Well, we can help you with the application process, but you need to sign up to take the PSAT." She explained what would come next— grants, scholarships, financial aid, and so on.

I later looked back on this guidance counselor as an angel. She was doing her job, of course, identifying which students were strong college candidates. But given the church's stance on higher education, my own belief that the world would soon end, and the fact that no female in my family had ever attended college, without her intervention, I doubt I would have continued past twelfth grade.

I knew nothing about any of the state colleges, nor did I visit any to make an informed decision. Instead, based on an algorithm all my own, I chose Indiana University in Bloomington. It was eighty miles away—close enough to easily visit Jasper but big enough to afford me the anonymity I craved. Having come from a small town where you couldn't buy tampons without your first cousin once removed witnessing it, privacy was paramount to me. And to my knowledge, no one else in my family or in my graduating class was applying there. I could reinvent myself.

Instead of spending the summer after graduation settling in and working in one of the local factories or becoming a bank teller, I was preparing for college. My mother bought me a typewriter and luggage from Kmart. At my age, she'd been cleaning houses and working in the cannery. She'd never had this opportunity.

In the fall, we loaded up the Cadillac with suitcases filled with bedding and clothing and toiletries and drove to Bloomington. I joined the other excited freshmen, all of us unloading our cars and eager to make our own homes away from home. I threw the blue hand-stitched quilt my mother had made over my bed, put up photos of family on the nightstand, placed the typewriter on the desk, and settled in. It was as easy as that.

CHAPTER 10

To look at me—playing euchre and drinking beer until 3 a.m. in my dorm room, vocally defending women's rights with my feminist friends, skinny-dipping in the quarries of Bloomington, reading Rita Mae Brown's lesbian fiction at the suggestion of a lesbian friend—no one would have believed that I was a fundamentalist Christian who privately believed that homosexuality was a sin, abortion was absolutely immoral, and Jesus was preparing to pounce on the earth. By the church's standards, Indiana University was the devil's playground. I was having fun on Satan's teeter-totter and jungle gym even as I privately denounced them.

Indiana University was vast in every sense. There were close to 50,000 undergraduate and graduate students, and the campus covered almost 2,000 acres, which meant I was often lost. There were times I found myself at a science or chemistry building or in graduate student housing asking an Indian woman wearing a colorful sari if she knew how to get to the student union. In between classes, I would buy trail mix, drink Tab, and sit in one of the lounges watching *General Hospital* with a crowd of students equally obsessed with Luke and Laura's tumultuous relationship.

I continued taking German and, very slowly, managed to read a short story by Thomas Mann. In the women's studies course, we looked at how women were often portrayed as ancillary characters in literature, something that had never occurred to me, but once pointed out, I couldn't stop noticing.

I tried my hand at writing poetry. My teachers were kind, but not exactly enthusiastic, nor should they have been. One poem from that time included:

> *If those who live are the livers*
> *Are those who die the gizzards?*

In addition to new academic subjects, at long last, I was with people very different from me, like Youssef, a Bahai from Iran, whose letters from home were filled with holes. The Iranian government strictly censored all correspondence.

All of the rooms in my dormitory were singles, and for the first time in my life, I had a room and a bed to myself. Bliss. The woman who lived next to me, Celia, was soft-spoken and somewhat shy. A staunch feminist, Celia told me that Judeo-Christianity had effectively succeeded in wiping out the worship of the mother goddess, which predated monotheism. This was all news to me and something I wanted to explore further.

When Celia's Lebanese boyfriend, Walid, came over, I overheard snatches of wild shouting matches, during which she accused him of being sexist and macho. Walid, equally soft-spoken when I passed him in the hallway, responded with a loud, heavily accented, "Then why you with me, huh? Why you with me? You crazy, you know that, Celia, you crazy girl!"

This was better than turning around in church and staring at people with scaly elbows.

I went to local bars on the weekends with my new posse of friends. Ye Olde Regulator, the "Reg," featured disco dancing and drew a lot of Middle Eastern guys, which I liked. "Eww, Angela," my friend Margaret said. "How can you stand those hairy guys?"

I could stand them just fine.

I was preoccupied with balancing the "me/not me, devil's world/God's world."

About once a month, I attended church services a half hour away, catching a ride with a Bloomington family. I didn't look forward to it. It felt obligatory, though I couldn't pinpoint why or to whom I was obligated. My parents never asked me about it. But I believed that if I kept plugging away and suppressed my intellectual questioning and instead read the church's free booklets and literature like *4 Horsemen of the Apocalypse* or *Easter Is Pagan*, then church doctrine would become clear. I would get baptized, make it into the Kingdom, and see Abby again. Period.

———

Home from Indiana University one autumn weekend in 1980, I went to church in Evansville on Saturday morning with my family. Without a welcoming smile, without even a "Good morning, brethren," the minister launched into "Brethren, Satan has been allowed a foothold in this church, and Satan has got to be rooted out."

Even though I was nineteen years old, and I no longer viewed Satan as I had as a child—a frightening, invisible personage—but rather as an evil energy, the minister made it sound as if Satan was actually sitting with us right there in the movie theater and needed to be forcibly removed.

"Again, just like in the Garden of Eden," he continued, "it's women who are leading the church away from God with their MAKEUP!"

What? I hadn't been prepared for this at all. Satan was *me* and all of the other women wearing eye shadow?

"WAKE UP! If you let makeup come between you and God, then I'm here to tell you—YOU WILL NOT MAKE IT INTO THE KINGDOM! Women, our apostle Herbert Armstrong is telling you through Jesus, it's because of YOU that Jesus cannot return! Your makeup is an abomination! Throw it out!" he screamed, as if my Bonne Bell lip gloss were a bomb ready to detonate and blow up the entire world.

His words were incomprehensible, despite being blunt and clear. My lipstick was wreaking havoc in the church? Jesus was loitering on the sidelines, refusing to return until I soaked a cotton ball in baby oil and wiped off my mascara?

In the complete and total silence that followed, a woman cried ever so quietly.

"Do you women think you can improve on God's work?" the minister finished triumphantly.

I *knew* I could, was my first thought. I had white eyelashes, white eyebrows, and pale skin. Makeup wasn't a luxury. It was as much a necessity as brushing my teeth. Without mascara, eyebrow pencil, eyeliner, lipstick, and a little blush, I looked like a white rodent with beady blue eyes. Makeup drew my features into definition: my eyes popped open, my lips became visible, and, perhaps as a result, my frowning visage and my opinionated voice did not fade away into the anemic world of dutiful women.

This makeup edict truly gave me pause. It seemed stupid and petty, if not ludicrous. Having spent over a year at Indiana University, I was far less willing to blindly obey the church's rules, though I worried that this was a sign that I'd let the devil into my life. In college, my feminist friends talked about female subjugation at the hands of organized religion, using words like "misogyny." I had to look that one up. I thought it might be a medical term related to gynecology.

In the weeks after the reinstated makeup ban, the other women, including my younger sister Liz, who was inordinately fond of red nail polish and lipstick, went to church with no color to adorn their faces. I refused. Technically the rule applied only to women who were baptized, because being baptized meant that you understood the truth and were willing to adhere to doctrine. However, the teenage girls, too, arrived at church barefaced. Even though the week before they'd worn as much or more makeup as I, they looked at me as if I had turned into a whore.

My mother, as was her way, never criticized me or even mentioned that I might tone down the fuchsia lipstick. I don't think she cared one way or another. My father made certain I heard many times that Jezebel had worn eye makeup, and look what happened to her. Pushed out a window and killed.

Even then, death seemed like a harsh punishment for wearing eyeliner. Later, when I studied the story in I Kings academically, I learned that while the church had created a cause and effect—wearing makeup would kill a woman—the kohl that rimmed Jezebel's eyes indicated that she was a priestess of the Phoenician god Ba'al. A Phoenician princess, Jezebel was not loyal to her husband, King Ahab's, God—the God of the Bible.

Not that I wanted to go to my death because of makeup, but the other women in church seemed diminished, and I, who would go commando to church before giving up my mascara, felt embarrassed for them. I ignored the makeup rule, much as I ignored or dismissed anything that didn't make sense to me. I sort of figured the church would soon see the error of its ways, like it had in 1974, and say, "Oh, forget it, makeup is fine. Our doctrinal committee convened, and feel free to slather on blush to your heart's content."

At the same time, I worried that these women, unlike me, were capable of putting aside their own carnal desires and needs to follow Jesus unconditionally. I didn't know which was worse: getting the Holy Spirit and becoming like them—pale, washed out, and obedient—or not getting it, remaining willful, and not making it into the Kingdom.

I called Alise in California to ask her what she thought. Ambassador College had temporarily shuttered the year before when the church was in receivership, but Alise had remained in Pasadena and now worked for the church's publication arm, churning out its monthly magazines, *The Plain Truth* and *Good News*, as well as free booklets like *Are We in the Last Days?* and *Did God Create A DEVIL?*

"Hey, Alise, what is going on with this makeup rule?"

"It's crazy," she said. "All the women here in Pasadena are pissed off."

It figured and made me feel vindicated that I wasn't the only one who thought her rights as a woman were being violated. My feminist friends in college said that the personal was political, and this was the perfect example of that reasoning. It also touched on all of the problems I'd historically had with the church: that Armstrong had better insight into interpreting the Bible than anyone else; that there was no room for disagreement, even when polite and respectful; and that men could make decisions about women's bodies, from the length of their dress and hair, to whether they had to carry to term a baby they didn't want.

Alise and I went back and forth, as we had for years, about church doctrines that we simply didn't understand and which seemed anti-woman and, frankly, stupid. When the church forbade us to see *The Exorcist, Carrie,* and *The Omen,* claiming they were demonic, Alise, who still loved to tell me stories about vampires, had fumed. "Of all people, we should be allowed to go because we believe in them!" Maybe, she'd suggested, it was because our church thought it knew demons better than the Catholics who were represented in the movies but who, in fact, were evil themselves and unqualified to perform exorcisms. We were proprietary over our demons, as we had grown up with them.

"How are things with Brad?" I asked her after we'd exhausted our complaints. Alise and I had just spent the Feast of Tabernacles together at the Lake of the Ozarks. Throughout the entire week, she hadn't stopped talking about Brad, her boyfriend of three years, whom she expected to propose to her in the near future.

"We just broke up," she said.

"What?" I was stunned.

"Yeah. I told Brad I wanted him to get tickets to go to the New Year's Eve ball with me. He said, 'I'm the man, and I'll ask you when I'm ready.'"

"Jesus. So sexist," I muttered.

"So I'm going with Michael," she finished, and her voice was light, airy, brazenly pugnacious, as if she hadn't just switched horses midstream.

"Who's Michael?" I asked, struggling to follow along.

"A guy I work with who's had a crush on me forever."

"Oh. Do you like him?"

"Kind of."

"Good. I mean, what a shitass. 'I'm the man.'" I heard my grandma's dismissive tone come from my mouth. Alise and I were both disgusted and annoyed by the pervasive sexism in the church, but there didn't seem to be any way to avoid it without leaving the church entirely, which neither of us could imagine doing. We were holding out, sucking it up, for salvation's sake.

"Yeah. I've waited for Brad long enough." Her words closed the subject with finality, and I didn't ask her anything else.

After talking to Alise and listening to her own private insurrection against male prerogative, I felt newly empowered to reject the church's makeup stance. I'd coat my eyelashes with layers and layers of navy-blue mascara, brush on sparkly, silver eye shadow, pencil my eyebrows brown, and apply a very pretty autumnal plum lipstick. Then out I went, on dates with guys who definitively didn't have the Holy Spirit.

A few months later, on a gray winter afternoon in 1980, I walked into Indiana University's Office for Overseas Study in Franklin Hall, a gracious old building on the far side of campus. As I had ever since I'd come to Indiana University, I appreciated the rural-like atmosphere of the campus, with its abundance of trees, the limestone and brick buildings, the Jordan River that cut through campus.

A girl from my German class mentioned to me that she was applying to spend her junior year abroad in Germany. I was unaware that students could study anywhere other than Indiana University but was intrigued and decided to look into it for myself. Given my background, Germany was a natural fit. We would be reunited after being separated by an ocean and 150 years. I fantasized that I would speak German fluently and establish myself as an authentic German, rather than a hyphenated German-American.

I looked at the brochure. Castles and cobblestones, the Rhine River and the Black Forest. Germany could simultaneously satisfy my wanderlust and appease my curiosity about where I came from and who I was. This was my ancestral homeland.

Then I spied another brochure. On it was a photograph of a stunning, golden-domed building silhouetted against a bright blue sky. The Hebrew University in Jerusalem boasted views of the Old City, as well as the Judean Desert and the Dead Sea. I imagined John the Baptist fasting in the desert and David fighting Goliath. During our family's Friday night Bible study groups, I'd read about Sodom and Gomorrah, Bethlehem, Nazareth and, of course, Jerusalem. Israel was the place that God had chosen for Abraham's descendants, the place where Jesus had walked and preached.

Apparently I didn't need to speak Hebrew, as classes like "Biblical Narrative" and "The Book of Jonah" were taught in English. In my imagination, Israel was imbued with holiness unlike any other place on earth. I was certain that merely stepping foot on the soil would bring me closer to God, closer to the Holy Spirit, and thus to salvation.

In addition to the brochure with the images of medieval castles on the Rhine, I took the one for Israel, which whispered to me conspiratorially: "Come! Come!" And just like that, on a dime, on a shekel, on a worthless German mark, I twisted, I turned, much as I changed lanes—swiftly, at the last second, and often without looking into my rearview mirror to check the traffic. Good-bye castles, hello camels. The Holy Spirit beckoned.

My parents were perplexed when I told them I wanted to spend my junior year in Israel. I was perplexed that they were perplexed. Hadn't we all sat in church for years and years listening to the minister and reading our Bibles and studying about the place in which God appeared, where the spiritual world met the physical plane? Wasn't Israel as much our spiritual home as Germany was our physical one?

Although going to Jerusalem to connect with my spiritual DNA made logical sense to me, it was considered a crazy, impulsive whim to both my parents and my siblings. In his end-of-the-world tone, my father warned me, "It's a powder keg over there! Jesus has to return lest all flesh should perish."

My mother, however, clipped a bunch of newspaper articles about Israel to try to help me prepare. But I wasn't interested in what was going on there at that moment. It was biblical Israel I planned to inhabit.

Alise, to my great surprise, had decided to marry Michael, whom she'd been dating for only four months. Now *that* was impulsive. First, she had to get baptized, because the church wouldn't marry a non-baptized person. I was both confused and jealous that she was able to take the leap and get baptized. Not so long before, we'd been decrying church doctrine to each other. I was still struggling with it, but apparently Alise had made peace. Or, if she hadn't, she was pretending she had.

I served as maid of honor at her wedding. Her husband, Michael, sixteen years older, was handsome and charming and did a really funny imitation of Herbert Armstrong. He screamed and pounded his fist, which was hysterical but also left me confounded that he could make fun of God's apostle.

Alise had changed. She was not going to go to France, not going to be a broadcaster, not going to finish college. At twenty-one, Alise was a married, baptized church lady living in Pasadena, California.

My parents threw me a big good-bye party at the 4-H center. Surrounded by my aunts and uncles and thirty-plus cousins, I ate fried chicken and my grandmother's sugar cookies and posed for a photograph with my grandparents holding a cake with an airplane drawn on it and underneath, written in blue icing, "Good-bye and good luck."

A member of one of the lost tribes, I was returning home. And my stars forever after would never be aligned quite the same.

CHAPTER 11

I dozed a bit during the long, cramped flight to Tel Aviv, then woke from my uncomfortable slumber and decided to go to the bathroom. From my seat, I saw that the aisle was crowded with at least twenty men wearing black suits and big black hats. Some sported ringlets of hair that dangled from the sides of their ears. Facing the same direction, the men stood swaying and muttering in the aisle next to the bathroom. It was as if they'd called a private meeting at daybreak. Impossible to get to the bathroom, I waited.

The flight attendant came around with a breakfast tray. There was a bagel, which I knew from college, a packet of cream cheese, and an orange thing not recognizable as fish or fowl. Was it sweet? Perhaps some weird jelly?

"What's this?" I asked the woman seated next to me.

"Lox," she answered, as if it were perfectly obvious.

Not helpful. I didn't know of any food-related word remotely connected to "locks."

I watched as she spread cream cheese on her bagel then methodically, precisely, lay her "locks" atop one half of the bagel, as if she were putting it to sleep on a white-sheeted bed, placed the other half on it to cover it up, and then took a bite.

I did the same, attempting to copy her discreetly. Delicious! It was some kind of salty fish. Always curious about a word's etymology, I wondered if it was related to "lochs," the Scottish lakes.

Fourteen hours after we'd left New York City, the plane touched down at Ben Gurion airport in Israel. A song in Hebrew blared over the intercom system, and the entire plane erupted in applause. They cheered and sang along as if it had been prearranged. There was a feeling of pure joy.

The plane did not pull up to the airport terminal, but rather came to a halt on the tarmac. There had been two terrorist attacks on the airport in 1972, which had resulted in changes to the airport security system. Planes parked on the tarmac, then a shuttle bus took passengers to the terminal, lest the plane be blown up next to the building or provide terrorists with easy access to the public space.

In New York, I'd already encountered what, at the time, felt like extreme security measures. Before checking in, an Israeli woman had asked me a number of questions: why was I going to Israel; had anyone given me a package to bring to someone in Israel; had my luggage always been with me or had I left it since I packed it; did I have relatives in Israel. Then she'd gone through my suitcase. She had removed everything—twenty rolls of film, the quilt my mother made, an electrical adapter, shoes and socks and jeans—then put it all back in. It had felt invasive, though the woman had explained, "You understand we have to ask you these questions for your own safety?" The truth was I really didn't. Had I read the articles my mother had clipped for me, I might have realized that Israel remained vulnerable to terrorist attacks from both inside and outside the country.

Finally I disembarked, and there I was: Israel. The Holy Land. Where Jesus walked.

At that time, Israel's airport terminal was a barracks-like building maybe the size of the Kmart back home. Eager to get my baggage and meet the Holy Land, I tried to walk quickly but could hardly get past the throng of people shoving, shrieking greetings at one another in Hebrew, and pushing huge carts of luggage around recklessly. A number of small children trailed behind women wearing long dresses.

There were men like those on the plane who wore long black coats. I slowed down just to take it all in. Young male and female soldiers about my age were positioned at each door, guns slung across their chests.

I was aware that there had been several wars in Israel, but this was the summer of 1981. I thought they'd resolved those problems, save for a skirmish here and there. Back in Bloomington, I had met with the university's advisor, Golda, and I'd received a packet of information about the Jerusalem program, but I hadn't read through it thoroughly. It had seemed so pedantic—the exchange rate of the shekel and the dollar, the importance of sturdy walking shoes and a canteen, an overview of the Ulpan, the intensive Hebrew classes in the summer before the main classes began in the fall, safety tips, and so on. I'd skimmed the parts about the recent history of the country. It was ancient Israel I was seeking.

I got through passport control, retrieved my luggage, and maybe I was paranoid, but it seemed like people were staring at me. Exiting the airport, I walked outside into the suffocating hot July afternoon and a distinctive smell of sun and pine. A barrage of male voices called out, "Yes, you need taxi?" and then "Yes, you have beautiful eyes," which I thought unexpectedly sweet. I smiled and the man said, "You want to have coffee?" I smiled politely again and said, "No, thank you." I hurried toward the taxi stand and passed quickly by men who stared at me and muttered, "Yes, you want maybe I show you Israel?" and "You are Swedish?"

After enduring what felt like being paraded in front of uncouth construction workers, I slid into the un-air-conditioned taxi, the seat burning the underside of my bare legs, and said, relieved in every respect and ready for the next adventure, "Jerusalem."

With the Mediterranean and Tel Aviv behind me, we drove inland, and the taxi climbed up, up, on winding roads into higher elevation. The driver took the curves aggressively, as if he were embroiled in mortal combat with them. Outside the window in the distance were barren hills with rocks sticking out of them and just a scattering of low, rectangular stone houses. The road signs were written in Hebrew on the upper right-hand side, with Arabic to its left and English below. Hebrew is written from right to left, thus the positioning. There was a sign for "Ayalon Valley" and for "Latrun" and "Bet Shemesh," a place mentioned in the Bible as a Philistine city, if I remembered correctly. We passed an old, rusted military vehicle on the side of the road. It looked as if it had been abandoned, though why such an eyesore hadn't been hauled away, I couldn't imagine. Who wanted to be reminded of the wars every time they drove on the highway, I thought, not realizing the importance of these symbols of the country's struggles.

Israel bore little resemblance to the country I'd expected to find. In my imagination, time had stopped after the first century. Though reason should have dictated that I wouldn't find men in tunics and sandals watering their camels at the wells, my emotional understanding of Israel was strictly connected to its past.

Aside from the Holocaust, I knew nothing about Jewish history. What had happened to Israel, or to Jews, in the 2,000 years since Jesus was crucified, I didn't know.

From my perspective, when the Jews rejected Jesus, God had abandoned them and created a new covenant with Christians. I couldn't even be certain that Jews had a Bible or believed in God. At least, not in the way I believed in God. But I wasn't in Israel for the Jews or for Jewish history. Modern Israel was just a conduit to the distant past, where I hoped to find the Holy Spirit.

CHAPTER 12

I dropped my suitcases in my dorm at Givat Ram and, without washing my face, brushing my teeth, or changing clothes after the long flight, I set off into the oppressive July heat to discover Jerusalem. I had my canteen filled with water, my guidebook, and some American Express traveler's checks in my daypack. I found enough people who spoke English to give me directions to downtown Jerusalem, and somehow I boarded a bus and got off on the main road, King George Street.

I pictured Jerusalem as spacious and silent and filled with holy people, people who were friendly and good and might even bear a likeness to the prophets. That expectation was soon proved wrong.

I stood at the window of a falafel stand on King George Street, excited to try one of those strange sandwiches in which salad and deep-fried balls—composed exactly of what, I didn't know—were stuffed into the pocket of a flat bread called pita. "Yes, you want to have coffee, maybe?" asked a young man whose dark coloring would have prompted stares in Indiana, as I waited for my sandwich.

"No, thank you," I smiled politely.

"You are from Holland? Sweden? Germany?" he persisted, the *r* rolling around his tongue.

"No, America," I answered.

"You have beautiful eyes," he said.

"Thank you," I repeated.

My falafel order came, and I tried it. The balls were bready and corn-mealish with unrecognizable spices, but a consistency similar to hush puppies. Delicious.

"You are not Jewish," the man pronounced.

"No." In my whole life, no one had ever looked at me and said, "You're not Jewish," or "You're not Christian," or made any comment at all about my faith, particularly based solely on my appearance.

"Excuse me," I said, continuing to keep my tone polite. "I have to go."

I started down the street to explore. He followed after me, calling, "I want you should have coffee with me."

"I have a boyfriend," I lied, as firmly as I could. I didn't want to hurt his feelings.

"Ah, I see," he sighed and finally left.

I took a right at the bottom of King George Street and continued walking on Jaffa Road, attracting more "Yes, you have beautiful eyes!" and quick intakes of breath from the male population. I stared straight ahead as if I knew where I was going.

Jaffa Road, the commercial center of Jerusalem, was neither imposing nor stately. The sidewalks were uneven and dirty, and many of the buildings were gray and squat. There was a pizza place, a small kiosk selling newspapers and various pastries, another falafel stand, an English bookstore, a few souvenir shops with olivewood camels and T-shirts proclaiming, "Israel Isreal." And then, in front of me, emerged a walled city.

From my guidebook, I learned that this was East Jerusalem, and the walls dated back to the 1500s from the rule of Suleiman the Magnificent in Ottoman times. I didn't know that, at one time, Israel had been ruled by the Turks. On my left, a tower peeked out from above the city wall. Called the Tower of David, according to the guidebook, it was a Turkish tower and minaret, and the Byzantine Christians had believed it to be the site of King David's palace.

I looked at the map of East Jerusalem to get my bearings. There, in black and white, I read the ancient names: the Mount of Olives, Jericho Road, the Kidron Valley, the Valley of David. The words themselves, representing the days of old, the world in which the patriarchs and matriarchs and Jesus had lived and died, sent a zing of exquisite pleasure through me. Ancient Israel was still there.

I entered the Jaffa Gate and edged my way into what the book said was the *souk*, the Arab marketplace. I peered into the open shops. "Yesss, you are German, come have a look!" "You my first customer, please, have a look!" "You have beautiful eyes, you want sandals, special sandals, very special sandals." From all sides came an onslaught of invitations, a cacophony of sounds, an assault of smells, which were a mixture of leather and spices and cinnamon-smelling coffee. I felt propelled forward, down the narrow, uneven cobblestone path. A small Arab boy led a donkey pulling a wooden cart, and the boy managed to adroitly dart through a crowd of tourists whose white caps identified them as tourists from a Baptist church in Texas.

There was so much to take in: the merchants selling carved-wood nativity scenes and brightly colored cotton skirts and blouses; the shouting and the calling out, "Yes, come in, I make a good price for you! Yes, you are from Denmark/Sweden/England/Germany!" The Arabs at the market could not have been more different than the stoic Germans I grew up with, who only got riled up when they'd drunk too much Falls City Beer or when the Patoka River was too dry or too high.

At one point, a young man about my age approached me. He had deep red hair and freckles, a startling contrast to his brown eyes and dusky skin. "Hello, you want to see something very special? I will show you," he said politely, not with the same aggressive sales pitch as the others.

"What?" I was wary. In less than a day, I'd developed more mistrust than I'd possessed in my entire lifetime.

"Come. I show you. Special, very special. Nobody see this."

I figured I'd walk with him as long as we stayed in the crowd. Apparently, my trust in humanity was more intact than I thought. And my curiosity outweighed my concern for safety. I was young.

His name was Khalid, and as we wended our way through the *souk*, he called out in Arabic to the vendors. This reassured me, that others knew him. He said he loved America and Americans. He asked me where I was from.

"Indiana," I said.

"Indiana Jones!" he joked. *Raiders of the Lost Ark* had just been released.

"What about you?" I asked. "Where are you from?"

"I am born here." He pointed his finger, as if everything within our gaze comprised the "here" where he was born.

"How long has your family lived here?" I asked.

He frowned. "Forever!" he answered with a little huff.

Not only had I been unprepared for Jews living in Israel, I hadn't expected Arabs, either. I'd vaguely imagined that after Jesus was crucified, some unknown, unnamed people had continued to inhabit the land, but in a very low-key way. Whoever they were, they hadn't been involved in the Middle Ages or the Renaissance or the Thirty Years' War or any of the other historical events and epochs I'd studied in school. Both the people of the Middle East and parts of Asia were irrelevant by the Western world's standards.

Khalid pointed out the Armenian Quarter, whoever the Armenians were, the Jewish Quarter and, finally, the Christian Quarter, where the Church of the Holy Sepulchre stood and where many Christians believed Jesus was crucified.

By this point, we'd left the crush of the market and, walking through a labyrinth of small alleys and streets, we exchanged information about our families. He, too, came from a big family—seven brothers and sisters. Two older siblings were married and had children.

I told him that my oldest sister, Wanda, was eight years older than me and my youngest sister, Rachael, was fourteen years younger and would start kindergarten soon.

Khalid asked me what I was doing in Israel, and I said I was taking an intensive Hebrew course for two months, then in the fall, I was going to study at The Hebrew University. He said he wanted to go to university, but it was very difficult for Arabs because of the political situation. I pretended to understand what he was talking about. How did the political situation preclude him from going to college?

We climbed a bunch of worn limestone stairs and made it to a spot where we had a spectacular view of that maze called the Old City. From up high, I could make out the tops of churches and rounded limestone roofs, as well as the long alleyways that twisted a sinuous path throughout. "You see? Very special." Khalid said to me. His voice was almost reverent.

I let the moment soak in: my first day in Israel and a redheaded Arab stranger was standing with me atop a building overlooking Jerusalem, a city we each felt belonged to us, for totally different reasons. I would have mentioned Willie Nelson's album, *Red Headed Stranger*, which I loved, but I guessed that Willie wasn't another point of commonality between us.

I opened my canteen of water and took several long swallows. Now that I'd stopped walking, it felt as if I'd been tossed into a dryer set on high. Khalid didn't have any water, so I offered him some of mine. "No, thank you," he replied.

"No, please." I pushed my canteen at him. His lips were really dry, almost flaky. I assumed he'd turned it down out of politeness. I was not one who cared about germs, but maybe he did.

"I can't," he said. "It's Ramadan. I'm fasting." At my look of puzzlement, he explained further. "We fast for one month. Just during the day, of course, and then at night after sunset we eat. We finish this week."

It was the beginning of July, so he'd been doing this for at least three weeks, during some of the most intense heat I'd ever experienced. "What else do you do?" I was curious about his religious practice.

"We study the Qu'ran, we give charity, we pray—you know." I was surprised to discover this level of piety and commitment in someone not in my church. Muslims, Buddhists, Hindus—I'd been taught that they were all ungodly, just by virtue of the fact that they weren't Christian.

Khalid pointed into the distance. "Over there, look, that golden dome? That is the Dome of the Rock."

"Wow!" It was the building that I'd seen on the brochure in the Office for Overseas Study. The Dome of the Rock seemed to throw off gold light from the top. It glowed and burned, a passionate building in the midst of others that were all white and rose-hued. "What is it?" I asked Khalid, assuming it was a church or something.

"Our prophet Mohammed took his night journey to heaven from that spot, and met Jesus and Joseph and the prophets as well as Allah. Now, we pray there."

"Oh, I see." I doubted that Mohammed had gone to heaven and returned to earth to tell everyone about it, but I understood that this was what Khalid had been taught. It was not clear to me if Muslims viewed Mohammed as a deity. I wondered if they believed that Mohammed, and not Jesus, had been the Son of God. If they worshipped a man, then they were certainly pagan. Unless they worshipped Jesus.

"How did you get red hair?" I asked Khalid as he walked me back to the *souk*, leaving behind talk of religion and history.

He smiled, as he often had in the hour or so we'd walked through the Old City, and he said, "The Crusaders. They came to Israel a long time ago, you know, and some of us, because of this, we have red hair."

First, I had found out about the Turks, then the Armenians, now the Crusaders. God, everybody had been here, and had left their mark.

"What about you?" he asked me. "You also have some red. Where is your family from?"

Yes, it was true, there were strands of red in my blonde hair, and my brother Jim loved to tease me that in the old days they drowned redheaded babies. "Originally from Germany," I explained, "but we've lived in America since the 1840s."

"Not long." Khalid dismissed my family's 140-year history in America.

"No, not compared to here," I agreed.

Khalid wanted to know more about America: What was my favorite television show; did I watch *Dallas*; had I been to Dallas; and did I eat hamburgers every day? Even though I thought American life was the most boring thing in the entire world compared to living in Jerusalem—Jerusalem!—I answered his questions: No, no, and no.

"What about President Reagan?" he asked.

"He's okay," I answered. I was not very political.

"He doesn't like us." Khalid said dismissively President Reagan. It took me several seconds to realize that by "us," Khalid meant Palestinians.

On our way back to the Jaffa Gate, we chatted as if we were two college students walking together after classes, and then Khalid showed me where to take the bus to return to campus. "Thank you." I held out my hand to shake Khalid's. He took it.

"You are welcome," he said. "Enjoy your time in my country."

CHAPTER 13

From Sunday to Thursday, I sat for six hours in "Kita Aleph" or "Class A," my beginning Hebrew class. During *hafsaka,* our midmorning break, we rushed to the bathroom or to the kiosk to buy chocolate or ice cream or chips or a "cheese sandvich"—melted white cheese in the middle of pita bread.

There were no classes on Friday, so we could prepare for Shabbat or catch a bus to elsewhere in the country for the weekend. And so, a few weeks after I'd settled in, it was time to go to Bethlehem. I had to see the Church of the Nativity.

Though still uncomfortable visiting Catholic churches, I figured since I was not there to worship, God would give me a pass. I had to duck my head to enter through its "Door of Humility," which was only about four feet high, originally constructed to prevent marauders on horseback from riding into the church.

Inside was a vast basilica with rows of pink limestone columns. The air was musty and redolent of centuries of incense. Guidebook in hand, I strolled through the church, pausing at the various altars: the Armenian Orthodox Altar, the high altar, and the Greek Orthodox Altar of Circumcision.

Spying a long line of people in front of a stairwell, I went over to investigate. I asked the woman in front of me what it was, and she said in broken English, "Jesus born."

Below was the spot where Jesus was actually born. Not a manger, like those I'd seen on television or on front lawns all over Jasper, but a grotto, a cave-like place where the animals had been housed.

My turn came to descend the narrow stone stairs inch by inch. Down below, the air was even mustier. It was evident from the low, uneven ceiling that this underground place had once been a cave, but it had been festooned with traditional Christian touches and looked more like an overdecorated crèche than a holy site. But I still hoped that the actual manger would be untouched, and it would be just as Mary and Joseph had left it 2,000 years before.

The line moved slowly, and as I drew closer to what lay ahead, I heard a woman sobbing. When I poked my head around the crowd, I saw a woman on her knees, forehead pressed against the floor, prostrate and weeping, as if she'd lost her only son.

I'd seen people overcome here in the Holy Land. In Hebron, standing in the Cave of Machpelah, I'd seen Jews, Christians, and Arabs in varying emotional states. The Jews would sway back and forth, faster and faster. Women dropped their heads against the cenotaphs that marked the burial spots of the patriarchs and matriarchs, eyes closed, lips silently praying. This kind of a visceral religious experience had yet to happen to me. I was both put off by the woman on the floor and also a little jealous of her. At least she was feeling something. Thus far, Bethlehem had not engendered much emotion, just curiosity.

Finally, I was at the grotto itself. Clutter marred the site of Jesus's birth—a marble floor, velvet curtains, little lamps hanging down, and on the stone floor, a silver star marked the exact spot where he was born. Instead of the star above that had led the wise men from the East to Jesus, the star was below. I'd seen the tourists ahead of me touching the silver star, so I did too. Cold. I did not feel a smidgen of spirituality. I made my way back up the stairs and went outside.

It was a bustling, bright, hot summer day. I walked toward Manger Square. Lining it were gift shops selling carved-wood nativity scenes and camels, as well as wooden boxes and jewelry and chess sets made of mother-of-pearl. I browsed around, trying (and failing) to avoid making eye contact with aggressive shopowners who called out, "Yes, come in, have a look." By virtue of being American, it was assumed that I had money, and could easily spend it. It was much easier to avoid eye contact altogether. Except when I forgot.

I reached for my camera to take a photo of a young boy on a donkey right there on Manger Square. The film, however, wasn't loading. I spied a camera shop and hesitantly went in. The owner, who was probably in his late twenties and wore a prominent cross around his neck, agreed to look at it for me. He slipped the camera inside a black bag to protect the film, took the film out, then opened the camera and sprayed it and cleaned it. "A lot of sand," he said. I had gone to the beach in Tel Aviv.

He put the film back in and returned the camera. I tried to pay him, but he backed away and refused. As much as I disliked the bargaining in the marketplace, I also loved the general sense of hospitality, with store owners offering you hot, sweet mint tea in a clear glass, or walking 200 yards to take you to another shop that might have what you needed.

He asked me what I was doing the rest of the day, and I said just walking around then going back to Jerusalem. "No bus on Friday after two," he regretfully let me know.

"Oh. Well, I'll find a hostel here in Bethlehem," I said. I didn't reveal that I also considered hitching a ride back. Jerusalem was just over five miles away. I was not worried.

"You stay with me," he said nicely. "My family. My mother and father," he continued to explain, even as I politely declined. He then introduced himself. He said his name was Eddie, he was a photographer, and he was scheduled to take pictures at an Arab Muslim wedding the following day. He asked if I wanted to go with him. What the hell? Like Khalid had offered, this was special, very special.

Eddie's family lived in a modest but charming stone home in Bethlehem a few blocks from his store. His mother came to the door when we arrived. Aside from her dark hair and complexion, she resembled my mother with her shapeless print dress and big smile. "She is an angel, knock wood! An angel, knock wood!" she said to me. She touched my hair, smiling even more broadly, took my hand and said, "Come! Eat!"

The table was in the kitchen, like ours was in Indiana, and food appeared, as if by magic, on the table. There were olives from their own trees, homemade stuffed grape leaves, hummus, salad, fresh figs, and pita bread, followed by a delicious chicken that had been simmered with olives, lemon, a lot of garlic and onions, and some yellow-orange spice, all served over rice. I oohed and aahed over the food, and Eddie translated what I said to his mother. She nodded and smiled and whispered, "An angel, knock wood."

After dinner, Eddie accompanied me downstairs and made up the couch for me to sleep on. He draped a sheepskin blanket over me, though it was not cold. "Goodnight," he said, and leaned down to kiss me. I offered him my cheek, but somehow, his lips landed on mine. I pulled away, not sure if it had been intentional or not, but I was willing to give him the benefit of the doubt. "I kees you," he said to me, and his lips descended.

"I don't want you to kiss me," I argued, and pulled the sheepskin blanket up over my face so he got a mouthful of hair.

"Eddie," I warned, "I don't want you to kiss me, so go upstairs to your own room."

"You don't want me to kees you?" he asked, and it occurred to me that perhaps he thought that I had been offering him sex since I agreed to spend the night in his home. Or at least an open-mouthed kiss.

"No, I don't," I said again firmly, but nicely.

"I don't understand," he said, but finally he went upstairs, leaving me to fall asleep in a strange house on a summer night in Bethlehem.

———

The next morning, the sun was barely up when I woke to normal household sounds and smells of breakfast being made and people showering. Before breakfast, Eddie took me up to the roof and pointed in the distance at fields that people claimed were Boaz's fields where Ruth had gleaned, picking up the barley that had been left behind by the reapers.

I was reminded momentarily of Khalid, who had brought me to an elevated point in the Old City and showed me the Dome of the Rock. A few kilometers away were small villages atop the Judean Hills. On Eddie's roof, I felt closer to the biblical Israel than I had in any of the churches I'd visited. In the early morning warmth and quiet, the world was incandescent and holy, and Israel felt like home.

———————

After breakfast, Eddie drove us to another village close to Bethlehem. Toting a big camera bag with various lenses, we made our way through the well-dressed crowd. I certainly hadn't packed for a wedding—I actually hadn't packed at all, because I'd planned to return the day before—so I was wearing a blue terrycloth dress with a white jacket that I buttoned around my chest to cover up any skin. While I noticed that people glanced at me curiously, everyone was unfailingly polite and said "Hello" in English, trying to make me feel comfortable. I appreciated it.

The bride wore a blinding white, voluminous dress. The person who'd made up her face had, even by my liberal standards, a heavy hand with eye shadow and blush. She seemed shy and happy and scared. She was about my age. She sat for a time on top of a stagelike area in a big chair and accepted gifts brought to her by the roomful of women.

Then we walked, dancing and singing, from the bride's village to the groom's home, where he and his party joined in. Friends and relatives hoisted the groom up in the air at various times. He, too, looked young and shy and at least a little frightened. The villagers ululated, and they sang and burst into dance.

This was quite different from Dubois County where, following the vows, there was a big, drunken reception at the Holiday Inn. Only after a good deal of beer, whiskey, or wine were we willing to offer a public display of noise or sentimentality.

I trailed along, and some of the girls put their arms through mine, as if we were best friends. I appreciated that gesture of female solidarity, and we smiled at each other with no other common language between us.

Eddie told me he was shooting another wedding the following day, and he asked me if I wanted to go with him. Absolutely!

———————

The Greek Orthodox wedding of the next day was more subdued than the Muslim wedding, and more traditional, because it took place in the St. Mary for Greek Orthodox church in Beit Jalah. Incense filled up the church, candles were lit, and people stood and sat. Very similar to the Catholics back home, I was sure.

This bride, too, was close to my age, maybe a year or two older, and she, too, had a face full of makeup. It occurred to me that she likely felt sorry for me because I was not married. Or maybe she envied me. It was impossible to know.

Now that I had my freedom, I couldn't imagine myself married, but I did sort of covet the happiness this young woman felt living the life that was expected of her, of remaining within her community and taking her place in this village that her ancestors had built and lived in for hundreds of years or more.

During the reception, Eddie was busy photographing, but he came over to me every half hour and solicitously inquired if I was okay. I was great. I'd been talking to a Greek girl a year younger than me who lived on the Mount of Olives. She planned to go to college the next year, but she wasn't sure where. She said that she was different. She didn't want to get married anytime soon.

When she was getting ready to leave, she spoke rapidly to an older man—her father—who then asked me if I wanted a ride back to Jerusalem. Yes, I said. Wonderful.

I said good-bye to Eddie, offered a kiss on the cheek, and asked him to please thank his mother for me again.

I felt as if I'd been away from Jerusalem and Hebrew and Jewish history and the Bar Kochba rebellion forever. That weekend was my first experience with the other residents of Israel, the Muslim and Christian Arabs, who lived in their own villages, their own worlds, in the territory known as the West Bank (a reference to the west bank of the Jordan River), which Israel referred to as "Judea and Samaria."

It was dusk as we wound our way up the Mount of Olives, past the golden, onion-shaped dome of the Russian church, past the garden of Gethsemane where Jesus was betrayed, to my new friend's home. How lucky they are, I thought, to live in Israel. To be able to say, "I live on the Mount of Olives." They invited me in, and we drank hot, sweet mint tea and talked about America and Israel and then, seeing how tired I was, her father brought me back to the dorm.

The Star of Bethlehem brought me to the greatest gift: the kindness of strangers.

CHAPTER 14

I stood in the long telephone line waiting to call my parents. The public phones in the basement of the dormitory on Mount Scopus required *asimonim*, round, coin-like tokens with a hole punched in the middle, which I'd bought waiting in another long line at the post office. As usual, a few of the bulky, 1960s-era, clunky silver phones were out of order, so there were about twenty people lingering to use the three working phones to call home.

The Ulpan, my immersive, six-day, all-day Hebrew classes, had just finished. I was now conversant enough in Hebrew to go to the open-air vegetable market in downtown Jerusalem and ask how many shekels the eggplant cost. It was three weeks before academic classes began at The Hebrew University campus on Mount Scopus and, like many other students waiting for the phone, I wanted to let my parents know where I would be spending the next few weeks.

I listened in on the chatter among the American students. There was a debate about whether the beaches in Netanya were superior to those in Haifa. A few others were talking about traveling in Egypt. I was going on a one-week archaeological dig in the north near Nazareth, then returning to Jerusalem to celebrate the Feast of Tabernacles, Sukkot, with the Worldwide Church of God.

Finally, it was my turn at the phone. Plink plunk, I dropped in my *asimon*. My mother answered and accepted the charges from the operator. "Well, hi, Tater!" She greeted me as she always did, her voice expressing how happy she was to hear from me. "Is everything okay?"

Since I rarely called, given the time difference and the difficulty making calls, she was concerned that something had happened. "Everything's fine. I just wanted to let you know I'll be on an archaeological dig for a week," I said. "What's going on at home?"

My grandparents were all fine, she said, but she thought Grandma Himsel was getting a little forgetful. My mother was working as a private sitter for an elderly woman. The woman had dementia, and she accused my mother of sleeping with her husband and of cutting up her slips. My mother laughed and said, "Well, that's how some people get when they get old." She said she'd found a chicken grinder at a yard sale, and I teased her, "I bet you found a lot of things at the yard sale!"

My mother had a self-deprecating wit and took my kidding in stride. "You got my letter about the Feast site in Jerusalem?" she asked me, and I said that I was looking forward to it. And I was. Aside from my time in Bethlehem, I hadn't been around any Christians, let alone anyone from my church, for almost two months. I'd been absorbed in everything Jewish—from the people, to the language, to the history. So it would be nice and meaningful to spend the week of the Feast of Tabernacles to hear sermons and fellowship with church people in Jerusalem, of all places.

Then my father got on the phone and almost immediately said he didn't know why the heck Mama needed another chicken grinder, she never makes chicken salad anyway, what's the matter with her, she must have something wrong with her.

As always, it was difficult to know how to respond. If I argued with him, he wouldn't change his mind, he would just get mad at me. On the other hand, I didn't like enabling my father's criticism and beratement of my mother.

"According to your father, I can't do nothin' right," my mother would halfway joke.

So I changed the subject.

"Looking forward to the Feast?" I asked him. My parents, my younger sister Liz, and my five-year-old sister Rachael were going to the Wisconsin Dells to celebrate the Feast of Tabernacles.

"Oh, yeah, it'll be nice. If the weather holds up, it should be real pretty this time of year. The leaves have already turned here."

As any farm boy would, my father kept close track of the weather, recording the temperature and rainfall on the calendar, every day of the week. Somewhere in one of the kitchen cabinets were calendars from the 1960s with my father's handwriting on them: "72, light rain." When my oldest sister, Wanda, accidentally backed her car into the rain gauge in the driveway, emptying its contents, my father reprimanded her, demanding that she park elsewhere. Farmers were proprietary over their rain.

"I'm going on an archaeology dig this week near Nazareth," I reiterated to my father. I couldn't trust my mother to let him know. I suspected she deliberately withheld information from him just to annoy him. A variation on slipping beef tongue into his soup.

My father perked up. Like me, he was fascinated by any new archaeological finds that might prove the Bible correct. "That should be interesting," he said.

I agreed. He asked if I'd had a chance yet to go to Ein Kerem, the birthplace of John the Apostle. For some reason, my father really wanted me to investigate this little village just outside Jerusalem. He'd mentioned it a few times in the letters he'd sent. "Not yet," I said. "But I will."

My father would love Israel, I thought then and many times in later years. To be physically close to the land on which the biblical stories had unfolded, and to walk the sites where Jesus and David and Samson and Rachel and Sarah may have walked, would have given him a thrill.

"So I guess you're twenty years old now," my father said, referring to my recent birthday.

I was always a little surprised when either my mother or father acknowledged my birthday. My parents still didn't have cakes, send cards, or give birthday presents to their children or family members, nor did they say the words "Happy birthday." The church's position on celebrating birthdays remained intractable. Because King Herod's daughter Salome had asked for John the Baptist's head on a platter as a birthday present 2,000 years prior, no one was allowed a birthday celebration. Like parents eating children, it seemed entirely possible that saying, "Happy birthday" would bring doom upon those I loved. And yet, it was nice to hear my father remember the day of my birth, my origin, and acknowledge that I had moved another full cycle around the sun.

We said our good-byes, and like all kids, I felt secure enough, after having touched base with my parents and heard their familiar and comforting voices, to zoom off into parts unknown.

CHAPTER 15

Ever since the 1800s, when Europeans arrived in the Holy Land, shovel in one hand, Bible in the other, people of faith have been looking for evidence of the veracity of the biblical stories. Did the flood really happen, and if so, was it possible to find remnants of the ark, or something else that might indicate a global deluge? To many devout Christians and Jews, the Bible was considered not just sacred but accurate, a historical document. If it was not true, then how could they justify their faith?

In 1896, the Merneptah Stele, an Egyptian victory stone, was discovered. It read "Plundered is the Canaan with every evil; carried off is Ashkelon; seized upon is Gezer . . . Israel is laid waste, bare of seed." Dated to 1208 BCE, during the rule of Pharaoh Merneptah, it was the oldest reference outside the Bible in which Israel was identified as such by its neighbors.

In the century since that discovery, the oldest surviving biblical text was unearthed in a grave in Jerusalem in 1979. Two tiny silver scrolls that served as amulets to ward off evil contained the priestly benediction mentioned in the book of Numbers: "May God [Yahweh] bless you and keep you and shine his light upon you." Dating to before 586 BCE, when the first temple was destroyed and Jews were sent into exile in Babylon, the text didn't necessarily confirm that the book of Numbers was in existence prior to the exile, but it is evidence that its scriptures were fundamental to the people's identity as worshipers of Yahweh—the personal name that God revealed to Moses at Mount Sinai.

The little scrolls were on exhibit at the Israel Museum, one of my favorite places in Jerusalem. The museum housed all things related to the archaeology of Israel, as well as its art and culture. There were 3,000-year-old arrowheads used in sieges on Jerusalem, as well as a stone tablet from the first century on which was inscribed in ancient Hebrew: "The bones of Uzziah, King of Judah, rest here . . . do not open!" Poor Uzziah—he'd had leprosy, and apparently his bones had been reburied around 700 years after his death in roughly 740 BCE.

Up north at the ancient city of Tel Dan, another exciting inscription was uncovered. On a large basalt stele, the ninth-century-BCE King Hazael of Damascus boasted of his victory over the house of Israel and the house of David, the first reference to David discovered outside the biblical narrative. Innumerable objects—from seals bearing names mentioned in the Bible, to entire cities like Lachish and Gezer—had been discovered in the past century that provided ample "proof" that, at the very least, the Bible was grounded in historical reality.

I didn't really expect to find a biblical inscription on my own dig near Nazareth. But I had my hopes. At the end of September 1981, I boarded the red and white Egged bus from the central station in Jerusalem, excited to physically dig in the dirt and perhaps find an ancient coin or a broken bit of pottery that would shed some light on the past.

Each morning, I got up before the sun rose, had a breakfast of tomato and cucumber salad, chunks of halvah (I came to love sesame seeds, whether baked into sweet halvah or bitten out of their salty shell in one graceful move that I never quite mastered), hard rolls smeared with chocolate spread, and canned tuna fish. Then our volunteer crew trudged the few hundred yards from our tents to Hurvat Tiria, the dig site farther up the hill where a number of rectangular trenches had been cut into the earth and sectioned off into a grid. We wielded trowels, filled the wheelbarrow with refuse to be carted away, and sifted dirt in a sieve.

We were a motley crew of volunteers. Ira was a Jewish guy from Staten Island whose parents had emigrated from Russia to the States. He had big, strange, blue eyes, which glazed over now and then, and he would say things like "Angie, I had a dream last night, and you were in danger." And I would say, "Oh my God, Ira, what?" But that was all he would tell me.

There was an older, quiet, retired Christian Dutch man for whom going on an archaeology dig in the Holy Land was a long-held dream come true. Lloyd was a fellow student at The Hebrew University who, like me, took a passionate interest in biblical archaeology, something that was incomprehensible to others who didn't experience a natural high when a Canaanite grave was uncovered.

Simon was tattooed and British and made me laugh. He delivered his curses—"bollocks sun" and "bloody mosquitos"—in a thick Cockney accent. Simon made the hard, tedious work, which reminded me of summers spent hilling potatoes at my grandma Himsel's farm, a little more bearable. One afternoon when we were scraping away in our quadrant, Simon revealed that he only had one testicle because of an accident in his youth. I made a mental note to use that in a story I would write one day. I was always on alert for telling details that might reveal character or motivation. Or just for anything interesting.

Two Norwegian girls, Turid and Astrid, were backpacking around Europe and the Middle East, and for them this was another adventure, like picking grapes in the south of France. Sally, a British woman my age, was sweet and pretty, and as a result of her time in Israel, she felt that God was calling her. She planned to get baptized in the Jordan River after the dig, and said she would invite all of us to come and witness it. I was jealous of Sally's newfound conviction, and it made me want to redouble my efforts to arrive at my own goal: unwavering, unquestioning faith that I believed would herald the arrival of the Holy Spirit.

In just one week, I became confident with the trowel and, without much discussion, knew when to haul the debris away in the wheelbarrow, and when to put something aside to wash it for a further look.

In the afternoons, when the sun was at its zenith, we took refuge in our tents. We lay on top of our sleeping bags, listened to music on portable cassette players, took a nap, read, or talked. I would scribble into one of my notebooks lofty poems about our shared humanity and how we could not allow fences to separate us—things that a twenty-year-old considered profound.

I was also reading Leon Uris's novel *Exodus*. I liked how he chose fiction to explore the founding of the state of Israel. As told through the eyes of an Israeli who was trying to bring Jews in post-World War II Europe from a detention camp in Cyprus to Israel aboard the ship *Exodus*, the novel delved into each character's life before the events took place. Uris brought to life the Holocaust, as well as Jewish life in Russia in the early part of the twentieth century, and provided a clearer explanation of British involvement in Israel prior to it becoming a state.

I was uncomfortable, however, with the depiction of Arabs as either rapists or murderers, and was a little surprised that he could get away with such a non-nuanced view of characters. The Women in Literature class at Indiana University had prompted me to consider the author's decision to portray women in certain ways. Was it to perpetuate stereotypes? Was it for the sake of accuracy? Wasn't it possible that women weren't the saints/sinners they were often presented as? It was an obvious question, but not one I'd thought about until that time. Now, I applied that same reasoning to Uris and his fictional depiction of Arab/Jew, good/bad, us/them. Writers were entitled to tell the story they wanted to tell, of course. But someone else might write a very different story, based on the same events.

On the last night of the dig, we sat around the campfire as we always did and told jokes and spoke a little more about our lives. I continued the conversation with Boaz, the director, about the biblical artifacts that had been discovered in Israel, and what he thought might still reasonably be found. Boaz hemmed and hawed. He said, "Angie, a good archaeologist isn't trying to prove or disprove the Bible."

I understood that he had to say that as an archaeologist first and foremost, but I couldn't imagine that as an Israeli and a Jew, he wasn't a tiny bit interested in finding out if the biblical text could be corroborated by archaeological evidence.

Like everything in Israel, archaeology was also a political issue, with Palestinians expecting to use archaeology to discount the Jewish claim to the land, while Jews used it to prove their long connection to it. Was there really a King David, and did he have a kingdom? If so, did that give Jews more of a right to Israel? And if not, did it give them less right to Israel?

Neither Jewish nationalism nor Arab nationalism was of great interest to me then. Despite my belief in God and in the Bible, I still longed for proof that the people and places and events mentioned in the Bible once existed. Unlike Sally, who told me one afternoon that her faith in God and Jesus didn't depend upon archaeological proof, I thought it was crucial.

It would be misleading to say that the historical value of the Bible didn't matter to those of us who believed that every word of the Bible was true. If it turned out that there had been no Ten Commandments from Mount Sinai, wouldn't that change things a little? Rooted in a specific time and place in history, the Bible went into excruciating detail as to who was on the throne and who did what to whom. If those events did not occur, if those places did not exist, if those laws and customs and rituals were inaccurate, then it prompted serious questions. The Judeo-Christian notion of God was based upon the premise that God acted within the confines of history, and that God had revealed Himself through the words of the Bible, as well as through the people that He had chosen to deliver His message to the world. So if the Bible—God's words—was inaccurate, it mattered. Whether you liked it or not.

Proof was what Constantine's mother, the empress Helene, was after in the fourth century when she supposedly found remnants of the true cross and part of Jesus's tunic. Archaeologists would say that it was impossible to prove that any of it had belonged to Jesus. True, it couldn't be proved scientifically. But using relics and other things left behind seemed to be the only way to get close to those who came before us. The arrowheads and tomahawks that regularly turned up when we plowed the fields on Grandma's farm were proof that the Native Americans had predated us.

————————

Hurvat Tiria didn't reveal any intact jars, bones, sarcophagi, or tombs, just some Roman glass and bits of pottery. I came to the dig hoping to find something—anything—but instead I met an interesting group of people who shared a curiosity and passion for the past. Maybe they were the people I'd been looking for when I was staring out the window at the Boone Township School. It felt like it.

In the week I was at Hurvat Tiria, it slowly occurred to me that it wasn't necessarily the pieces of the biblical past I was trying to put together and make whole again. Nor was it the country and the soil that I'd set out to explore. I was digging around in my soul, trying to excavate the answers buried there. I had a whole new set of questions, in addition to the ones I'd set out with a few months before. It wasn't just how can I get the Holy Spirit, but what *is* the Holy Spirit, and who exactly was Jesus, and was I really doomed if I didn't stay on this path, this one path to God? But even considering the possibility that there might be another path made me worry that already I was being influenced by Satan.

On the final morning of the dig, we rolled up our sleeping bags, packed our backpacks, exchanged addresses, and said our good-byes.

I stood on the grassy expanse that overlooked Nazareth in the distance. I loved everything about archaeology except actually doing it. I was no Indiana Jones, seeking the Ark of the Covenant. I preferred excavating in other ways—intellectual, experiential—to breathe life into the written texts of the Bible and animate them in today's world. I wanted to find an answer to the questions that troubled my parents: Where are we from, and where are we going?

CHAPTER 16

The following week, my academic advisor, Golda, invited me to have dinner in her *sukkah,* the Hebrew word for hut or tabernacle, which she, along with most of the other Jews in Israel, erected for Sukkot or, as I called it, the Feast of Tabernacles.

Golda lived in an airy, book-filled, rose-gold limestone home in Jerusalem. She and her husband had moved to Israel from Brooklyn with their four young children just before the war of 1967 broke out. Her mother, whom everyone called Oma, German for "grandma," lived with them and offered quiet and funny commentary from the sidelines.

I arrived early for dinner, and was in the kitchen eating some of the little pretzels that I loved while Golda checked something in the oven. She turned and asked me about the church and its connection to Israel. I told her that we believed that England and America were two of the lost tribes.

"How is that?" Golda faced me, towel in hand.

"Well, for example, the British people got their names from two Hebrew words, '*brit,*' covenant, and '*ish,*' man. So the British are 'people of the covenant.' And the Bible says that 'in Isaac shall thy seed be called.' The son of Isaac would be Isaacson. Drop the 'I' and you have 'Saacson' or 'Saxon.' The Anglo Saxons are descended of Isaac."

"That makes no sense." Golda dismissed what I believed was a scholarly explanation. "In Hebrew, the son of Isaac is '*ben Yitzchak*.' Yitzchak is Isaac, and it means 'he laughs.' The Torah wasn't written with English in mind."

I would have to rethink this.

"Do you give this church money?" Golda pressed.

"Yes, of course. We tithe."

"Your parents give the church ten percent of their income?"

"Well, that's the first tithe. The second is to be used during the Feast of Tabernacles, and the third is for the widows and the poor."

"I would imagine everyone in the church is poor if you're giving them all your money!" Golda laughed. I was uncomfortable. "They sound nuts. Absolutely crazy, Angie. It's one of those cults that just want your money."

I felt a whoosh of something disturbing, but before it had a chance to properly land, I pushed it away. I couldn't afford to listen to any criticism of the church. Like my Catholic and Lutheran families, and my older siblings who had also left the church, to me God just hadn't opened Golda's mind.

Sensing my discomfort, Golda changed the subject. "Angie, taste this, does it need more salt?" I took a spoonful of Israeli salad, the finely chopped tomatoes and cucumbers tossed with lemon juice, olive oil, and salt that was a staple for breakfast, lunch, and dinner.

"It's good," I said.

I wandered out to see the *sukkah* that had been built using the garden's walls, on top of which they had laid long bamboo poles as a roof. Golda had set up several tables in the garden underneath bulbs that were strung from the roof, which provided just enough light to cast shadows and make it feel as if we were in our own secluded world.

Golda's family, several of her ex-pat American friends, and some of her students sat around the tables; the conversation was lively and bounced back and forth effortlessly. I listened to opinions about everything from the West Bank settlements to Anwar Sadat's assassination the week prior.

Sadat was assassinated by members of the Egyptian Islamic Jihad. I'd read in the English newspaper, the *Jerusalem Post*, that Sadat had been attempting to crack down on Muslim fundamentalists who refused to recognize Israel's existence, and who felt betrayed that Sadat had made peace with Israel in 1979 in the Camp David Accords. Sudan's president, Gaafar Nimeiry, was the only Arab head of state to attend Sadat's funeral. Even in death, Sadat was being ostracized by the Arab world.

The Israelis were concerned that the new president, Hosni Mubarak, might not honor Sadat's commitment to peace with its neighbor. Security in Jerusalem was tighter than usual. The bus drivers took more than a moment to pat down my bag when I boarded, and the old man outside the grocery store, whose face looked like a dried apple and who typically sat half-asleep on his wooden stool, showed more than a perfunctory interest when he searched my daypack.

There were also a few dissenting thoughts on Moshe Dayan, the military leader whose famous black eye patch provided the world with an image of fighting Jews. Dayan died the same week that Sadat was killed. After the Six-Day War in 1967, when Israel took back East Jerusalem, he was the first Jew to pray at the Western Wall, atheist though he was. An amateur archaeologist, he'd also entered Hebron in the dead of night and lowered a skinny twelve-year-old girl down into the narrow shaft to explore the Cave of Machpelah. She hadn't found Abraham's or Sarah's bones, but she had taken photographs of the cave. I was so jealous.

"This must be very weird for you, Angie," Golda addressed me.

"Not weird," I said. "But different."

I liked different.

In the two and a half months I'd been in Israel, slowly, slowly, I was starting to understand that a Jewish culture separate from the Christian world I grew up in had existed and thrived for 2,000 years. Jews were scattered across the globe, yet remained connected by a shared past, a biblical text, and a yearning for their ancient homeland, Israel.

Until I went to Israel, I hadn't realized that it was created as a Jewish homeland, in part, as a result of the Holocaust. According to Israeli law, anyone with one Jewish grandparent was granted the "right of return" to Israel. This served as a slap in the face to the Spanish and Portuguese governments who, for hundreds of years until the nineteenth century, had demanded documents attesting to people's "purity of blood," and to the Nazis, who'd marked for death anyone who had one Jewish grandparent's blood running through his or her veins.

With the creation of the state of Israel in 1948, diaspora Jews were no longer safe in the Arab world; eventually, two-thirds of the 900,000 Jews from Arab countries immigrated to Israel. My roommate Talya's family was from Mexico, and prior to that, from Lebanon. My friend Leora's mother was from Baghdad. Leora's family had locked up their home and said good-bye. She claimed her family had lived in Iraq since 586 BCE, the time of the Babylonian exile at the hands of Nebuchadnezzar.

While the congenial conversation and laughter continued around me under the *sukkah*, I looked up at the Jerusalem sky peeping through the poles and recalled the stars at daybreak when my family would start our journey each autumn to the Feast. Without believing in Jesus, I thought Jews were missing out on a big part of the meaning of the Feast. It didn't just recall Moses wandering in the desert for forty years; it also represented the Second Resurrection. If I remained in the church, I would be there when the last trumpet was blown and the dead were resurrected from the ground.

I wanted to be there.

CHAPTER 17

Every day during the Feast of Tabernacles, I attended services at a hotel in downtown Jerusalem. The hotel chairs in the conference room were more comfortable than the hard folding chairs I was accustomed to, but the hymns and the opening prayer and the sermons were the same as those I'd heard my whole life.

On one of the last days of the Feast, an American woman named Eve came up to me. She lived in the West Bank with her two teenage children and husband, a Palestinian Muslim whom she'd married before she came into the church. Originally from Texas, Eve was tall and thin and strikingly pretty with dark hair, pale skin, and bright blue eyes. She spoke quietly and with a bit of diffidence. Eve suggested that we meet at her house some Sabbath and listen to the sermons on tape that the church sent her.

I said that would be great, and she gave me her phone number.

"By the way, Angie, did you know that the church doesn't allow us to wear makeup anymore?" Eve asked softly.

I was aware that she was genuinely concerned for my eternal salvation, so I didn't get my feathers ruffled. I replied, "Yeah, I know. But I'm wearing it anyway."

"Oh, okay. I just wanted to make sure you knew."

"Thanks." I could tell that she wanted to help me be a better Christian.

Living primarily with Jews, I thought that going to Eve's house in the West Bank and listening to church tapes would help me maintain my connection with the church and with Jesus. I was a little worried that Eve would preach about my makeup and God knows what else. In fact, Eve became a dear friend.

On many Saturday mornings, after a cup of hot tea and toasted pita slathered in butter and honey, I walked out of my dorm past the small, ramshackle house of an Arab family whose shy son was often outside tending his sheep. I waited nearby on Damascus Road for the Arab bus. There was no discernible schedule—the bus happened along whenever it happened along.

On the bus, older women wore traditional long, black, embroidered dresses and sat wearily in their seats. Middle-aged men smoked cigarettes while teenage boys talked loudly and laughed. A few curly-haired, shy-eyed children with young mothers stared at me in that way that children do when they see someone so foreign.

The bus was a microcosm of Arab society, just as the Jewish buses I rode in West Jerusalem were a microcosm of theirs. Hebrew music blared from the radio, at least one woman crocheted a *yarmulke*, Israeli soldiers in green uniforms stood shoulder to shoulder, and several men and women bent over their pocket-sized, well-worn prayer books, silently mouthing prayers or psalms.

Several times on the Jewish bus as the doors were about to shut, there was a loud "*Nahag, tafsik! Tafsik!*" or "Driver, stop, stop!" that came from someone chasing the bus outside on the sidewalk. Despite the fact that the bus was completely full, the chorus was taken up by a stranger in the front seat, then repeated by another, until the entire bus seemed to be screaming, "*Tafsik!*" The bus driver inevitably stopped, the relieved traveler squeezed onto the bus, and the passengers who'd shouted allowed themselves a satisfied smile at one another.

I'd started to get used to the loud talking and screaming in Israel in general. It was not necessarily rude, which had been my immediate judgment, but rather an effective means of making your needs known and of speaking up for yourself or for others. The notion that we are all responsible for one another was quite something to take in. In Jasper, we wouldn't dream of interfering in anyone else's affairs, not even a neighbor who beat their kids, nor a family member who drank too much.

The Arab bus went up the hills and around curves, and about twenty minutes later I pulled the string to ring the bell at my stop. I got off and walked up the hill to Eve's house, a modern, white stone home set on a hillside in Beit Hanina.

When the kids were young, Eve's husband, Suleiman, had moved the family from Texas to the town he'd grown up in on the West Bank. He was intent on removing them from corrupt American values. Now teenagers, the kids hated the lack of freedom in the Arab culture, hated not being able to buy cornflakes, hated the gossiping villagers, hated their mixed bloodline, neither really American nor Palestinian, hated the way Palestinians treated their animals, hated learning a new language, and especially hated the Israeli occupation of the West Bank.

Many Saturdays I sat at Eve's kitchen table, drank Turkish coffee, and listened to a male minister's voice emanating from the cassette player and droning on about the end of days, prophecy being fulfilled, and the five keys to understanding God. The usual.

Eve was churchy, but in a nice way, even as I challenged her about Mr. Armstrong and his new truths. Eve would softly explain, "He's God's apostle, Angie, so we have to follow him." This, I knew, was standard church-speak, and the ministers would often say, "If Mr. Armstrong asked me to jump off a cliff, I would do it."

I was feeling even more unsettled than usual at blindly following Mr. Armstrong and the church, but the specter of the Resurrection hung over me, and I feared my impatience was the work of Satan, trying to keep me from the Kingdom, and from my sister.

Suleiman was a tall, wiry, polite man. His kids and his wife hated his country, even though he'd tried so hard to make a nice life for them. In the living room, Suleiman's mother sat clad in her traditional long, black dress. She lived a few doors away, but was usually at Eve's house. Eve communicated with her in basic Arabic and brought her tea or Turkish coffee and sweet things to eat. She reminded me a little of Golda's mother, Oma.

Eve's daughter, Laila, had just started high school. Like Eve, she was tall with black, wavy hair, fair skin, and hazel eyes. Laila had the soul of an activist. She yelled at her fellow Palestinians who beat their donkeys, took in stray cats, and dropped shekels into beggars' palms. She'd already decided she wanted to be a lawyer when she grew up and bring justice to those who had no voice.

On one of my Saturday visits, Laila said, "Mom, I'm going to tell Angie. Angie, somebody offered for me. My cousin."

"What? Offered what?"

"Laila, you know we're not going to let you marry your cousin," Eve broke in.

"Oh my God!" This was like a soap opera.

"Yeah, exactly. I mean, I'm an American. I'm not one of these Arabs. I'm going to college. I'm not staying here."

Eve continued to reassure Laila that it wasn't going to happen, but the more she tried to reassure her, the more incensed Laila became. Her father's sister thought Laila would be interested in her first cousin, Mohammed! Laila told me that several girls at her school had already been offered for.

My father had often said it wouldn't be a bad idea if a father chose his daughter's husband, just like they'd done in the times of Abraham. The thought of anyone making such a choice for me was maddening. I could only imagine that Laila, who was feisty and smart, but also sensitive to her family, was genuinely terrified that her future was not her own. She could be engaged to her cousin, and if she opposed it or ran away, that would be the end of her relationship with her family.

Eve finally had enough of this talk and put in the next tape. My mind wandered as the words of some faceless, nameless American minister filled the kitchen, preaching about how Jesus, like Abraham, had had perfect faith, which we should strive for ourselves. Yet again, I found myself thinking about how surreal it was that I was actually living in Israel. I was sitting in a friend's house in the West Bank. It felt as if I was in the beating heart of the world, the place where every conflict large and small, political and personal, jostled for attention and demanded to be acknowledged and discussed. I felt alive in a way I never had before. And it was because I'd become a part of this world, not apart from it. And this world that I truly inhabited was far more fascinating than all of my speculations on the next world.

Laila's older brother, Aziz, was as reserved as Laila was passionate. Aziz had been arrested once and sent to jail because a kid near him threw a rock at a soldier. As was Israeli policy, all of the kids around the culprit were arrested. Palestinian parents lived in fear that Israel would simply decide to keep their kids incarcerated. This was mirrored on the Jewish side by parents who feared that Arab kids would not stop at just throwing rocks, but also detonate bombs. What became clear to me was the universality of the fear and mistrust on both sides of this raging issue.

I felt as if I needed to take sides. Choose one and demonize the other. Either the Israelis were absolutely right, and the Arabs were absolutely wrong, or vice versa. It was uncomfortably similar to the church's attitudes, where we were told that you couldn't be lukewarm in your faith. You were of this material world—or of God's world. A perennial fence-sitter, I wanted to say to Laila, "No, no, you don't understand! They're wonderful!" and to Golda, "No, no, you don't understand! They're wonderful!" They were both wonderful to me, and the heartbreak was that they might never know it.

I told Aziz I was really sorry about jail. He shrugged it off, but I couldn't fathom how awful it must have been for a sixteen-year-old boy, just a little younger than my sister Sarah. I felt hopelessness for those on both sides whom I'd never met. This wasn't going to end anytime soon.

Laila once said, "I mean, I'm sorry about what happened in Europe, but it wasn't my fault, it wasn't the Arabs' fault, and why do the Jews just think they can grab our land? Because they lived here thousands of years ago?" Her calm, even-toned logic was like a slap in the face.

Until then, I believed, like most Evangelical Christians, that Israel was the Promised Land, which God had promised solely to Abraham's descendants, for eternity. Laila saw it from another perspective: once you left a country, you couldn't expect to come back a few thousand years later. The nest egg was long gone. The wren had flown away.

CHAPTER 18

I was immersed in modern Israel. Heated political discussions broke out over Shabbat dinners or at lectures at the university or in line at the grocery store.

There was gossip that Yasser Arafat was gay; a debate over whether Reagan was committed to Israel or if he was just acting; a disagreement over which falafel stand was best. These were quite different conversations from the ones I'd had with church friends such as "Who is the Beast that the book of Revelations refers to, and what does the number 666, the mark of the Beast, signify?"

At the same time, as observant Jews and Christians had for thousands of years, I looked for answers in the biblical text. My classes analyzed the book of Ruth from a literary point of view, investigated medieval Jewish philosophy, and compared the ancient Far East legends and myths to the stories in the Bible.

One professor said that the literary structure of Genesis was reminiscent of other Near Eastern creation myths. He maintained that Genesis provided two different, often conflicting, accounts of the creation of the world that were written by two, perhaps three, different authors—not Moses, not God. The Mosaic Law, my professor asserted, had been assembled over a long period of time. It was not "the truth," but "a truth."

I had never before questioned the veracity of the Bible. I had only been concerned with its correct interpretation. There was one right answer, one right religion—mine.

But things were changing. I was changing.

I was studying the Bible academically, not spiritually, and it felt heretical and wonderful and exhilarating. I had fascinating new friends, both Jewish and Palestinian. Latife was a Druze woman, in love with a Muslim man. "If my family finds out, they won't kill me, but it will be very bad," she told me. My study partner, Patty, quizzed me on the barren women of the Bible, and spoke fondly of her Moroccan Jewish mother and her repressed American father who had converted to Judaism.

In many conversations with my friend Louise, who was a social worker, she explained that she believed therapy was about the concept of "lost and found." In the process of talking to a therapist and remembering the past, a patient "found" pieces of him- or herself that had been lost. Over time, I was losing some of my faith in the church. What I found, however, was not at all what I'd expected.

I found modern Jews. Regular people. Not Jews who rode on camels, but people like me who complained if it was too hot or too rainy, who told jokes and swore and had their own opinions. On a trip to the Negev, the desert in the south, I sat around a nighttime campfire with a child of Holocaust survivors, another from a long line of Hasidic rabbis, and one whose ancestor had been burned at the stake during the Spanish Inquisition. These new friends were a bit different from my childhood pals, with whom I'd chanted from the basketball stands, "Sauerkraut, sauerkraut, pretzels, and BEER! All for Jasper, stand up and cheer!"

I started looking at the biblical text with my head, not my heart. I came to view the Bible as originally having been transmitted orally, but then written down on parchment and papyrus, patched together by human beings, not by God.

Studying commentary on the Bible challenged me and made me consider new possibilities and ideas. The Bible was not just a holy book, or a book of laws, but it also contained literature: poetry, laments, and love stories: books that contained literary themes and subplots, metaphors and puns, as well as complex and often irrational characters, including God.

I lost my ability to read the Bible with an uncritical eye. And I found that many books of the Bible were actually lost: the book of Jasher, the book of the Wars of the Lord, a book of songs, and many others referred to in the Bible.

Israel itself felt like one giant lost and found. Jews from the nethermost corners of the earth found themselves, after an absence of 2,000 years, back in Israel. Excavations uncovered scraps of ancient texts, seal impressions, arches from Roman periods, remains of Byzantine churches, mosaic floors, and much more.

Then there were the Arab and Jewish lives lost in Israel's many wars and conflicts. Lost, the Palestinian people's claim that all the land between the Mediterranean Sea and the Jordan River was theirs. Found, a new country, based on what others had lost.

Lost, my certainty; found, ambiguity and ambivalence.

Lost though I may have been, I was happy losing myself in Israel.

Yet I also knew that, in a way I couldn't yet articulate, my lost-ness was only beginning to surface. Which meant that my found-ness was still in the future.

CHAPTER 19

Out of the blue, one day I realized that the central dilemma in the television sitcom *Bridget Loves Bernie* that aired from 1972 to 1973 had been that Bernie was Jewish and Bridget was Irish Catholic. I was eleven when *Bridget Loves Bernie* aired, and I'd recognized that Bernie's parents had a problem with his wife, but in my naïve mind I'd attributed the dilemma to the family deli, an odd grocery store in which salami hung from above the counter.

Even though it was a hit, *Bridget Loves Bernie* was canceled after one season. In 1973, *The New York Times* described the brouhaha in the article "*Bridget Loves Bernie* Attacked by Jewish Groups." Orthodox, Conservative, and Reform rabbis, as well as other members of the Jewish community, were infuriated by the depiction and acceptance of intermarriage and met with the management at CBS to have the show canceled. The lead actress, Meredith Baxter, later said, "We had bomb threats on the show. Some guys from the Jewish Defense League came to my house to talk with me about changing the show." A member of the Jewish Defense League was actually arrested.

That random realization was one of many I had in Israel. I also discovered that Barbra Streisand, Leonard Nimoy of *Star Trek*, Simon and Garfunkel, Neil Diamond, Freud, Einstein, and Jonas Salk were

Jewish. It was surprising to my friends that I hadn't known, and equally surprising to me that I was supposed to have known.

As the dominant majority, Christians were perfectly comfortable expressing their beliefs externally, or inserting openly Christian characters in television shows or movies. Even though *The Flying Nun* didn't sit well with my own family because a flying nun connoted demonic powers, at least Sally Field prayed in church.

On the other hand, I learned that *Bridget Loves Bernie* seemed to reflect a trend of that time—that for many American Jews, their identity was less about religious practice and more of a cultural definition. For people like me, who were unaware of what it was to "be" Jewish, Bernie's Jewish identity didn't register without the mention of "synagogue."

While contrary to the teachings of the church and therefore a totally alien concept to me, I did come to understand this important distinction. The notion of "being Jewish" was not based purely on spirituality. It could be a deep-seated attachment to history or the way you parent your children or your penchant for certain foods. Once at a party in Israel, one of the guests said she grew up identifying strongly as a Jew, but wasn't at all religious. "For me," she said, "being Jewish is a bagel."

I knew it wasn't for me to judge, but given my religious background, I couldn't help feeling a little sad. She probably knew more about Shakespeare than she did about her own faith. That didn't make sense to me.

I had another epiphany on top of Masada. Sixty miles south of Jerusalem, Masada wasn't exactly a mountain, but more of a rock plateau, looming 1,800 feet above the Dead Sea. On top were the ruins of King Herod's palace and fortification, which he'd built in 31 BCE as a safe place in case of a revolt. Jewish zealots later used the palace when they fled Jerusalem in 66 CE after the Romans destroyed both the city and the temple. In 73 CE, the Jews on Masada realized that the Romans were going to attack, so to deny them a victory, they committed suicide rather than be sold as slaves and prostitutes. The Jews would not be subjugated to the empire of pagan gods.

A few hours before sunrise, my classmates and I climbed the Snake Path that slithered its steep way around the side of the red rocks and up to the top of Masada. Sunrise was a dramatic unfurling of fire and light. A sliver of pink appeared on the horizon, then the sun seemed to burst into red and orange, slowly revealing the mountains across the Dead Sea to the east.

My friend Louise and I walked around the site. The 2,000-year-old Roman attack ramp that ran up the side of Masada was intact. I noted that a group of guys had gathered facing east. They had strapped leather bindings around their forearms and a small black box on their foreheads. They swayed back and forth, bending and muttering over small books they held in one hand, just like the men on the plane. Louise casually said to me, "They're praying."

Oh, so that's what that was!

In the gentle, early morning light, walking through the ruins of the storerooms and torn-down palaces that were little more than stones outlining what had been rooms, I conjured mental images of bearded men and long-robed women going about their domestic lives: baking bread for the Sabbath, the men standing and facing Jerusalem and praying, just like the American men were doing in front of me. Here, words and prayers were the bridge between the past and the present.

The Bible was a portable temple, a spiritual home in exile that could reside in the hearts of anyone, anywhere, anytime. The text replaced the temple as the place where people could come close to the Divine. Prayer replaced blood sacrifice. In Hebrew, the word for sacrifice, *korban*, meant "to come close."

The purpose of any sacrifice, any prayer, was simply to bring you closer to God.

In Christianity, Jesus was the blood sacrifice.

Without belief in Jesus, could you come close on your own?

CHAPTER 20

Before I went to Israel, I thought I knew all there was to know about my Savior. As I studied, I discovered that much of what I had been taught about Jesus was actually disputed, even within the Christian text itself. This included his ancestral bloodline.

Both Matthew and Luke traced Jesus's ancestry back to King David, with Luke saying it was through his mother Mary, while Matthew said it was through Joseph. Mark claimed that Jesus became God's son at the Baptism, while John said Jesus preexisted and became flesh.

Quoting the second-century pagan Greek philosopher Celsus, the Catholic writer Origen repeats Celsus's claim that Mary was "convicted of adultery and had a child by a certain soldier named Pantera." In early Jewish writings, Jesus was also said to be the son of Pantera, a Roman soldier. In the nineteenth century, a tombstone bearing the name Tiberius Julius Abdes Pantera, a Roman soldier who served in the Galilee during the time that Jesus was conceived, was discovered in Germany.

Of course none of that proved anything. But the Bible didn't prove anything either. It wasn't scientific fact. It was belief.

I'd accepted it as a given that Mary had given birth to Jesus as a result of the Holy Spirit, not by having sex with a man. God had somehow artificially inseminated Mary with His DNA, thus making Jesus both a god as well as God's son.

I hadn't viewed it as either inconsistent or pagan—that Jesus was both fully human and fully God, much as the Greek demigods had come into being through a god mating with a human to produce mankind. I recalled my friend Celia at Indiana University, who'd spoken extensively about how the goddess Isis nursing her son Horus paralleled the image of Mary nursing Jesus. Celia, in her quiet way, was confrontational. "It's strange that there are two male gods—God and Jesus—instead of God and a wife, don't you think?"

I was so used to the Christian status quo that not only didn't I think it was strange, I'd thought it was wrong and blasphemous to question it.

In Israel, I started to see Jesus as a first-century Jewish man. Many Jews then were chafing against Roman control and hoping for a Messiah, someone who, like King David, would reestablish a country run by Jews, and not existing as a client state of Rome.

Even my mental image of Jesus had shifted. He couldn't possibly have been a fair-skinned, light-haired, European-looking man. Rather, he must have looked like the olive-skinned, black-haired, Middle Eastern men of average height and weight. As a man, Jesus walked and talked, bathed and ate. He felt pain, and was part of the foment against the Roman rulers.

The apostle Paul had believed that Jesus was going to return imminently. Paul would have *plotzed* if he'd known that 2,000 years later, Jesus still hadn't returned to earth.

"What's Jesus supposed to save you from?" Louise once asked, curious.

"Everlasting death."

"Oh." My answer did not impress her.

"You must feel very conflicted," Louise commented, which I immediately denied. It was Louise who was always conflicted—over her boyfriend, over whether she should swim or study, over her relationship with friends back home. Not me. I dealt with conflicting desires easily. Israel or Germany? Israel. Go to the Sinai? Sure. Falafel or schwarma? Both. Being conflicted was just short of a moral failing.

Still, I couldn't deny that Louise was right.

In Israel, I started to feel uneasy with the notion that God required a human blood sacrifice to appease Him. Would it be so awful, I wondered, if Jesus had been fully mortal, with a flesh-and-blood mother *and* father? How much human could you have and still be a deity? Christianity, I started to think, was fixated upon two things: Jesus's virgin birth and his death. Since then, those obsessions—sex and death—had played out in everything from trying to regulate people's private lives, to being concerned that women remain virgins until they were married, to fetishizing martyrdom and the afterlife.

But what about all those years in between? Weren't we supposed to do more than just wait around to die, or wait around for Jesus to return? Christianity seemed death-centric. Modern Christians were obsessed with dying and getting into the next world, and the only path to that was accepting that a dead Jew nailed to the cross 2,000 years prior was your Savior. His death ensured that the rest of us would have a chance at eternal life. He'd died, so we wouldn't have to.

According to the book of John:

Who is the liar? It is the man who denies that Jesus is the Christ. Such a man is the Antichrist—he denies the Father and the Son. No one who denies the Son has the Father; whoever acknowledges the Son has the Father also.

Denying Jesus would make me the Antichrist.

I'd long hoped for a bolt out of the blue that would provide me with deep certainty that Jesus was my Savior and that I would be saved from everlasting death, and granted everlasting life. After seeing a vision of the resurrected Christ on the road from Jerusalem to Damascus, Saul was transformed to Paul and from a persecutor of the new Christians to the most zealous Christian missionary.

Without intending to, and without even knowing it myself, I was turning spiritually south, toward Jerusalem and toward the first-century rabbinical Judaism that Saul/Paul had left behind. Instead of the Christian view that this world was the devil's, and Jesus alone could swoop in and save it, I was drawn to the possibility that this world was God's and that we, as God's partner, would perfect it.

I felt at odds with a faith that emphasized the world to come more than the world we live in. One that ignored many of the current world's woes with a simple shrug and, "Only Jesus can fix that when He returns." And mostly, I couldn't prevent myself from being curious, which was decidedly antithetical to the kind of Christianity I grew up in. Curiosity meant asking questions, and asking questions meant rebelling against authority. Encouraging Satan.

CHAPTER 21

The church had long declared that, "This world is Satan's playground."

But Satan wasn't always the Satan of the church and of Christianity. Modern-day Satan was a shibboleth. In the Bible, "shibboleth" was the password used by the Gileadites to sift out the enemy Ephraimites, who could not pronounce the "sh" sound. The word "shibboleth" in Hebrew originally meant stream or flood, but in English it became synonymous with a catchphrase or slogan. I loved the way the word began as one thing, a password, but then, like a stream, it twisted and turned, its original meaning disappearing in the tides of history.

In Hebrew, Satan simply means "adversary." In the book of Genesis, the snake that tempted Eve was just that—a snake. But then in the second century, a thousand years after the book of Genesis was written, Christians identified the snake as Satan. The snake had slithered across history, shibboleth-like, and become Satan. The book of Revelation referred to "that ancient serpent, who is called the devil and Satan, the deceiver of the whole world," being thrown from heaven along with his fallen angels. In the book of Luke, Jesus says: "I saw Satan fall like lightning from heaven."

Both of those passages undoubtedly alluded to the book of Isaiah: "How you have fallen from heaven, *haylel, morning star*, son of the dawn!" When the Bible was translated into Latin in the fourth-century

Vulgate, the Hebrew word *haylel* became the Latin word for morning star, *lucifer*. And that added another layer to Satan's identity—Lucifer.

Neither Satan nor Lucifer was anywhere on Isaiah's radar. The prophet was taunting the Babylonian king as having fallen from heaven and lost his political power. Reminding him that the God of Israel transcended nature. God could never be a star in the sky. The prophets were excellent at taunting.

It wasn't exactly Satan or Jesus I was grappling with. It was 2,000 years of a European, Christian mind-set. It was the ancient battle of good and evil, God and Satan, West versus East, Us versus Them, the Cowboys versus the Indians, Bridget versus Bernie, Christian versus Jew. It emphasized the polarities that pit people and nations against each other, making them adversaries—satans in the original sense of the word— insisting that if you cannot pronounce *shibboleth* like I do, you are an enemy.

For Christians, however, Satan was an external being and responsible for evil. Satan was jealous that we'd been made in God's image, and Satan was also in a competition with God. And God was letting him contend.

If there was no Satan, no evil force in the universe that I was struggling against, then the evil in the world, and the struggle against it, was my own.

CHAPTER 22

People judge one another based on the way they look. Everybody does, and everyone balks at being judged, whether by their skin color, their body shape, how they dress, walk, and talk. As a non-Jewish, blonde, white woman, in Israel I was perceived as slutty.

Every day I was reminded in ways large and small that I was different, that I wasn't deserving of respect, that I was an object. I didn't actually care if they thought I was a loose, blonde bimbo. But I wished they would keep their opinions and hands to themselves.

I was walking up the narrow stairs of the Tower of David, Eve and Laila ahead of me, and I felt a hand behind me reach up and grab me between the legs. The passageway was chock-full of people, and we were wedged together without an inch between us. I couldn't turn around, couldn't even bat his hand away, and so I very loudly said, "Get off of me!" Nothing. All the way up the stairs, a stranger's hand remained firmly between my legs as I continued shouting in English, "Get off!" I could hear Laila saying, "Angie, what's happening?" and I said, "Some schmuck has his hand up my crotch." At the top, when I was finally able to turn around to find out who'd violated me, I couldn't tell which of the several men coming up the stairs had been the culprit, so I glared at them all.

Many women accepted that this kind of sexual (or verbal) abuse was something men did. Meaningless. Impossible to change. But to me it was just like the church's rhetoric about women being helpmeets to men and men ruling over women. I was incensed by it.

I had no one to complain or talk to, because it appeared that I was bragging about being followed, hissed at, catcalled, and grabbed. Women should be flattered by the male attention. Any male attention. And, of course, there was a casual acceptance of sexual harassment. It wasn't called misogyny. It was called "boys will be boys."

So I wrote a poem about the daily dance between men and women, comparing it to bargaining in the market:

GIVE AND TAKE

She appraises the
Merchandise while the
Owner rushes around
"It is good, yes? The
best in the market."
"How much?" she asks.
"Six hundred shekels."
"For that! I'll give you 250."

The owner sadly shakes his head.
"How can you be so stingy?" he asks.
"Look at it." He displays it in his hands.
"It is beautiful. I wish I
Must not part with it. But I know a
Woman like you will use it
More than I would."
Woman hesitates.
"Actually, I don't really need one."

Man puts his arm on woman's arm.
He looks into her face and softly says,
"You a very beautiful woman.
All beautiful women need one."

Put like that . . .
"For you," he continues cajolingly,
"I make special price.
Five hundred shekels."

"I'll give you," she softly returns,
"275 shekels."
Sadness fills his eyes.
His shoulders slump.
He is the bewildered little boy.
Man wearily argues,
"450."
"275."
"450."
"This is ridiculous!" woman snaps.
"I'll give 300."
"400."
"300."
"400."
She turns to walk away.
"Wait! Wait! Come back."
She allows herself a small,
Triumphant smile then
Turns around. "Well?"
"325."
"300. That's it."
They stare at each other stonily.
He shrugs.
She gives him
300 shekels.
She walks out of the store, satisfied,
Taking a piece
Of the storekeeper with her and
Leaving a piece of herself for him.

Later, alone, she wonders if
She was taken.

Another time, on an early morning bus to Be'er Sheva with Louise to check out the Bedouin market, my Ephraimite status was made abundantly clear. When we boarded, there hadn't been two free seats next to each other, so Louise was sitting with a woman across from me, and I'd been sitting next to a young guy. He got off, and in his place an ultra-Orthodox man wearing a long, black coat, pants, and black hat sat down next to me. I'd learned from Golda that for an Orthodox Jewish man, any physical contact with a woman who wasn't his wife was forbidden.

A few minutes later, I felt a hand against my leg. He must think it's his leg, so I'll just move over, I thought. I moved my leg. His hand followed. Maybe it's my hand on my leg, I thought. Something crept under my backside. Impossible! Religious clothing presupposed religious behavior! Despite all evidence to the contrary, I continued in denial. I believed that my perception of the situation had to be wrong. In my shock, I did nothing. When his hand began squeezing my butt, I finally looked him in the eye and said, "You have to move." Wordless, he got up and moved to another seat.

Louise leaned across the aisle and asked me what had happened. "He was grabbing my ass!" I was still half-convinced that it hadn't happened, and I'd misunderstood the encounter. That it had been my hand.

"Prick," she blurted out.

As I learned, religious garb didn't necessarily indicate moral behavior. On the contrary, it could serve as a guise to blind people from reality—like me, like Father Schroeder's choirboys, like all of the people in the church who never knew about Herbert Armstrong's sexual abuse of his daughter. Looking "religious" instilled trust in others, making them that much more vulnerable.

Louise had a theory that a religious Jewish man wouldn't make inappropriate overtures toward a Jewish woman, so the following week, when I went to meet Eve on King George Street, I wore a dress, thick tights, and clogs, and wrapped a scarf around my hair, careful to tuck all of the blonde strands underneath. I was trying to pass for Jewish, but also married.

An Orthodox man in his thirties approached me and asked where I was from. Since I was incapable of ignoring someone, nor did I want to walk away from where I was to meet Eve, I replied. I lied and said New York City. Indiana would have definitely given me away. He said he knew New York City, where did I go to school? I said, "Yeshiva."

He looked at me more closely, but I maintained a completely straight face, still hoping that both my long-skirted attire and my lie had been convincing.

He asked me which yeshiva. I said, "Brooklyn."

"Yes, but which one?"

Oh, no. There was more than one yeshiva? I'd thought it was the name of one, specific Jewish school in Brooklyn. So I said, sharply, "Brooklyn," and walked away.

I had never been to Brooklyn and knew only vaguely that a yeshiva was a place of Jewish learning. From my Hebrew class, I understood it came from the root word "*yoshev*," "to sit," so I assumed sitting down and studying was what a yeshiva was all about. Apparently, there was more than one.

I realized that despite my frequent invocation of "*Oy vayz mir*" and headscarf, I could not pass. Those Gileadites could see straight through my Ephraimite disguises. They assumed that like all Westerners, especially the Dutch, Scandinavian, and German women who often hooked up with Arabs and Israelis, earning them a certain reputation, I had loose moral standards. Sometimes I was able to block it all out, walk down the street, and barely hear the hisses piercing the air around me. My learned obliviousness again worked in my favor. Growing up in a chaotic household, I had developed the ability to block things out. It was my go-to coping mechanism.

When I told Louise later about the incident on King George Street, trying to pass for being Jewish, she said casually, slightly dismissively, "Oh, Angie, you've never belonged anywhere, in Indiana or with your family. You've always been an outsider. You're very complex. You're not black and white."

I must have frowned, because her tone softened, and she said, "No, trust me, it's more interesting."

Not being black and white to me meant lukewarm. Wishy-washy. Very, very gray and murky. You couldn't get into the Kingdom with one foot in this world.

And in some sense, I still wanted to belong. And to be saved.

CHAPTER 23

Had I gone to Germany instead of Israel, I would have belonged. Instead, I'd seen the brochure for Israel featuring the Dome of the Rock and heard another call. "Lech lecha!" God had told Abraham. "Go!" My Bible professor explained that this was an internal call. No one had forced Abraham to leave. It was a call only he heard, in order to go find himself.

The Dome of the Rock was one of the first sites I visited when I arrived, and a place I returned to several more times. Built as an Islamic shrine by Muslims in 691 CE, the Dome of the Rock preserved the sanctity of the Temple Mount, where both Jewish temples had once stood. The first temple was built by King Solomon and destroyed by the Babylonian king Nebuchadnezzar in 587 BCE. The Jews were sent into exile in modern-day Iraq.

In the eleventh century, the Catholic Church said that anyone who helped recapture Jerusalem from Muslim rule would receive immediate remission of sins. The Crusaders pounded across Europe to the Middle East, where they enthusiastically murdered both the Jewish and Muslim populations, not only with impunity but also with the belief that they were doing exactly what God wanted them to do. An anonymous eyewitness to the Crusaders' siege on the Temple Mount in 1099 recorded in the *Gesta Francorum*, *The Deeds of the Franks:* "The slaughter was so great that our men waded in blood up to their ankles." Another source, Raymond of Aguilers, said that the blood was "up to their knees and bridle reins." Whether ankles or knees, it was bloody. There seemed to be a link between godliness and bloodiness.

The Crusaders set up headquarters on the Temple Mount, immediately erecting a golden cross on top of the Dome and repurposing the other Muslim buildings. When Saladin recaptured Jerusalem in 1187, it was returned to a Muslim site once more and has been ever since.

Inside the Dome was a huge limestone rock, much like the limestone that bathed the entire city of Jerusalem in its magical white-rose aura. Jewish tradition maintained that the rock was the one that Abraham laid Isaac upon when called by God to sacrifice him. The Ark of the Covenant, carved in stone and containing the Ten Commandments, may have rested upon the rock within the first temple. Stone on stone.

Each time I stood in front of the railing encircling the rock, I recalled how Abraham had been willing to sacrifice Isaac, a testament to his obedience—or perhaps to his faith—that his son would be resurrected from the dead. Isaac is not recorded in the Bible as ever speaking to Abraham after being placed on the altar as a human sacrifice. In fact, he remained fairly mute and passive after the event unfolded.

As a teenager, whenever I argued with my father about why there were "girl" jobs and "boy" jobs, his response was, "When God told Abraham to sacrifice Isaac, his only son, he didn't ask why. It wouldn't hurt you to be a little more like Abraham."

I was not Abraham and doubted I would ever be able to summon up that kind of no-questions-asked subservience.

It was the spring of 1982, and the academic year would be over in another six weeks. However, I had gotten permission from Golda to extend my time in Israel and to finish my bachelor's degree at The Hebrew University. It was another of those snap decisions. I'd overheard another student explaining that she was able to finish her college credit requirement in Jerusalem. It sounded like a great idea and, also, I couldn't imagine returning to Indiana after living in the Middle East. So I asked Golda, and she worked it out.

Happy, I walked across the Temple Mount toward the Dome of the Rock. An Arab family sat in a grassy area, mom wearing the traditional long, black dress and headscarf, dad in jeans. Their two young children speaking rapidly in Arabic, and though I didn't understand it, I thought one of the kids was tattling on the other. The mom smiled and pulled the aggrieved one close.

The Temple Mount was a complex of buildings, fountains, minarets, and arches, all overlooking the Old City below. Throughout the vast space, Muslims, Jews, and Christians walked past each other, intersected, stared at the al-Aksa mosque, spoke, and took photos. Being there meant something different to each of us.

For some Jews, it was inextricably linked to the first and second temples and where they had stood, and where God had once dwelled, demanding sacrifices.

For Muslims, this was their safe space, the heart of Muslim life.

For me, it was a touchstone to the biblical past.

Just below the Dome of the Rock was the Church of the Holy Sepulchre, where Catholics believed Jesus had been crucified, buried, and resurrected, and nearby was the Western Wall. They were a trinity within a triangle, the three faiths resting upon these three rocks.

The Wailing Wall was divided into a men's and a women's section due to the jurisdiction of the ultra-Orthodox population. "The Shekhinah [God's presence] has never departed from the Western Wall," said the midrash, and Jews from around the world stuck prayers and hopes written on paper into the cracks of the wall, as if God would read and take note of them more directly.

I visited the Wall many times. I placed my hands against the hewn stones that Herod erected 2,000 years before, not as a part of the temple but as a retaining wall, the outermost wall surrounding the Temple Mount. I closed my eyes and offered a general prayer for peace, for health, for my family.

There was always one woman, and usually more, who sat in a chair or stood with a little prayer book, eyes closed, swaying back and forth in a long-sleeved dress that covered her knees, even on the hottest days of summer, intensely addressing God. Often the women cried.

Golda had told me a joke: "So Shmuel went every day to the Wall to pray, for thirty years, he went and he prayed but nothing ever changed in his life. He was as poor as ever. His friend said to him one day, 'Shmuel, every day you go to the Wall and you pray, but your life doesn't get better. How does that make you feel?' and Shmuel said, 'I feel like I'm talking to a fucking wall.'"

I thought this reverence for an old wall verged on idolatry. The veneration for Jerusalem, and for Israel, for any place at all, did as well.

I wrote:

> *Jerusalem, where mountain met desert, brooded.*
> *People loved her with a love that bordered on idolatry.*

I was one of them. An idolater.

CHAPTER 24

The Dome of the Rock was a part of my everyday landscape at The Hebrew University on Mount Scopus. Going to and from classes, I glimpsed it below. It was a golden beacon that had been intended to commemorate and mark the spot where the temples stood, much as an "x" on eggs marked them as nest eggs, not to be disturbed.

One day I was walking with my friend Bruce after class, and as we passed the vista overlooking the Dome of the Rock, Bruce came close to me and half-whispered, "Angie, I'm Christian."

I was stunned. "I thought you were Jewish!" At this point, I knew what it meant to "look Jewish," and Bruce looked Jewish. I was careful not to make a "you look Jewish" comment because I knew this was in poor taste. Louise and Talya and all of my friends could say that of other Jews, but it wasn't appropriate coming from me. Although I noticed that people had rarely refrained from telling me that I *didn't* look Jewish.

On buses, in the street, in my classes—wherever I went in Israel, I was asked at least once a day, "Where are you from? You are not Jewish?" In the United States or elsewhere, you would never ask a stranger, "Are you Christian? Are you Jewish?" I remained nonplussed when others, including strangers, made comments about what I looked like. One Jewish friend once said, jokingly, "Hitler would have loved you!" I was stunned that he thought this was funny.

But, like being hassled by Arabs and Israelis, I also kept to myself the frequent side comments like, "You don't look Jewish. Why did you come to Israel?" which felt very much like I was being accused of not having a right to be there. My reality was different than that of my friends. Things changed in Israel after 1989, when there was a huge wave of fair-haired, Russian Jews escaping the former Soviet Union and making *aliyah* to Israel. But back then, I felt as if I was required to define myself to others.

"Yes, I am," Bruce confirmed. "But I'm Christian. I believe in Yeshua."

I couldn't get used to people referring to Jesus with his Hebrew name, Yeshua—Joshua. It seemed pretentious even though I knew it wasn't.

"Oh. I see."

"And I'm gay."

"Oh."

He looked at me as if he were waiting for more of a response, but the unexpectedness of him confessing to being both Christian and gay was overwhelming. So I said, "Why did you become Christian?" I was most interested in that anyway.

"I was praying and asking God to give me faith," Bruce was saying. "I felt Judaism lacked spirituality. It was just—empty, spiritually."

I listened and understood. In the Jewish practice I'd seen, praying was by rote, and it appeared that those with the most direct connection to God were the ultra-Orthodox. And that world was, to me, unappealing to say the least.

"I mean, I like being Jewish, and I like the holidays," he said, "but I was studying and reading the New Testament. I was quasi-Buddhist for a while in high school, you know, and I was vegan and stuff."

This I disapproved of. Buddhists were pagan. Heathen.

"But then I started going to church, and I had this amazing dream. Jesus came to me and said He loved me. The next morning, I realized I'd received the Holy Spirit. And I've been Christian ever since."

"That's really cool," I said. I knew my response was lame, but I was kind of at a loss for words.

A gay Jewish guy got the Holy Spirit. Not me. Goddammit.

CHAPTER 25

One Saturday, I was sitting at Eve's kitchen table in Beit Hanina, and Eve told me she'd received a coworker letter, a letter sent only to baptized members of the Worldwide Church of God. She didn't know what to make of it. She handed it to me.

I skimmed through the opening of the letter:

> *Very frightening, very sobering, yet very reassuring news! . . . Prophecies . . . 35 countries already have or will have by 1985 the technological know-how and the capacity to produce nuclear weapons . . . NUCLEAR TERRORISM—nuclear MASS MURDER . . .*

It was almost three single-spaced, legal-sized pages devoted to nuclear war. The usual fare. And then, tucked in the end of the letter:

> *. . . with deepest regret I have to say to you now, Mrs. Ramona Armstrong has refused to be at my side here in Pasadena headquarters or in further travel, but has insisted on living separately in Tucson. It has been determined by events, facts and fruits that I am not spiritually bound by God and only by man's law of this world . . . God HATES divorce. So do I . . . This determination SHOULD NOT BE USED AS A PRECEDENT TO ENCOURAGE OR JUSTIFY OTHER*

DIVORCES IN THE CHURCH. With much love, in Jesus' name, Herbert Armstrong.

My father had overheard from one of the church gossips that the makeup ban had been reinstated because Mr. Armstrong's wife loved makeup, and if Armstrong took it away but she continued to use makeup, he could justify divorcing her. However, she had abided by the no-makeup rule, foiling his plans.

Honestly, nothing made sense to me anymore.

Eve didn't know what to think. She thought Mr. Armstrong's wife had been much too young for him, and she'd likely manipulated him. But he was a man of God. How had he let this happen?

In the end, Eve and I considered the possibility that demons had come between Mr. Armstrong and his wife. Laila entered the room during the last part of the conversation and said, "You guys are crazy."

We also learned that Mr. Armstrong would be in Israel the following month. Because Eve was baptized and in touch with headquarters, she'd asked if she could meet with Mr. Armstrong during his visit. It was confirmed, and she invited me to join her. As much as I criticized the church and questioned why only Mr. Armstrong could interpret scripture properly, I still believed that he was holier, more spiritual, than the rest of us. Given my childhood, Mr. Armstrong still loomed large. He was a booming, angry, threatening, almost godlike figure who determined if you were saved—or not.

Out of respect, I wore a dress and my lace-up, brown Israeli Nimrud sandals. I also wore black mascara, eyeliner, eyebrow pencil, and lipstick, but not so much as to be rebellious or disrespectful. It had always been God's opinion of me I worried about, not any human on earth, not even Mr. Armstrong's.

I had a vague notion that just by being in Mr. Armstrong's presence, some holiness would transfer itself from him to me. I wasn't like the devout Catholics, who worshipped the pope and wanted nothing more than to kiss his hand. But there was a long historical precedent in religion whereby the man or woman of God might mysteriously convey some of his or her holiness to others, whether alive or in death in the form of relics. They were sort of like a physical manifestation of a prayer cloth.

Eve and I waited in an adjoining room in a hotel suite while men in formal suits conferred quietly with one another. Having lived in Israel for a year, to me the fair-skinned, clean-cut, Western men who traveled with Mr. Armstrong seemed foreign. They weren't gesticulating with their hands, their crisp white shirts were buttoned up to their necks, and they wore black wing-tip shoes instead of loafers or sandals. Funny how one's perception of what was the norm could change in just one year.

Finally, the men motioned for us to follow them. It was time to meet Mr. Armstrong. We entered another well-appointed room with a couch and chairs, an area with what seemed to be a bar, and a beautiful view out the window of the walls of East Jerusalem.

Gentlemanly, Mr. Armstrong stood when we walked in and extended his hand. In turn, we shook it. I expected to feel a jolt of spirituality just by touching his big, dry, old, pale hand that looked as if it had never participated in a minute of hard labor. I was disappointed to find that this small, nondescript, white-haired man in his mid-eighties did not emanate an aura of godliness. He asked me what I was doing in Israel, and I said I was studying, and he nodded and smiled. That. Was. It. For a man who'd had such a large impact on my family, he seemed ridiculously, improbably irrelevant.

Eve said a few more words to him, expressing her gratitude as if he were a rock star and she a groupie. Her eyes were shining. I had never seen her quite so excited.

I didn't begrudge her having had a spiritual moment. I just wished it would happen to me. There was something clearly lacking in me that both Bruce and Eve could get the Holy Spirit.

CHAPTER 26

I followed through on my original plan to go to Germany when I arranged to spend the summer there in between years in Israel. As much as my parents might maintain their Germanic distance, when I told them I was going to Germany, I knew they were glad that I was leaving what they viewed as war-torn Israel and heading to a more civilized country. Indeed, when I spoke to them on the phone, they asked if I was anywhere near what was happening up north in Lebanon.

"No," I reassured them. "I'm nowhere close."

It was the first week of June 1982, and war had broken out in Lebanon. But, with no bombs falling on Jerusalem, no skirmishes taking place anywhere nearby, I didn't feel personally at risk.

In 1948, when Israel was established after a United Nations vote as a homeland for the Jewish people, hundreds of thousands of Palestinian refugees fled from Israel into Lebanon, shifting the population from mostly Arab Christian to mostly Arab Muslim. The Palestine Liberation Organization, or PLO, under Yasser Arafat had set up its base in southern Lebanon, on Israel's northern border.

In 1982, Prime Minister Begin and the Israeli government wanted not only to push back and marginalize the PLO, which planned and carried out terrorist activities against Israel, but also to attack the Syrian forces that aided the PLO and instate a pro-Israel, Christian government in Lebanon. When Israel's ambassador to the United Kingdom was shot in an assassination attempt, Israel decided, under Ariel Sharon as the defense minister, to invade Lebanon.

In the year I'd been in Israel, I hadn't spoken to my family often. We relied on aerograms, thin blue letters that we sent back and forth. I sent them postcards from places I visited, making sure to choose fun ones with camels baring their yellow teeth in a big grin, or religiously significant ones. My father was delighted when I finally sent him a postcard of Ein Kerem, the town where John the Baptist was born.

In turn, both of my parents wrote, updating me on who was pregnant in Indiana, who had shot a deer, which great-uncle was in the nursing home, and how far the basketball team had advanced in the state championship.

My father told me that this war breaking out indicated that time was short, the future Armageddon was around the corner, and the world had to end soon, just like Matthew 24 predicted. My mother asked how my classes had gone and if I'd gotten her last letter. My father wanted me to call when I got to Aunt Margaret in Hamburg, and I promised I would.

––––––––––

What a pleasure to be ignored! No hisses, no stares, no propositions. Oh, the sheer joy of polite nothings. It was the end of June 1982. In a few months, I was turning twenty-one. I was mentally and physically and spiritually carefree.

I flew into Hamburg and took a train to Lubuck on the North Sea, where Aunt Margaret had a vacation home. After her husband, Walter, had died, Aunt Margaret had returned to Hamburg. She'd visited Grandma a few times, and I recalled her as a kinder, gentler, happier version of my grandmother. The two sisters were very close, and every Christmas, Aunt Margaret sent her Asbach Uralt chocolates filled with liquer. They spoke each Sunday afternoon, when the telephone rates were down. Grandma was a different person when Aunt Margaret was on the phone. She spoke in rapid German, her words punctuated by laughter.

Aunt Margaret was the only person from Grandma's family that we'd had any connection with. Her other siblings had died, and my father had only one first cousin, who lived in England. "They were a weird family," my father would say.

Aunt Margaret and her friend Gretel met me at the train station. She talked as if she had known me my whole life. She asked me about the family, about Israel, what I was planning to do in Germany, and how long I would stay with her (making sure I knew I could stay as long as I wanted). "Although we are old and maybe not so much fun for young people!" she laughed—the exact same laugh as Grandma—which was comforting.

I settled in for a week. In the mornings, Aunt Margaret made soft-boiled eggs that she placed in little eggcups, and I learned to tap the shells with a spoon and eat out the runny yolk. I spent afternoons walking along the beach and venturing into the still-cold water. We went out for dinner then stayed up late playing cards.

One evening when Gretel and I were alone, waiting for Aunt Margaret to join us to play cards, Gretel turned to me and in her heavily accented English said, "You know, I loff your aunt."

"I know," I said. "Everyone loves Aunt Margaret. She's wonderful."

"No," she said, as if she hadn't made it clear. "I loff your aunt."

"I know," I reiterated. "We all do."

Gretel looked at me and said nothing more.

Five days after I arrived, I bought a two-month German rail pass so I could crisscross the country. I hugged Aunt Margaret and Gretel good-bye and thanked them for everything.

Years later, many years later, I recalled Gretel telling me she loved Aunt Margaret. Only then did I realize what she'd been saying: they were lovers. I wondered if Grandma had known or suspected. No one had ever said anything over the years. And so, when I had my suspicions, I first asked my aunt Viola. "You know," Viola said slowly, "I wondered that myself." And then I asked my father. And he said, "You know, I wondered that myself."

Keeping things quiet, sweeping them under the carpet, was alive and well in my family. And yet, I like to think it also said something about my grandmother, my father, and my aunt that they'd been capable of loving and accepting Aunt Margaret even as she'd married a Jewish man and then had a lesbian relationship.

———

I'd long been curious about the world my grandfather's family had left behind. To be clear, there were no big mysteries about them, no questions about my family's past that urgently needed answering. But since I was curious about origins in general—personal, national, spiritual—I'd joined my father at the local library many afternoons, poring over newspapers and census records and other documents that had been preserved on microfiche. I was seeking the Himsel name and trying to put together a narrative of their history in America. Aside from it being a straightforward narrative of birth, marriage, and death, I found that our history mirrored much of the history of America.

America's successes and struggles, its wars and social upheavals, were also those of my family. My great-great-grandfather's brother was killed in 1863 in the Battle of Champion Hill, the famous, pivotal battle of Vicksburg led by General Grant that culminated in Vicksburg's surrender. Another brother survived the Civil War but met his end in a drunken gunfight in a bar. His wife gave birth to their fourth child the day after his death. Both my grandfather and my great-uncle served in World War I, my father in World War II, and my uncle Robert in the Korean War.

The big flu epidemic of 1919 claimed the life of my father's great-aunt. Another of his great-aunts, Margaretha, and four of her children drowned crossing the White River in Haysville, Indiana. When trying to drive the wagon onto the ferry, the post broke, the ferry went forward, and the horses and wagon with the entire family went into the water. I'd read that over 2,000 people attended the funeral and burial, and the article made mention that there had been two sermons, one in English, one in German. The funeral procession from the church to the cemetery was over a mile long.

Then there were the oral traditions I'd heard, stories of how the gypsies had taken a child, how the parents of my great-great-grandfather seemed to have disappeared, perhaps they'd gone west during the gold rush. My father's great-uncle was born with dwarfism, and my father said that the old-timers claimed that his mother believed it was because when she was pregnant, a gypsy came to the door begging, and she'd closed the door and turned her away, so the gypsy had put a curse on her.

In the twentieth century, the combination of the invention of the automobile and the tendency to drink excessively had led to my grandfather's death. The women's movement sent women to work, gave them financial stability and birth control and, not coincidentally, choices to not get married or to get divorced. Jasper lagged behind the rest of the country on the feminist front. It was a religious county, and we didn't give up our traditions so easily. They had to be wrested from our fists.

In Germany, I wondered if there was more to the immigration story than I already knew. I was compelled to return to the village my ancestors had left those many years before. Of course that had been the original plan when I'd gone to the Overseas Study office at Indiana University a year and a half earlier. I'd taken an unlikely, long detour to Israel, but at long last I was back where my family had begun.

Another train took me to Bayreuth, where I boarded a bus and gazed out the window at a mostly unspoiled vista of rolling hills, green open fields, and small farms and villages tucked into valleys. It was not unlike southern Indiana. The bus driver called out "Glashuten" to me as he came to a stop, then I walked down the steps and onto the street, returning not in wooden shoes, but in my brown, lace-up leather sandals.

There was a tavern in front of me, and so I decided to go in, introduce myself in German, and see if I could find out if there were any other Himsels around. When I said my name and that I was from America, it was as if I were a ghost come back to life. The people I met were trying to comprehend this information. I realized my arrogance—that because I'd known about their existence, I'd assumed they'd known of mine. They tossed a few comments to each other in their Bavarian dialect. One of them said, "Frau Schmidt, Frau Schmidt." I gathered

Frau Schmidt ran a bed-and-breakfast. I thanked them all profusely in broken German that had suffered from disuse over the past year. On my way to Frau Schmidt, backpack on my back, a very polite, middle-aged man approached me, smiled, and said, "You are the Himsel girl?" Already, word had gotten out. This was truly a village.

Frau Schmidt lived in a two-story, well-kept home, and the front yard was rife with flowers. When I rang the bell, it was clear she'd been expecting me. Frau Schmidt could have stepped out of *Grimms' Fairy Tales*, with her apple-dumpling cheeks, her silver hair parted down the middle and wrapped in a bun on top of her head, and her cotton dress topped with a full, crisp white apron.

She showed me to one of the available rooms upstairs, and when I returned to the kitchen, she offered me hot chocolate, which was more like chocolate soup, and then pulled out the phone book. She called the Himsels, who lived in the nearby town of Pettendorf. I overheard a lot of "*Ja, ja, das stimmt*," that's true, that's true. She arranged for one of my cousins to pick me up the following day so I could meet the family.

———

Freddie was in his forties, had taught in England for several years, and spoke English perfectly. It was as if I'd known him forever, like he was one of the cousins I'd grown up with and caught fireflies with on Sunday evenings at my grandparents' farm. I hopped in his car, and we chatted about when my family had left Germany, where we lived now, and also about my grandfather and great-grandfather Himsel.

My newfound cousins and I enjoyed a hearty lunch of potato dumplings with rich brown gravy. It tasted like my childhood. I looked at the people around me whom I had never met, but who bore the same name and, for the most part, the same blue eyes and fair skin. I'd been welcomed into so many strangers' homes over the past year—Golda, Eve, Eddie in Bethlehem, Talya's aunt who'd invited me several times for Shabbat dinner, a Jewish family in Tzfat that Louise and I met at the bus stop one Friday afternoon, and now this family with whom I shared a bloodline.

They were ordinary village folks, modest of dress and manner. Their intonation seemed familiar to me—plain and straightforward. Almost deadpan. Kunigunda, whom everyone called Kuni, was in her late seventies, probably as old as Grandma Himsel, and she recalled that someone once said that some Himsels had emigrated to America. It was odd to imagine that this parallel life was happening here in Germany—people growing up, getting married, and dying—unaware that an entire offshoot had taken root elsewhere. Though very much hyphenated, they definitely felt like family members. My visit was one of the more unusual things to happen in the village—cousins from America didn't typically turn up out of the blue.

When I said I wanted to look at church records, they were startled. Looking up family history was apparently not as popular in Germany as it was in the United States. Since the miniseries *Roots* had aired, Americans' interest in their own ancestry had been piqued. In Germany, they lived next to their churches and cemeteries. The past was their present.

My cousins indulged me and got on the phone with the pastor. The next day, they drove me to the church in Gesees, a mile or so away. The church was uncannily similar to the former Evangelical Lutheran Church in Haysville, from the tall, thin spire to the clock on the exterior of the white stone just below. Even though I'd visited innumerable churches in Israel, I felt a quick tinge of guilt and fear sitting in a pagan place of worship, like I had when Alise and I had visited St. Joe's.

The minister took me around the interior of the church. There were vaulted ceilings and long, narrow Gothic windows that let in some light. Hard, brown wooden pews. A sober sanctuary.

After I looked around and took a few photographs, the minister settled the old book containing the church records on a table in the back. Notebook next to me, I began recording every time the Himsel name appeared, drawing lines to indicate who the parents were, which town they were from, when they'd been born, and when they'd died. They weren't terribly creative with their names, which made figuring out the relationships even more difficult. Sometimes there were two children in the same family named Margarethe or Georg or Katharina.

I became curious about the female lineage as well, and in addition to the Himsel name, I added Retsch and Schatlin and Nutzel and my great-great-great-grandmother's maiden name, Teufel ("devil" in German, which amused me no end—I literally had some devil in me!). The papers grew. The lines linking the generations branched off at awkward angles, or bumped up against one another. My family ancestry was an untidy, sprawling, crooked, unwieldy tree whose branches reached up and over and down, laden with Neuners and Meyers, Harders and Himsels.

I asked the minister why some of the entries were written sideways in the church records. He explained that was to indicate that a child was illegitimate. The baby's parents weren't married, and, in fact, there had been a special section in church for women who were unmarried but had children. "Why weren't they married?" I questioned.

I was told that sometimes they weren't allowed to marry someone from another village. I could hardly believe it and thought that I had misunderstood his German. No, apparently not. At the time, Germany was a series of fiefdoms, each run by an individual prince who controlled and decided the fate of its inhabitants. Some of the princes had chosen to become Lutheran, and thus their entire communities had been ordered to switch from Catholicism to Lutheranism. This particular area in Bavaria had gone back and forth between Catholicism and Lutheranism over the centuries. The landowners hadn't wanted their serfs to marry those in other villages, but to stay local and swell the population of their own village.

Born, christened, died—so many babies died young, a few days old, and then a year later, another was born. By the end of the day, I'd examined the books and created a web of relationships. I found the entry for my great-great-great-grandfather, Georg, who'd immigrated to America with his second wife, Anna Keller. The German script was practically a different language, and the sharp, vertical, and elegant scratches on the yellowed pages gave me a primal thrill, as exciting as when I was standing on the hilltop in Nazareth looking at broken pieces of pottery. I recalled another thing Boaz, the director, had said on the dig when we were talking about archaeology and why it mattered: even if we were only doing it for ourselves, that alone was a higher purpose. If we transform ourselves personally, we can possibly transform the world. Archaeology puts the self into part of the grander whole, and gives you a perspective on where you stand, and you can feel as if you are part of humanity.

Similarly, sitting at the table next to the minister with the church records in front of us, then walking through the church graveyard seeking an ancestor's name on the thin stone slabs buried deep in the German soil, gave me perspective about my heritage. From the church records, I traced our family back to the early 1700s, to Georg's great-grandfather who was married to Barbara Schatlin. They had been "day laborers," poor farmers who hadn't owned their land but had worked the property of the local landowner—people who hadn't had the right to marry the person of their choosing, who'd suffered the personal loss of children and endured the decisions of the local prince. But my immediate family had been different from them in at least one respect: we'd decided to leave, taking a chance that we would be free to make our own choices. Reinvent ourselves. Become who we wanted to be.

On the last day of my visit, I said my good-byes to my newfound family, who'd been so kind and generous and helpful, who'd showed me the exact site where our ancestors' home had once existed, who'd fed me and had brought out old photos of people who would have been my great-great-grandfather's cousins.

And then, I brought up World War II. I couldn't help myself. I wondered if they knew what was happening when it was going on, and if so, did they care or even express consternation. "It was a terrible thing," they said. "Terrible, terrible." They shook their heads, and their bodies seemed to go slack. One of the Himsel women was married to a man, Wilfred, who had lost an eye in World War II. He'd been the most jovial and engaging throughout the days I'd been in Pettendorf, and he said to me, slowly, in halting English, because he wanted to make sure I understood, "We didn't know what was happening. We didn't. We had to go to the army, or we would be sent to Russia. Or shot." He held a make-believe gun to his head. "We had no choice. But we didn't know." I nodded. I didn't pass judgment. It was a dark, ugly time, to put it mildly, but still I wondered.

I understood this culture that was based on blindly, obediently following orders, doing as they were told, and thus saving themselves. Here in this tiny village, I could understand how they hadn't realized that one day Jewish families suddenly started to disappear. There were no Jewish families anywhere near them. I understood their inability to scream out in outrage. Sort of.

As much as I was interested in my own origin in Germany, I had also become curious about the Jews' origin in the country. According to my guidebook, Jews had lived in Worms since the end of the tenth century. I hopped the train to explore the small town on the banks of the Rhine River in southwest Germany. Around the year 1000, about 400 Jewish families left Northern Italy for Central and Eastern Europe. Worms was one of the early places where the Jews settled and became a thriving community. The Jews who'd left Italy came to be known as the Ashkenaz, named after the great-grandson of Noah. Ashkenaz was the son of Gomer, and rabbis later suggested, using linguistic associations, that Germania was related to Gomer. I was not the only one who leapt to tenuous etymological linkages.

Though much of Worms had been destroyed in World War II, it had been rebuilt and boasted a cathedral and town hall. The clean and manicured homes and streets gave the whole town a very pleasant look. I headed first to the Rashi Synagogue, named after the great Jewish scholar who once studied in Worms. The first synagogue was built on the site in 1034 and had been central to the community of Jews throughout the medieval period and into the modern era. In the Jewish cemetery, the headstones were brown and weathered, but it was still possible to decipher the Hebrew on many of them.

Worms could also claim the famous Edict of Worms in the sixteenth century, which denounced Martin Luther as a heretic. Martin Luther, I'd learned in Israel, was horribly anti-Semitic. His book *On the Jews and Their Lies* claimed that Jews were the devil's people. Having attained a status almost that of a prophet, Luther's views had a profound influence on Germans at the time and for centuries afterward, and it was with this underpinning that I started to comprehend how this hatred eventually contributed to the Holocaust. When the Nazis came to power, they used Martin Luther's works as "evidence" that Jews needed to be expelled from Germany and all of Europe, and this thinking culminated in the Wannsee Conference of 1942, when the Nazis formally adopted the Final Solution.

Anti-Semitism was irrational, Golda once said, yet I continued to think there had to be some underlying logic, lost to the rest of us, but justifiable to the anti-Semites. It clearly had to do with jealousy, fear, and hatred of anyone who was different. I recalled the story of my uncle looking up to the sky and calling out, "Heil Hitler!" He had never known any Jews.

At times in Israel, it felt that if people weren't talking about who was Jewish, they were talking about who was anti-Semitic. It was hard for me to understand at first why modern Jews appeared to be, to my mind, hypersensitive about it. It was as if they feared a Hitler or a pogrom hiding around the corner, and they had to be on constant alert in case they had to pack their bags and find a more hospitable country.

My complete lack of understanding of the Jewish historical experience was made clear to me in a joke Talya told me: A Frenchman, a German, and a Jew were taking an English class and had to write about the elephant. The Frenchman wrote about the elephant and his mating habits; the German wrote about the elephant and his weight and how much he ate; the Jew wrote about "the elephant and the Jewish question"! Talya laughed hysterically when she got to the punch line, but it took me a while to really get it. I was still learning that for many Jews, everything, including elephants, had to do with being Jewish. Of course, Talya didn't understand my joke any better:

Did you hear about the zoo they're building in Indiana? They're putting a fence around Kentucky.

But now that I was outside Israel, I understood Talya's joke much more clearly. I felt as if I was almost seeing the world through Jewish eyes. I wondered if one of my Jewish friends was the one visiting— Louise or Talya—would Germany have been as kind to them?

The German trains were punctual, clean, and spacious. A quality that I appreciated as a tourist, but one that also felt eerie given the role efficient trains had played in the Holocaust. The trains were ominous.

Americans backpacking around Europe were the loud ones, laughing at anything and everything, shouting, "Oh, hey, man, look outside! Check out those mountains!" They put their feet up on the seats, which earned them admonishments from the conductor. Because I'd been away from the States for a year, Americans seemed big and loud and confident and happy—determinedly happy.

I was happy too, to gaze out the window and drink in the green summer forests and the castles on the banks of the Rhine that popped up like pictures from a book of fairy tales. From the tops of cathedrals in Cologne and Munich and Heidelberg, you could see how the spic-and-span streets were laid out in an orderly fashion. The summer sun's heat didn't oppress, but peeked out and warmed you. There was no talk of the war in Lebanon on the radio, no silence on the bus at the top of the hour when the news came on, just Nicole, the Eurovision winner, singing in a sweet, innocent voice, "*Ein bisschen Frieden,*" or "A Little Peace."

But I couldn't avoid the elephant in the country forever. The concentration camps. Just ten miles north of Munich was Dachau, the first of the camps in Germany, originally intended for political prisoners. Its 200,000 prisoners later included Jehovah's Witnesses, homosexuals, immigrants, the Roma, political opponents and, of course, Jews.

"*Arbeit macht frei.*"

Work makes you free. These words greeted me on the gates. Those same words had greeted its prisoners forty years before. I walked around the deadly silent, somber camp. My steps were slow and reluctant, because I could hardly bear to see what I knew I would see.

I felt as if I were holding my breath. Or barely breathing. I peered at the barracks and their narrow bunks. How many people shared that one narrow bunk? As many as they could pile on. I could only look briefly at the brick ovens where the corpses were burned. Several visitors remained there, as if they couldn't look away, as if they couldn't will their feet to move.

The watchtower was a looming, leering presence. Barbed wire surrounded the entire camp. There was a black sculpture that looked like skeletal arms and legs all jumbled together. I didn't linger. Some things you can just absorb and feel, not intellectualize and ponder. It was all I could do to be there and bear witness in my own way.

Two-thirds of Europe's Jews were murdered in the Holocaust.

Every Yom HaZikaron, Israel's Memorial Day, a siren went off throughout the entire country, and people remained standing, motionless, exactly where they were. Cars pulled to the side. Buses stopped. People remained still as if in a game of freeze tag. Then, when the siren stopped blaring, everyone resumed what they'd been doing. The two-minute silence honored the victims of the wars and conflicts in Israel over the past century. It was a human memorial that took place throughout all of Israel. A memorial of quiet and peace, in the presence of ever-present war.

A few months before when I was back in Israel, I'd visited Yad Vashem, the Holocaust Museum in Jerusalem. The literal meaning of "yad vashem" was "memorial and name," and the museum took great care to memorialize the names of those who'd perished, in part because in the Holocaust they'd been just numbers. Museums and memorials—even the rusted military vehicle on the road from the airport—were all about holding within each of us the memory of others and of events that should never be forgotten. Personally, I didn't need a memorial to remember. I had not been back to Abby's grave since she was buried, even though it was just a few miles down the road from where we lived. I could never forget.

As I sat on trains that crisscrossed Germany—Hamburg to Bayreuth to Worms—all on time and meticulously clean—I couldn't help but mentally review everything I'd seen and done and experienced in the past year. So much of what I'd thought I was sure of had been challenged. At almost twenty-one, the most important question in the world seemed to be: Who was I?

I was:

Borderline judgmental.

A little know-it-all.

Somewhat oblivious to things that were obvious to others.

Occasionally impetuous (okay, more than occasionally).

A mess of contradictions.

Conflicted.

A poet.

Fascinated by the first century of the ancient Near East and my newly discovered Josephus.

Inordinately curious about people and willing to give everyone the benefit of the doubt. Over and over and over again.

A guffawer and a giggler.

A Christian woman from southern Indiana.

A person with doubts.

A young woman who continued to believe and have faith that if I had the Holy Spirit, I could get saved.

And so back to Israel I went. To finish my last year of college and, hopefully, get closer to salvation.

CHAPTER 27

I fell in love in Israel. Deeply, madly in love. It was a love that never ended, despite the flaws that I discovered.

There are always flaws. Which is why it's good to be in love first.

I also fell in love with Jerusalem.

Actually, I was mad about Jerusalem.

In the Middle Ages, a map was created in which Jerusalem was the center of the universe—the belly button. Even then, the mapmaker knew that this was patently untrue. But when you love, your love is the center of your world, the umbilical cord that connects you, a conduit for the blood that gives you life.

For almost two years, every day from my perch on Mount Scopus, I looked down into the bleak but beautiful landscape of the Judean Desert. It was a hard, stony land. Ancient olive trees were scattered here and there, and in the spring, the almond trees' pink blossoms smiled, "hello, we've awoken."

Whether it was the Romans contemplating from this vantage point how to conquer the walled city below or Jews gazing at the destroyed temple with tears in their eyes, there it was. Jerusalem. The light was pure, crystalline, dry, distilling the sunset in an orange and red that was painful and beautiful at the same time.

When you live there and have an everyday life, the past is a back-drop against the present. Some would say the past is also the present. But when you are trying to get to the post office to send an aerogram back home, the 4,000 years of the past is the past, and the present is the bank teller who ignores customers and speaks in rapid Hebrew to a family member on the phone. Still, I saw how the ancient and the modern converged.

Every Friday afternoon, downtown Jerusalem was congested with green-uniformed soldiers home for the weekend buying *challah* and flowers for the Sabbath, and an assortment of young and old, Ashke-nazi, Sephardic, and Mizrahi Jews rushing to get last-minute cucumbers and tomato for Israeli salad or cookies or okra or nondairy cheesecake for their meat meals. I came to love Friday's burst of purpose, which was followed by an abrupt cessation of activity. On Saturday, an almost holy silence descended upon the city, which was devoid of shoppers and cars. Every week Shabbat commemorated God's rest from His creation, and I loved feeling that we moved not just linearly forward in time, but also cyclically. Time was holy, as holy as the space preserved for churches, mountains, synagogues, and mosques.

Sometimes I walked down from Mount Scopus then entered the majestic Damascus Gate of East Jerusalem, flanked on either side by towers on top. Inside was the bazaar, the *souk*, where I bought *sahlab*, a sweet drink made of rose water and topped with pistachios and shreds of coconut.

Sprinkled on the periphery of the Old City, outside its walls, were hundreds of tombs dating from 2,000 and more years ago. They were an exploration unto themselves. The Tomb of Absalom was a rock-cut tomb with a pillar that was identifiable from afar. However, it was not the tomb of King David's rebellious son Absalom, but rather dated to 1,000 years later, to the first century CE, and may very well have belonged to King Herod's grandson, Herod Agrippa. All roads led to Herod.

There was also the Tomb of the Kings, which did not, in fact, house the bones of the kings of Israel but those of Queen Helene of Adiabene (currently Iraq), a first-century queen who converted to Judaism and chose to be buried in Jerusalem.

Mahmoud Darwish, the Palestinian poet whose family had been uprooted in 1948 when their village was razed, wrote, "*Standing here, staying here, permanent here, eternal here, and we have one goal, one, one: to be.*"

Just to be. What a simple request.

The Jewish poets wrote of Jerusalem too. The modern poet Yehuda Amichai wrote passionately about her in his 1968 ode, "Jerusalem is a Port City":

> *She is always arriving, always sailing away . . .*
> *And the commerce and the gates and the golden domes:*
> *Jerusalem is the Venice of God.*

City of blessings and of bloodshed. City of stone, ancient Salem.

CHAPTER 28

One special night in April 1983, Golda's table was even fuller than it was at the many other dinners I'd attended over my almost two years in Jerusalem. I'd finished all of the coursework for my degree and, after Passover, I would be returning to Indiana to look for a job. I'd said my good-byes to Eve and her family one last Saturday at her kitchen table in the West Bank. I went to the Wall one more time with Talya and stuck my tightly folded paper into its cracks. But finally, I attended a Passover seder, my second at Golda's house.

Before the festive meal, the men slapped on their small, round head coverings called *kippot*. There were many variations of what they looked like, when they were worn, and what they indicated about their wearer. Some men wore theirs all the time, some just in synagogue, and some for meals.

In Indiana, cars and trucks sent a silent message about their owner, while in Israel, *kippot* could be read as smoke signals within the Jewish world. A hat-like, brightly woven Bukharan *kippa* most likely indicated a hippieish, liberal-leaning Jew—unless a woman was wearing it, in which case she might be a Reform rabbi or a feminist/observant Jew. The Hasidic and ultra-Orthodox men reached for the large, black-velvet *kippot,* while Modern Orthodox men wore hand-crocheted ones or maybe a big black or white satin *kippa*. In

Israel, the *kippa* also reflected a man's political beliefs, with the larger, knitted ones indicating a more right-wing bent.

Golda's husband, Bob, stood at the head of the table and picked up the Haggadah, the book that tells the story of Passover, and began the service. I opened mine from right to left, as I'd become accustomed, then tried to follow along. For well over an hour we took turns recounting the story of the Exodus, sometimes in English but mostly in Hebrew.

Each part of the Passover story was represented on the seder plate: small bowls containing saltwater represented the tears of the Hebrews as slaves in Egypt; a green vegetable—spring, and hope; a chopped-up apple, cinnamon, and nut mixture called *haroset*—the mortar that the Hebrew slaves used to build the pyramids; horseradish—the bitterness of slavery; an egg recalled the circle of life; a lamb's shank bone represented the paschal lamb that was offered during Passover; and in the middle of the plate, a large cup of wine to welcome Elijah, the harbinger of the Messiah. On another plate were three matzahs, covered with a cloth. We dipped our fingers in wine and put drops on our plates symbolizing each plague.

There was more dipping and eating as we continued reading from the Haggadah. When it was my turn, I read a paragraph in English then we all sang the traditional song "Dayenu," which translates to "enough." If God had only taken us out of Egypt, it would have been enough; only given us the Ten Commandments, it would have been enough. And so on. The philosophical questions that were raised in the Haggadah offered me a whole new perspective of Passover than those I'd learned growing up.

When it was time to eat, Rosa, Golda's Russian housekeeper, fluttered about bringing out platters of chicken marinated with unfamiliar spices. When she came to me, Rosa asked in Yiddish, "*Vullst du ein bissele?*" It was close enough to German that I understood the meaning: "Do you want a little?"

Since Yiddish originated initially as a dialect of German, though it was written with Hebrew letters, I'd devised my own fairly intelligible Yiddish by slurring the ends of my German, changing a final "t" to an "s," and dropping the umlaut altogether. What a funny twist of fate that, instead of speaking German with my *landsmen,* I was in Israel combining Hebrew and German to speak the language that Jews had once spoken in Germany and Eastern Europe. "*Ein bissele,*" I replied. Rosa and I understood each other perfectly. A few people looked at me with curiosity. It amused me to think I'd fooled anyone—that they thought I could speak Yiddish.

"You know the Samaritans today still slaughter a lamb and roast it and eat it," I overheard somebody saying.

"Where are the Samaritans?" My heart beat faster. There were Samaritans out there somewhere? Real *Samaritans?*

"Here in Israel. There's a small group of them. Not even a thousand. Most of them live in the West Bank. They broke away from Judaism when the Jews came back from exile from Babylonia, and they claim they are descendants of Ephraim and Manasseh." Apparently, not just the Worldwide Church members claimed to be descendants of Ephraim and Manasseh. They were a hot ticket.

It was explained that the Samaritans only have the first five books of the Bible, the Torah, and they still follow biblical customs. They sacrifice a lamb on Mount Gerizim—which they believe is the original Holy Place, not the Temple Mount in Jerusalem—and then they roast it and eat it with matzah and bitter herbs. I wondered if they still dressed in the biblical manner. The Amish in Indiana wore garb similar to that of the seventeenth century when their founder, Jakob Ammann, broke away from the Mennonites. The dress of Hasidic Jews was similar to eighteenth-century Eastern Europe when Rabbi Israel Baal Shem Tov founded the movement. Observant Muslim women continued to wear the *burqa* and *hijab* that Mohammed instructed them to wear in the seventh century.

Conversations broke out in clusters. I overheard my tablemate Paul, a psychiatrist, speaking about patients whom he'd treated for "Jerusalem syndrome," a term applied to people who, upon coming to Jerusalem, suffer from the delusion that they are John the Baptist or the Virgin Mary or some other mystical person.

"There's a British woman with two young daughters who sits on Jaffa Road and begs," I interjected. "The mother thinks that her dead husband was Jesus and will be showing up in Jerusalem anytime, so she brought the kids to Israel to wait for him."

Patty had taken the family into her dorm during cold days, and she'd tried to get them help. But the mother had brainwashed the kids into believing that their father was Jesus, so they sat and waited on the street for him to return.

Paul shook his head. "Sad."

I didn't think the dead father was Jesus, but it did occur to me that half the prophets might be diagnosed with a psychiatric disorder if they were alive today. Including Jesus.

At Passover, of all times, when Jesus had been betrayed and crucified, I should not be having the same recurring thought: that Jesus was irrelevant. I worked hard to push it aside. At the end of an April evening, without a scent of burning lamb flesh, a sacrifice, *korban,* nor a flat cracker representing human flesh to be consumed, we opened the door to welcome Elijah to drink the wine at the center of the table.

Door open, I sang along with the repeated chorus welcoming Elijah, "*Eliahu Ha Navi, Eliahu Ha Tishbi . . .*" Elijah, the prophet, who would herald the coming of the Messiah. When? "*Bimherah.*" Fast, let it be fast! No, Elijah, I thought. Not so fast. Keep your distance. Don't come too close. Let me have a future.

CHAPTER 29

The reverse commute back to Indiana was tougher than I antici-
pated. How hard could it be to slip back into my smile-at-strangers,
obey-the-speed-limit, Midwestern life?

Hard. Very hard. Harder than the culture shock I'd experienced two
years previously when I left for Israel and, at times, confused Mai-
monides with Nachmanides.

I wanted to drink Turkish coffee in the afternoon with Talya. I
said "*ken*" for yes and "*lo*" for no. When I threw my sister Mary's
one-year-old son, Ryan, up in the air, I said, "Ooopah!" Eventually,
those more superficial changes would revert to my Indiana norm—
saying yes and no and drinking Diet Pepsi. But the internal changes
remained.

Just before I'd returned to the States, the US Embassy in Beirut was
bombed by an Islamic terrorist, killing sixty-three people. It was all
people talked about in Israel. That, and when Israel would withdraw
from Lebanon.

In the States, people were mourning the finale of the TV series
M*A*S*H.

I missed the ever-present political discussions in Israel: debates
about the ultra-Orthodox being exempt from the army, or why we
should never give back the Golan to Syria. I missed how real people

were. Even the nasty, crappy kind of real. All of the "Have a nice day!" chirpiness seemed fake. Pushing my grocery cart at the local IGA in Jasper, I bumped someone's heel, and instead of throwing up his hands and loudly saying, "Nu?" the guy apologized to *me*, "Whoopsie! Sorry!" as if he'd been guilty of walking too slowly.

Yet I settled back in. Liz and I shared one room upstairs, my younger brother John, who'd just finished high school, was in another room, and Sarah, home from college for the summer, and seven-year-old Rachael shared another bedroom. Including my parents, there were seven of us in the house. Practically empty.

My mother worked as a private caregiver, and my father, at fifty-eight years old, was still pouring concrete and working a jack-hammer and doing all kinds of construction work. On Sundays, we visited our grandparents, and on Saturdays, we went to church. Sarah and I wore makeup. Liz didn't. Since Alise was married and living in California, I realized that I had no other real friends in the church. I'd been gone a long time—four years, including Indiana University—and while the other girls my age were perfectly nice, they were also perfectly obedient and wouldn't dare object to any church rulings. So I felt ostracized from the kids I'd gone to socials and baseball games with. Still, week after week, I made the drive to Evansville with my family, as I always had. Thinking I would finally get the Holy Spirit.

Until I decided what kind of job I wanted, I worked at the Older American Center, as I had a few summers prior. I helped set up the weekly Bingo games, trimmed the hedges in the yard, made six different kinds of homemade ice cream, cleaned splats of tobacco off the front porch, and otherwise kept the seniors company, like John, who sat on the front porch swing with me and advised me, "Sweetheart, trust everyone, but cut the deck."

All I wanted to do was run far away. Far from the silos and barns and rolling hills of southern Indiana. Far from where the radio aired the Heinold Hog Market, "Gilts are down three, sows are up one."

Sally Ride, the first woman in space, had just shot off into the heavens. That sounded good to me. I wanted to pack my bags and move somewhere else, somewhere where everyone didn't speak English, where everyone wasn't white and Christian, and signs along the highway and church marquees didn't proclaim, "Try Jesus. If you don't like Him, the devil will always take you back."

My older siblings had long established their lives: married with children, or in serious relationships. Wanda had two kids, Mary had one and was pregnant with her second, and Jim and Ed were both seriously involved with the women they would eventually marry. Paul had moved to Terre Haute, had a job, and was dating. I felt a little bit of self-pity. Where did I belong? If not here, where? I took long walks in the woods and stood overlooking the creek where I'd spent so many summer afternoons with my siblings.

It was a vast, relentless, endless Midwest horizon.

My friend Patty called one day and said, "Angie, move to New York!" She lived in Queens and said she could help me find a job and an apartment. Her enthusiastic voice was as enticing as the brochure with the gleaming Dome of the Rock.

So in August, I shot off into space on an airplane and landed in New York City.

Patty arranged for me to live with her friendly neighbors Ralph and Laura, an older, childless couple in her apartment complex. In exchange for providing Laura with some minor, unspecified medical attention, I could sleep on their pullout couch until I found an apartment. Considering my time spent at the Older American Center, this did not seem difficult.

I envisioned a kindly couple in their seventies or eighties who made hot tea at night and needed help remembering which medication to take. Ralph was a dapper man in his sixties who dressed in crisp cotton shirts tucked into his Bermuda shorts. Laura, also in her sixties, had short silver hair and, the first time I met her, wore a shapeless cotton robe.

Ralph explained that he was going in for a hernia operation, and he wanted someone to put the eye drops in Laura's eyes every night, and sometimes rub ointment onto her chafed skin. I heard the word "chafed" more times that summer than in my entire life. Her elbows, her hands, and her crotch were in a perpetual state of being chafed. It was a hot, muggy summer, but Ralph kept the space heater turned up high so Laura wouldn't catch pneumonia. Instead, she was chafed.

I placed my suitcase next to their couch in the living room, much as I had taken up residence in Aunt Margaret's apartment by the sea. I was happy to have found a rent-free place with a nice married couple until I got a job and could save up money to be on my own.

The morning after my arrival in New York, I had coffee with Ralph and Laura at the kitchen table, and they wished me luck finding a job. Patty went with me on the subway to Manhattan, explaining the subway system, how to transfer, and what uptown and downtown meant.

From the second I hopped on the subway car to the second I exited onto Lexington Avenue and Fifty-Ninth Street near Bloomingdale's, I was drawn in. People of every hue, some dressed in suits for work, others wearing traditional clothing from Africa or Asia or South America, gathered for a few minutes on the train. It was truly a microcosm of the macrocosm, and I was a part of it.

I registered with employment agencies, filling out applications and setting up interview appointments to be an administrative assistant or receptionist. In the bargain basement of Alexander's Department Store, I bought a gray business suit with padded shoulders to wear on interviews. I was a professional.

That evening when I arrived back at the apartment, Laura greeted me at the door. She was stark naked. Stark.

I blinked several times. She'd been wearing a cheerful, caftan-like housedress that morning. Perhaps I was mistaken. Maybe she was clothed. It was a terrible habit of mine, insisting that my perspective was right, despite all evidence to the contrary. No amount of blinking or turning away changed the fact: Laura was buck naked.

"Oh, hi," Laura greeted me. "How did it go?"

"Good!" I said. "I found a suit."

"Let me see," she said, and I showed her my conservative gray suit. She complimented me on it, and I pretended I didn't notice that her breasts were hanging down to her belly button.

Then I ran over to Patty's apartment and squealed, "Laura is walking around the apartment totally naked!"

———

For almost three months I would continue sleeping on Ralph and Laura's couch in Queens. After work and on weekends, I walked or took the subway to Chinatown, Little Italy, the Upper East Side, Chelsea, and the Village. I sat in Greek coffee shops, where I ate moussaka and filled up notebooks with short stories, vignettes, and bad poetry.

This was my new normal in New York City: homeless people camped out in the lobby of a bank; a guy in a fedora speaking gibberish to himself on the street; classical violinists playing Schubert in smelly subways; Laura sitting naked in her recliner reading her horoscope; and Ralph wondering if Patty was a prostitute because she was living with her boyfriend.

It was New York City in 1983. I felt like I belonged. I was home.

———

On the evening of Rosh Hashanah, when I returned from the job I'd gotten at a small real estate company, Ralph and Laura called out, "We're lighting the candles, Angie, do you want to join us?"

In the kitchen Laura stood wearing a big, blue velvet *kippa* on her head, and slippers on her feet. Nothing in between. She was a large expanse of drooping white flesh, a white flag that had called it quits. I'd lived with them for almost two months. As usual, neither Ralph nor I commented on or referred to Laura's birthday suit. My capacity to tune things out—from my father's pervasive yelling and preaching to the church's obvious corruption to an Orthodox man's hand under my ass to Laura's nudity—enabled me to survive.

We lit the candles together, made the blessing in Hebrew, and wished each other a happy new year.

CHAPTER 30

It felt like I was playing dress-up with the *click click click* of my new gray pumps against the sidewalk of Third Avenue. I entered the twenty-three-story building, showed my ID to the building attendant, then took the elevator up to the eleventh floor, where I worked as a receptionist at a corporate real estate company. I sat at my very own desk, where I could see everyone who got on or off the elevator, a wonderful thing for someone who was still staring at people, hoping for a glimpse of the equivalent of someone scratching her dry elbows and sending white flakes down her dress.

I assumed a professional tone over the phone: "How can I help you? May I take a message for him?" And I wrote down on a pink "While You Were Out" message pad, "Mr. Tucker, 9:36 a.m., please call back when you can." At twenty-two, I was almost as confident as I seemed.

I was a chatty girl. Friendly. I made eye contact with people on the street. I couldn't help it. I was friendly with everyone from people asking for directions to the Metropolitan Museum to my new work colleagues to the lawyers who called my boss. One of those lawyers, Selig, was chatty in return over the phone.

Naturally, it was his name that first intrigued me. Its etymology, its meaning. Selig was Yiddish for "blessed." Then one day he came to the office, and I met him for the first time. In his mid-thirties, Selig wore the usual corporate uniform: light gray suit and red tie. He had a genuine and nice smile, which crinkled his blue eyes. I thought he was cute. We bantered in a flirty manner, and the next day he called me at work and asked me out for dinner.

We went somewhere downtown in the Village, and I sort of gathered from the way Selig talked about the restaurant that I was supposed to be suitably impressed by where we were going. I tried to be enthusiastic, but fancy restaurants and hovering waiters did not excite me.

Still, it was a wonderful first date, and not because of the restaurant but because we fell easily into a conversation, interspersed with flirtation. I told him entertaining Ralph and Laura stories, and he told me a little about growing up as an Orthodox rabbi's son in Canada and in Chicago. In turn, I briefly mentioned that I'd just returned from Israel after going to school there for two years, but no, I wasn't Jewish.

My background was fascinating to Selig. You would have thought I was from some exotic place featured in *National Geographic* where women went topless and men pierced their genitals, instead of the rolling hills and farms of southern Indiana.

After that first date, we went to off-Broadway shows and listened to jazz in the Village. We both loved okra and Indian food. Okra didn't make us soul mates, but we quickly forged a deep, emotional connection.

We talked on the phone at night for an hour about absolutely nothing, but it felt like something. I told him my mother bought dented cans with no label because they were cheap and she figured whatever was in it—kidney beans, peas, corn—she could still use. Selig said, "Your mother is a dented can," which was so profound that I jotted it down.

On the surface, Selig was clearly an unlikely choice for me, and I for him. But we had a number of things in common, not least a predisposition to make choices that were somewhat unconventional within our families and communities.

Selig became a lawyer instead of a rabbi as all of the firstborn sons for at least the past four generations had done. He also had a track record of being involved with non-Jewish women. Selig liked self-taught art, art by untrained and often marginalized people, and his apartment's walls were filled with somewhat crudely executed but passionate drawings and paintings.

Ironically, many of the artists had a fixation on Christian, end-of-world prophecies. In the hallway there was a painting of a red heifer over which a helicopter hovered and on which were written phrases like "WORLD'S NUCLEAR POWER BEYOND CONTROL" and "ISAIAH 64-2 THE MELTING FIRE BURNETH" and other similar biblical sentiments. I wasn't so enamored by those paintings. I was trying to distance myself from the End Times, not stare them in the face on my way to the bathroom.

But as much as Selig broke the rules and thoroughly inhabited the modern world, he also had a strong sense of history and rootedness. Like me, his traditional past often collided with his adventuresome present.

Getting a job had been easy. I could answer a phone, type ninety-plus words a minute, speak professionally, and look presentable. Finding a roommate was a different matter.

Real estate in New York City was brutal. For the pleasure of renting a small room that contained a twin bed and a dresser, I had to pay half my salary per month. But only if the potential roommate liked me or if someone else hadn't already scooped up the place.

Finally, after months of searching the "Apartments/Houses to Share" real estate listings in the *Village Voice*, a downtown paper that contained everything from personal ads to indie film reviews to articles on the AIDS crisis, I found an unfurnished room to rent on a bucolic, tree-lined street on Avenue P in Brooklyn. Almost three months after I'd arrived in New York City, I hugged Ralph and Laura good-bye. Laura had the decency to put on her housedress for the occasion.

I schlepped a foam mattress onto the subway in Chinatown and dragged it to my new apartment. My roommate Marcia's aunt was getting rid of a couch and some chairs and wanted to know if I could use them. The chartreuse velvet couch circa 1965 and matching chair were free. Of course I could. I was my mother's daughter.

It was a family neighborhood, and our building was composed mostly of middle-aged to elderly people, Jewish and Italian, from what I could gather. It was not the cool place to live in New York City, not the Village with its bars and nightlife, not the gritty East Village, not Alphabet City on the Lower East Side where the punks with bright blue spiky hair hung out and crack addicts crashed in abandoned buildings. But for a year, it was home.

On Saturdays I took the subway to a strip mall in Queens, where I attended church services in a rundown rented building that could have been the Owl's Home. For several months when I'd lived with Ralph and Laura and then when I moved to Brooklyn, I went every week.

It was 1984, but it could have been 1968 or 1975 or any year, for that matter—the ministers were still bombasting about the world coming to an end and speculating about the Antichrist.

I was sick to death of hearing about the end of the world. How this world was Satan's world and we had to avoid everything in it. The thing that continued to make me seethe, though, was the church's attitude toward women. The ministers incessantly reminded the congregation that it was Eve who'd heeded Satan, taken the fruit, and tempted Adam, Eve who had disobeyed, Eve who was responsible for the world's ills.

I was sick of the lack of any real intellectual inquiry on the part of the ministers or the congregants.

Having studied the Bible as an academic subject, I now recognized more complexities and more contradictions within it than I had before. And the church made no attempt to reconcile any of them. Not once had a minister admitted that when God created the first human, it was not technically a "man," it was an "earth creature," the real meaning of *Adam* in Hebrew. A being created from earth. Only when that earth creature was split in two were both man and woman created, at the same time, equally, from the same creature. That was the understanding of many Hebrew scholars.

"God created man in His image," one of my professors had joked, "and man, being a gentleman, returned the favor." At the time, his words had seemed blasphemous. Now, I was beginning to see how we all projected onto God whatever values we ourselves had. Our god was a reflection of ourselves, not the other way around.

No, the church hadn't changed. I had. Gradually, and without a conscious decision, I stopped going to church. I overslept. Or felt it was too far—over an hour from Brooklyn. I hadn't made any friends in church. What I still wasn't willing to admit to myself was that the church itself, its beliefs, had become indefensible.

Yet, inexplicably to Patty and Selig, I continued practicing many elements of the church's teachings, in my own haphazard, inconsistent way. I didn't eat pork or shellfish. I took off work for the high holidays, staying home and reading the Bible. Despite all of my very real, ongoing questions and concerns about the church, and even about Jesus as a god, and despite my desire to straddle Satan's world and the church, I expected that one day I would figure it out, get baptized, and make it into the Kingdom.

This expectation was incomprehensible to my roommate, Marcia. A Jewish atheist who was a therapist and dealt with delusional patients and drug addicts every day, Marcia and I spent many Sunday afternoons talking about our pasts. In her therapeutic, nonjudgmental manner, Marcia listened when I explained that, just as the angel of death had "passed over" the doorposts of the Israelites marked with the blood of a slaughtered spring lamb, if you accept Jesus's blood as your sacrifice, you will be "passed over" for death, and given eternal life.

I could have quoted Matthew 26:26, "Take, eat; this is my body." And verse 27, "And he took the cup, and gave thanks and gave it to them saying, 'Drink ye all of it. For this is my blood of the new testament which is shed for many for the remission of sins.'"

But the power of Jesus's blood and my stubborn refusal to completely let go of the church were not easy to explain, especially to a Jewish atheist who had not grown up needing to be raptured to Petra, to salvation, and to my sister.

CHAPTER 31

New York City was a revelation around every corner. Everything delighted me: browsing the Columbus Avenue street fair and gazing at its Australian sheepskin hats and gloves and filmy black scarves; crunching my way through the bed of multicolored autumn leaves that blanketed Central Park and taking special note of the squawking birds flying south for winter; spending long afternoons in the Metropolitan Museum, walking slowly through the Temple of Dendur, and peering as closely as possible at the wizened, hardened, chestnut brown mummies in their cases.

Clad in a purple disco shirt with silver thread woven throughout, I danced at the Limelight, a church that had been converted to disco. Foreigner's "I Want to Know What Love Is" blasted loudly over the sound system.

I rode the subway and listened in on a cacophony of conversations, which I committed to memory or quickly wrote down on the back of a receipt, for use in a story I might write:

"Anthony, do you think I'm 'nave'? Somebody told me I was 'nave.' What's 'nave'?" Harvey asked.

"The clock keeps on ticking, Harvey," said Anthony. "My father's been dead twenty-four years now. Fell off a scaffold."

"Shut up! I don't wanna hear about your father no more!"

Harvey caught me staring at him. I had not yet acquired the ability to avoid eye contact. "What's 'nave'?" he asked.

"Naïve?" I said. "It means 'innocent.'" Oh, how I loved people asking me the meaning of words and me being capable of providing it!

"Do you think Irene loves me?" Harvey turned to Anthony. "She said she loves me, but I dunno . . ."

"Twenty-four years."

And just then, I heard a voice. "Harvey!"

"Irene!"

Irene appeared to have Down syndrome. Her face was all smiles, and she hugged Harvey. "Irene, do you love me?"

"Yes, Harvey."

"The clock keeps on ticking," said Anthony.

"I don't wanna hear about it no more, Anthony."

What this conversation was all about, I had no idea. I jotted the exchange down as fast as I could, a quintessential New York City moment with strangers pondering the fragility of life.

Indeed, the clock kept on ticking. I vividly recalled looking at the clock on the day my sister died. Her time on earth had come to a stop, but those minute hands just kept moving. I was twenty-three years old, time continued to pass, and I began to feel cautiously optimistic that the world would not soon come to a screeching halt. Maybe this wasn't the End Times.

In Indiana, the passage of time was indicated by birds heading south in the fall, the return of the martins to the bird box, and the sound of leaves in the backyard kicking up a fuss; in spring, the early potatoes were planted; May brought blueberries; and in June the strawberries blossomed. In July, I got up at sunrise with Grandma and put on one of her old, long-sleeved shirts and pants, sprayed bug spray all over to keep the chiggers from biting, and went down to the creek to pick blackberries before the sun rose hot and hard in the sky.

In New York, spring was nigh when the Bloomingdale's windows displayed mannequins frolicking in bikinis. New York University students sat on park benches in Washington Square, soaking up the sun and watching a street performer dance hip-hop to a boom box in between classes.

A year after I'd arrived, I'd changed jobs and apartments. Marcia was getting her master's degree, and I didn't want to take over the lease. I spent at least two hours a day commuting.

I moved to the Upper West Side and in with a new roommate, a Brazilian woman, Julie. We stayed up until the wee hours, drinking Brazilian coffee and talking about John Lennon's music and Gabriel García Márquez's books and waxing versus shaving. A spiritual person, Julie liked to say, "God writes straight on crooked lines."

My job at the corporate real estate company had become excruciatingly boring, and so I took another, better-paying and more interesting job as an assistant to a vice president at an ad agency on Madison Avenue. With my fast typing skills, pleasant phone manner, and basic common sense, my boss, Brian, seemed to value me. One day, four months after I'd been hired, Brian asked me to have drinks to discuss things, and I said sure. Married with two kids, Brian was a quiet guy in his mid-forties who typically schlumped around the office.

We had drinks, but didn't discuss much, and when Brian said goodnight, he leaned over to kiss me on the cheek. Like expense accounts and leg warmers, kissing on the cheek was a ubiquitous 1980s thing. But his mouth landed on my mouth, and then his tongue attempted to make its way between my lips. I was so shocked that I pulled away and said, "Oh, g'night," and ran down the subway stairs. It was déjà vu—the Orthodox man's hand was again under my ass. How was a woman supposed to see these things coming? A religious man, one's married boss—did they all think they had carte blanche when it came to women?

The next day, Brian's office door was closed. I settled in at my desk and decided I would just pretend nothing had happened. No point in upsetting the applecart. My job was more interesting than the previous one, and there was even potential for growth.

Pam from HR called and asked to see me. Pam wore her usual boxy suit and a blouse bow tied at the neck. She sat behind her big desk and made small talk for about forty-five seconds, then went straight to the point. She said that Brian felt I wasn't the right person for the job. It took me a few minutes to realize that I was being fired.

Pam's barracuda smile remained pasted on her face. "We no longer need you. You may take whatever you have, and we'll send you a check for the past two weeks."

Back then I didn't understand that I'd been fired because Brian had tried to kiss me. Giving people, and institutions like the church, the benefit of the doubt, or being unwilling to see what was clear to others, was a quality I found difficult to shake. I trusted everyone, and hadn't learned to cut the deck.

CHAPTER 32

I was not a poet. I was a writer, but not a poet. This took me quite a few years to accept. I still wrote poetry, and sent it out to journals. And it was rejected. A sample:

> *Iamallone*
> *Iam*
> *Allone*
> *Alone*
> *One*

My former roommate Marcia, who had become a very good friend, asked if I'd ever considered getting a master's degree in creative writing or literature. No, I hadn't. But, like the guidance counselor, this suggestion turned out to be fortuitous. I applied and was accepted into an MFA program at City College, where I could take evening classes and work during the day.

———

Terry, a woman in my fiction writing class, was in her forties, and one day the teacher asked her exactly what she was trying to say. Her stories contained some powerful elements but were somewhat didactic and, even though it was fiction, we assumed it was based on her childhood with a father who beat her with a belt.

"I'm trying to say," Terry said, frowning, "that my parents never really loved me, and all my life I've been trying to get someone to love me. And I've suffered."

The entire class was silent. It felt as if we were in a group therapy meeting, not gathered around a long table in a fiction writing class in which we attempted to transform our material into something greater than tattling or venting or bitching and moaning.

The teacher compassionately but professionally said that he admired her writing, and the complex emotional world she was traversing, but felt Terry needed to remove herself a little bit from it so she could better shape the story.

I, too, vacillated between being too close to the material I was working on, and being way too distant. Where was that in between, as a writer? Where was a place that was not "the truth," because this was fiction, but "a truth"? Unlike Alise, I had no interest in writing nonfiction. That was no fun.

A man named Burt sat next to me every week because he thought I needed protection from the harsh world, just as he insisted on walking curbside to shield me from traffic. Thirty years older than me, he was fond of quoting, in a dramatic and sonorous voice, "Unless she is willful, and full of disastrous genius, she will sink into convention."

Burt and I talked about being writers, the relationship between the creator and the created, the object and the subject, and as a reader, how do we let our defenses down and enter into a world that is made up?

"What does this character want, Angela? That's what all writing is about—somebody wants something they don't have," Burt lectured when we met for breakfast at a diner on Seventh Avenue.

I often stayed up until two in the morning, working on short stories and then a novel inspired by *Lolita*. In it, an older woman had an affair with a teenage boy. At the time, it felt fresh and original, something no fortysomething woman would ever do. What did the protagonist, Stacy, want? She wanted the child she'd never had.

I wrote and revised, time and again, a short story called "Leo." In it, a young woman named Darlene is working at the Senior Citizen Center when Leo, one of the seniors, confides in her that the seventysomething Lillian, whom everyone called Miss Hollywood because she'd modeled nude in 1930s LA, was interested in him.

Yep, I don't know if you know it, but I went over to her house one night. Yep, red silk sheets and the incense was burnin'. She was hot for me and I was hot for her. She was wearin' hot pants—and I mean hhhot pants, ooh, doggies, they was so-ome hhot!

This conversation was lifted directly from memories of my summers in Jasper, with Leo following me around as I clipped the hedges or dusted. I went on to write about how Leo had told me a few days before his wife died of cancer, "I asked her if we could, you know, do it, one more time. She said yes. So we made love right there in the hospital bed. And that was the last time we did."

I was twenty-one years old when Leo confided this information to me, coming down the stairs of the Older American Center. There was a quiet hum of chatter in the center—the quilters were upstairs, and several men sat playing at card tables in the living room. I knew that, though it was just any other summer day in Jasper, his words were important and said something about love and life and hope.

Though over the years I wrote and rewrote the story, with every revision feeling as if I was getting closer to its soul, I was never satisfied with it. None of the versions captured an old man's heartbreak. Leo would never have what he wanted—his wife's warm body lying next to his.

Throughout the roommates and the friends and the writing and the master's degree and four different secretarial jobs, I veered back and forth between Christianity and Judaism.

I hadn't been attending church and instead was taking classes at the Ninety-Second Street Y and the Park Avenue Synagogue. While

Madonna was wearing a black corset as an outer garment and singing "Papa Don't Preach," I was studying Kabbalah, the Jewish mysticism text that she became an ardent follower of years later.

According to the Kabbalah, God was One, but at the outset of Creation had withdrawn into Himself, splitting Himself in two—the Revealed God and the Infinite God. This reminded me of Christianity: God in heaven, Jesus on earth. When the explosion outward occurred, it split the Revealed God from the Infinite God, which was described as a vessel shattering, sending *sephirot*, emanations, into the universe. Thus, the mystics concluded, the reason there is suffering in this world could be traced to the very beginning. The vessels holding the God-stuff broke as they emanated from God, so creation was imperfect from the outset.

The Kabbalah teacher explained that the Jews were in exile because the entire world is in exile. Why do they suffer? Because everyone suffers. And, if the world is in exile, then God, who is the world, is also in exile.

I found this notion of God in exile both reassuring and deliciously subversive.

Man's beliefs and goodness, however, could repair the vessels and thus redeem not only the world, but also God. God's sparks were floating throughout the ten levels of the universe, lost, needing to be found and put back together.

Perhaps these "lost and found" quests were universal, and everyone from Jewish mystics to American immigrants felt a sense of homelessness, of having been torn from a place long, long ago. Lost in the universe, humanity was in exile from God, from themselves, and from one another.

———

Still, my internal war raged. And it was impossible to separate it from my ongoing relationship with Selig.

"I never realized that you still believed in that church," Selig once said, over one of our many dinners at a downtown hotspot. It was clear that my religious issues were impossible for him to fathom. He was understandably perplexed, given my choice to live in Israel and my studies of everything from the historical roots of the Exodus to the Khazars, that I was unwilling to entertain the possibility of converting to Judaism.

My fear of allowing my hard-won identity to be obliterated was so deeply entrenched it was almost obsessive. To belong to a group of people, to be forced to follow rules, to be afraid of doing the wrong thing, to give up even a tiny bit of personal autonomy to a religion or to a man. To be sucked back up into someone else's definition of who I was and who I should be.

And deep down, I continued to believe that there had to be one right faith, one that I had yet to find or commit to. It was my everything-is-black-or-white, German, judgmental background. I had not given up my search for the Right Answer, the Right Faith, the one that God approved of.

I felt as if I was suspended somewhere between the dew-kissed grass that covered the rolling hills of southern Indiana and the hard, hot concrete sidewalks of New York City. I was in a place where the smell of autumn leaves and manure battled against the fumes of car and bus exhausts. In exile. Like God. And all I wanted was to be whole.

CHAPTER 33

In 1985, when I was twenty-four, I attended my last church service.

I stopped attending services and stopped believing in the church as the only way to make it into the Kingdom.

I thoroughly enjoyed my classes at the Park Avenue Synagogue and the Ninety-Second Street Y. I didn't have to force myself to go. I looked forward to it; it was as if they were an extension of the classes I'd taken at The Hebrew University in Jerusalem. Nothing was more thrilling than spending an entire Sunday in a roomful of Jews examining the Song of Songs through the lens of Jewish mysticism.

It was therefore not unreasonable that Selig was confused when, after a year together, he asked if I would ever consider converting and I said simply, "No, I'm Christian."

"But you take all of those Jewish classes," he said. "And you don't even go to that church anymore." To him, I was kind of like a woman who said, "I love you" to two different men—and meant it.

Over dinners at an Indian restaurant on East Sixth Street, a Greek restaurant in Queens, or a slew of other places in Manhattan, Selig and I continued to spend time together and grow closer. And, while we were drawn to each other, there was an underlying wariness that at least I felt. Neither of us really wanted to commit to each other long term. We couldn't envision how that would work. There were just so many differences between us. There was the age difference, the religious differences, and the worldview differences. I avoided ownership of anything—I didn't have an iron or a TV. I had one skillet and a few forks, knives, and spoons. Selig liked stuff. Disturbing paintings, hobo picture frames, antique furniture, stylish coats and shoes. He was an eclectic collector.

I was very concerned with the meaning of life. He wanted to score the best tickets to *Starlight Express*.

Selig and I were always on the verge of ending it. Our relationship sputtered along, and when it was good it was great. But relationships can continue for an awfully long time when both people are ambivalent and not willing to set some boundaries, as my shrink friends would say. I couldn't commit to an eight-hour lipstick. Selig wanted a Jewish wife and family.

And then, after one of dozens of breakups over the years, I went out with a plastic surgeon whose facial muscles did not move the entire evening. He wanted to give up Manhattan, move to Vermont, and live the simple life. Having only narrowly escaped the simple life myself, this was of no interest. There was also the best-selling author who wrestled with me on his couch, trying to convince me that he had women begging (*begging!*) him to perform oral sex on them; a cute Indian guy with whom I had absolutely nothing in common, but who called me for months after our one and only date; a divorced man from California who came into town every month on business and only wanted to go to dinner, hang out, and kiss—which got old fast. There was also a sexy Greek guy (*very* sexy, dark and swarthy, my weak spot) and a struggling actor who called me and whispered, "What color are your panties?" To get rid of him, I described the white, cotton granny panties that I was actually wearing.

Through all of this, Selig and I continued to return to one another, chicken to egg, wren to nest.

"Some people *do* have futures," Selig once said during one of those conversations in which we poked at, danced around, suggested the possibility of a future together. "Some children do not die. I'm not asking you to be anything you don't want to be. I'm asking you to have a life. A future."

A future. What a concept.

CHAPTER 34

I picked up the gray prayer book, discreetly peeked at that of the woman next to me to find the correct page, and flipped forward, following slowly in Hebrew on the right side, then looking over at the English translation on the left page so I could understand what I was saying.

I was in a synagogue on the Upper West Side on a Saturday morning in December 1987. Selig and I were taking another break. I had decided the night before that I wanted to know what it felt like to go to synagogue. No underlying pressure. It was just me, going to have a spiritual experience, like people climbed the Himalayas or smoked peyote in an attempt to arrive at the Divine.

People continued to filter into the synagogue, the women whispering to each other, chasing after their children, chanting off and on as the spirit took them. The cantor boomed away like an opera singer.

I'd been to an inclusive and cool Conservative synagogue on the Upper West Side for Friday night services, and I'd also gone to a Reconstructionist synagogue with a friend. I hadn't been to a Saturday synagogue service in several years, probably not since Israel, which was quite different than this Western version of worship. In Israel, even in the Orthodox synagogues, men wore slacks and shirts, and many sported sandals.

I wasn't sure yet how I felt about this Orthodox ruling that men and women had to be seated separately. On the one hand, there was logic to it because, as I'd noticed at parties, men and women often naturally split up, the men hanging out in front of a game on TV while the women congregated in the kitchen.

On the other hand, the fact that in the Orthodox world women were relegated to the wings, with not as good a view of what was going on, the fact that women were not allowed up front, on the *bimah*, to participate in any meaningful part of the service, upset me. It reminded me of the ministers' words: "Women were made for men, not men for women. Women should not teach. Women should learn in silence." I wondered if the men would agree with being put in second-class seating.

We sat, we stood, the Torah was taken out of the ark and carried around the synagogue. During the service, when the words *kadosh, kadosh, kadosh* ("Holy, holy, holy") were spoken, everyone lifted their heels on saying each word, as if striving to pull up closer to God. The ancient ritual felt like a fossil of another, ancient world, whose imprint had traveled across time and place and had turned up embedded in the collective memory of this sophisticated, well-dressed crowd in a New York City synagogue.

The men's section was separated from the women by a low, wooden wall. An older man whispered loudly to a few toddlers: "Here, have one. Have two. You want green? I have green." He held out a handful of lollipops, and the children politely chose one each. Synagogues usually had a "candy man," whose pockets were filled with sweets for the children. Golda's husband, Bob, had been the candy man in their synagogue in Israel.

We sat, stood, then prayed out loud, a melodious mesh of voices. Then, during one of the silent prayers, a child burped. Automatically, a few men nearby pronounced a fervent "Ah-*men!*"

The rabbi delivered his sermon, tying together Thanksgiving and Hanukkah in an interesting way: the Native Americans had helped the intruders in their land, saving them from physically starving, only to later have their land and spirit crushed by the descendants of the white men. He reminded us that we celebrated Hanukkah, which was coming up that week, because the Greeks, too, were foreign intruders and had tried to crush the Jews, physically and spiritually. But we had proven victorious in that battle, with God's help.

The rabbi neither exhorted us to repent and change, nor warned us that the End Times were coming. Ironically, the discordant music, the jumble of Hebrew and English, the mishmash of people coming and going soothed me.

I closed my eyes and thought about Jesus.

He was like an old boyfriend I still felt fond of but couldn't quite commit to. Couldn't quite accept that his blood had been sacrificed to give me eternal life. I thought of him but didn't miss him.

CHAPTER 35

The years were a shibboleth in the original sense of the word. The Iran-Contra scandal dragged on, Whitney Houston belted out "The Greatest Love of All," and the space shuttle *Challenger* blew up seventy-three seconds after it launched. The clip was aired again and again, a precursor of the relentless twenty-four-hour news cycle.

My friend Louise had gotten married, and I attended her wedding in Toronto. Talya, who was getting her doctorate in psychology, was dating a Lebanese-Jewish man. Like her, his family had fled Lebanon after the state of Israel was created in 1948, and they'd ended up in Brazil. Laila was in law school in Washington, DC, determined to right wrongs and tilt the world toward justice. Eve's husband had divorced her without letting her know. She had been in the States for the summer, and he informed her she shouldn't come back. Patty and her boyfriend had broken up, but she remained in New York City, happy and optimistic. Alise and Michael had divorced, and Alise returned to college and confessed she'd never believed in the church. She'd only gotten baptized in order to get married.

My mother's parents died a month apart. My grandfather died in the living room of the farmhouse, where he had a clear view out the window of the pond and the cows in the pasture. "As long as he could see his cows, he was okay," my mother said.

A month later, my grandmother's heart stopped beating. Just like that. No more Sundays at my grandparents'. We all felt as if we'd been orphaned.

It was 1988, and Selig and I were back together. My sister Sarah had just graduated from college and moved to New York City to pursue acting. Coincidentally, my roommate had moved out, so we were sharing a basement apartment in Queens, my fifth apartment in five years. They all resembled each other. Wood-paneled walls. Mattress on the floor. In the corner now was a desk where my new word processor sat. A nicked hand-me-down filing cabinet contained my socks and underwear. On the floor next to the mattress was a stack of books, some used for research, some for pleasure, most for both because I found research deeply pleasurable.

I'd published a few stories but was now writing a novel that referenced the Jewish theologian and philosopher Martin Buber. Even though I only needed a mere two lines of text to display the protagonist's philosophical bent, I'd read all of Buber's *I and Thou*. On top of it was the medieval writer Judah Halevi's book *The Kuzari*, an imagined conversation between a rabbi and a pagan. And then there was Josephus's tome, *Antiquities*. The title itself I found beyond delightful and thrilling. Josephus was mostly for fun. However, after reading his account of the first-century-BCE King Herod looting King David's tomb, I'd been thinking it would be interesting to write something about that. Even if there was no audience in America in 1988 for Herodian grave robbers.

In the midst of my books and papers was an empty coffee mug, a mostly eaten bar of Toblerone, pink nail polish, and a pair of socks that might or might not be dirty.

I lived in a messy, spartan nest. The kind of place you could flee from quickly, should catastrophe arise.

———

"You're keeping it," Sarah said as a statement, not a question, after I peed on the stick and it immediately, without hesitation, flashed the plus sign.

"Yeah."

There were some things in a family that were understood, not up for discussion. I wasn't opposed to others getting abortions, and if I had become pregnant by someone I didn't love, or had just met, then yes. But in this case, the pregnancy seemed almost miraculous, since Selig had been told he was practically infertile.

"What do you think you'll do?" Sarah asked.

Unlike me, Sarah was someone who liked to have a plan and know what her next step—preferably next five steps—was. I understood what she meant: Would I stay with Selig and make it work? Would I convert to Judaism? Would I move back to Indiana temporarily? Would I stay in New York and be a single mom?

"I'll keep the kid. And I'll figure the rest out."

I lost count of how many people I told I was pregnant before I told Selig.

First I called Alise, who still lived in California and knew all about the excruciating back and forth with Selig over the past several years. She answered with a cheerful, "Hey, Ang!" Her voice always sounded as if she were thinking of a good joke that she couldn't wait to tell you.

"Hey, so I have some news."

"What?!" she answered breathlessly.

"Well, I'm pregnant. And I'm thinking about converting," I said, because it was something I could say to her.

"You may as well," Alise advised almost airily, as if it were a matter of choosing which pair of shoes to wear.

"I don't exactly believe in Jesus, but if I'm wrong, I'm screwed. And so is the baby."

"I don't really believe in God, so I'm screwed, too."

It felt almost like a blow to hear Alise, of all people, say she didn't believe in God.

"The other thing," I barely dared to confess now to Alise, "is what if I convert to Judaism and then somebody like Hitler comes back? My kid would be doomed, and it would be my fault."

"Nah," Alise said. "They would come and get him even if he was half-Jewish. And you too." She let out her unmistakable cackle, and I cackled with her, because she was right, and it was a crazy relief to realize that I could not predict what kind of a world my child would be born into.

———————

Patty had been privy to my New York City life for the past five years—from the crazy Ralph and Laura stories to my various jobs, apartments, roommates, and relationships. So when I called and said, "Patty, you won't believe it, I'm pregnant," she laughed and said, "Mazal tov!" As if it had been planned and as if it were any ordinary, commonplace pregnancy. Which comforted me and made me feel like maybe it was.

"So are you thinking of maybe converting?" she asked.

"I don't know," I sighed. It was a legitimate question, especially coming from Patty, my study partner who had quizzed me on the similarities and differences between the ancient Babylonian creation myth, the *Enuma Elish*, and the book of Genesis.

"You have to do what's right for you, Angie," Patty said.

"I know," I said, but after I hung up the phone, I realized that wasn't entirely true. I also wanted to do what was right for the baby.

CHAPTER 36

I called Selig (having already told the guy at the deli where I bought my morning coffee that I was pregnant) and said I wanted to see him for dinner. I had it all worked out. I would tell him quietly, gently, ease into it.

"Okay, but is there a reason you want to meet for dinner?"

"Just to talk." I didn't realize it, but it probably seemed weird to him to so formally ask to meet for dinner. However, I somehow didn't want to have a conversation in private about this. I liked having an exit strategy.

"About what?"

He was a lawyer. Relentless. I hadn't planned on his questioning my motive, so I stammered, "I have something to tell you."

"You're pregnant."

"How did you know?" I was incredulous.

"I just figured what else would you want to tell me."

I failed to see his logic. How could he have thought that I would be pregnant, given his presumed infertility?

We met for dinner at an Upper East Side restaurant near his apartment. It was the end of September, and we'd just celebrated my twenty-seventh birthday over dinner. As always, we greeted each other with a kiss on the cheek, a smile, and a "Hi, darling."

The maître d' led us to a table. People were seated around us, chatting, eating soup, doing the usual things that people do at a restaurant.

I looked across the table. Without Selig saying a thing, I saw all of the concerns and questions in his face.

"Well, this is exciting," he said, but it seemed forced. Not terribly reassuring.

The bread arrived. I was starving and buttered it with enthusiasm. I agreed, yes, it was exciting.

"Did you see a doctor? To confirm? Like, how far along you are?"

"No. I don't need a doctor to confirm it. My boobs are sore, I missed my period, and I'm exhausted. I'm guessing I'm about a month pregnant."

"You don't think you should see a doctor?" Selig persisted. It was as if a doctor might provide a different answer.

"I do need to see a doctor. But there's nothing a doctor is going to tell me now. I'm pregnant. I know it's not planned. It's not like this is easy for me, either." It was difficult to be reasonable when I felt he was being unreasonable. Couldn't he just ask me how I was, for Christ's sake?

"Oh, I know, I know," he tried to reassure me. "I don't know how these things work. I thought you needed to see a doctor. That's all. To make sure everything is okay."

The waiter appeared and we ordered, thank God, because I needed protein.

"Have you told anyone yet? Your family?" Selig had many questions.

"No, of course not," I lied. I felt like he really didn't know me at all.

"Are you having any morning sickness?" The inquisition continued. It was as if, now that I had a speck of a lentil inside me, I'd become someone else, someone he needed to more closely examine. Which was kind of true. I was not the same person I was just a month ago.

"No," I answered. "I feel fine."

"Good, good. I'm glad. As long as you're healthy and the baby is okay."

The food arrived. I ate every bit of my chicken and mashed potatoes—comfort food.

"Are you—thinking about maybe converting?" he asked. According to Jewish law, if the mother was born Jewish, of Jewish blood, then the child would be Jewish. Though my bloodline would never be ethnically Jewish, if I converted under an Orthodox rabbi, the baby would be recognized as Jewish in the Orthodox Jewish world that Selig's family inhabited.

On the other hand, if I actively rejected Jesus, whose blood had been sacrificed to give me eternal life (maybe? I think?), the door to the Next World would be forever shut to me. I would never see those I'd loved and lost and who resided there.

In the past, every time the conversion conversation had come up, it had seemed theoretical. We weren't committed and didn't have a kid together. Now, conversion would have to be a discussion. I understood that. Nonetheless, it also pissed me off. What I wanted Selig to say was "I'm so happy, and as long as you're happy and healthy, and we're together, that's all that matters. We will work everything else out." Those were the words I'd written for him in my head. He was woefully off-script.

A few tears fell down my cheeks, which shocked both of us, because I rarely openly displayed my emotions. The German in me. However, the pregnancy had kicked in with a vengeance, and if I wasn't eating, I was crying.

"No, no, Ang, it's fine. We don't have to talk about it now. It's okay. I love you and everything will be fine." But by then I was furious, even though he'd finally said the words he should have said an hour earlier. I could go from heartbroken to livid in a split second. It would serve him right, I thought, if I raised the kid a devout Christian. In Indiana.

No sooner had I puffed myself into a tizzy of self-righteous anger than I deflated. I regained perspective. This wasn't about Selig. It was about the baby.

———

Selig and I went to our first doctor's appointment together. The doctor rubbed cold goo over my exposed and ever-burgeoning abdomen, then moved the Doppler up, down, and all around. On the screen was a vague, grainy outline of a curled baby. The doctor said, "And there's the baby's neck, and look at this, the baby is yawning!" Selig and I looked at each other like the proudest parents. Our baby was yawning!

CHAPTER 37

"Are you getting married?" Patty asked me when we met at one of our favorite Israeli cafes in the Village. I overheard Hebrew being spoken at several tables. It comforted me.

"No time soon," I said, scarfing down a huge bite of falafel that I'd smushed around in a plate of hummus. "What I need to do is buy some maternity shirts. And pants."

Patty looked at me more closely. "Really?"

"Yeah. I can't button my jeans." I lifted my loose shirt to show her.

"And are you moving in together?" she asked.

"I guess. Eventually. I mean, we basically live together. But I like to know I can go back to my apartment. You know. Good to have an escape route," I joked.

"When are you telling your family?"

"Eventually," I said again. Again, with all the questions.

"What do you think they'll say?"

It was difficult to predict how my parents would react to my pregnancy. Whatever they privately thought about my relationship with a Jewish man fourteen years older, they had kept it to themselves. I always thought this was an excellent quality.

My mother would probably roll with my situation. She had not a bad word for anyone. Her criterion for judging others was "as long as they're a nice person."

I imagined my father would say, "Well, we taught you kids right, and when I meet my Maker, I believe He will say, 'Well done, my good and faithful servant.'" He quoted that line from the book of Matthew for everything from when my older siblings married Catholics to when Ed spent the weekend in jail.

My father adhered to his own version of strict Christian standards. Eight years before, when my older sister Mary had become engaged to Ray, a divorced man, my father had threatened not to attend the wedding or walk her down the aisle. In the end, my father not only attended Mary's wedding but also walked her down the aisle. Family came first, and perhaps he also recognized himself when he saw his children taking paths antithetical to their parents' ways.

The truth was, I did things on an as-needed basis, and I told people things on a need-to-know basis. Right now, they didn't need to know.

To Patty, I said, "I think they'll be okay with it. Or if they're not, they'll keep it to themselves. As they should. Selig told his parents. They're very happy about it—his mother said it's a miracle. But now they're bugging him about me converting."

If I didn't convert to Judaism, Selig's family would be deeply disappointed and potentially keep the baby and me at arm's length. They believed they were entitled to a vote.

"That's a lot, Ang," Patty said.

"Yeah. That's why maternity clothes and food are good distractions for me."

———

Selig and I weren't talking about marriage. It was understood that he wouldn't marry me unless I converted. Though most everyone assumed that marriage was important to me, they were wrong. I didn't think a piece of paper proved that we were committed. To be committed you had to *be* committed, accountable to one another. I was trying to get used to being accountable.

I spent most nights at Selig's apartment. We made the bed together in the morning, throwing the duvet across and sort of settling it in place. We took a taxi downtown together, and Selig dropped me off in midtown, where I worked as an administrative assistant to a lawyer. Then we met after work and had dinner. On weekends, we had brunch together or with friends. Selig picked up the Sunday *New York Times* on Saturday night. I got the book review section; he took the arts and leisure.

We commented on what we were reading. My literary tastes ran the gamut from P. D. Wodehouse's Jeeves books, which had me laughing out loud, to Rainer Maria Rilke's poetry. Selig liked thick biographies of political figures.

Selig still wanted to stay out late and go hear music, but I needed to be in bed by 10 p.m. We were adjusting to a new reality, but we were comfortable and happy together. As long as we could avoid talking about conversion, commitment, and marriage.

It was still not easy for me to commit to remaining in the same place with the same person for the rest of my life. There remained a tiny part of me that continued to believe that, any day, the world would end, and I would be fleeing.

CHAPTER 38

In the chill of an autumn evening on Park Avenue, after Selig and I had eaten dinner, he said, "You know, Ang, there are exercise classes for pregnant women?"

"You must be kidding me!" I turned on him when I realized what he was insinuating. "I'm starving all the goddamned time, I'm *pregnant*, too bad if you wanted a thin woman and now I'm a fattie . . . !"

On and on I went, standing on the sidewalk facing him while other people shuffled past us in typical New York fashion. Words tumbled from my mouth of their own volition. "You can go fuck yourself! I'm exhausted and starving! I don't have the energy to do one fucking jumping jack!"

Selig apologized. "No, I didn't mean it as a criticism, and of course you should eat whatever you feel like eating. No, really, Ang, if you're still hungry, I'll get you something," he said, with terror in his eyes.

Of course, I had totally overreacted. I didn't think that an argument over my asking for his pizza crust would sink our relationship. However, I felt like nothing was about what I wanted or needed. Selig worried about what his parents, his family, his friends, and his business colleagues would think.

I'd spent too much time as a child riding in a pink-finned Caddy to care if people thought I was a little too chunky. Instead, it was still

God's judgment that mattered. But I wasn't sure what God wanted me to do. Convert? Get married? Do nothing? I was certain that God had an opinion about it. Probably the same opinion as mine.

"The baby can choose whatever he or she wants to be when he gets older," I suggested once to Selig. I thought that was a reasonable solution, letting me off the hook and dumping the responsibility on my child.

"It doesn't work that way." He shook his head.

"It could," I argued. "People do it all the time. They let the kid decide when they get old enough."

"But they can't make a decision unless they have some grounding in their parents' faith."

"I understand, but we can celebrate all of the Jewish holidays. I never celebrated the Christian ones anyway, and I can be kind of de facto Jewish without converting."

Again, he shook his head. "I'm not telling you that you have to convert. I can't and won't do that. But I'm telling you that no child of ours will be considered Jewish within my family's Orthodox world unless you convert."

I had trouble truly determining if Selig truly believed in God or if Judaism was a kind of heirloom, like Shabbat candlesticks, something to be passed down. And he didn't understand that given a choice between his family and God, I would choose what I thought God wanted.

God, however, remained silent.

CHAPTER 39

One time, out of nowhere, my father said to my mother, "I guess you really miss your frog legs. I know you liked 'em an awful lot, and now you can't have 'em anymore."

My mother replied, "Maybe there will be frog legs in heaven."

"No, there won't be," he said, shaking his head. "They aren't clean."

"Maybe God will make them clean in heaven," my mother countered.

"No," my father insisted. "He can't."

"With God, all things are possible," my mother concluded.

"Yes, all things are possible, but God wouldn't do that."

My mother was ever hopeful, ever trusting in the power of God to make the unacceptable acceptable. Just as she didn't like when distinctions were drawn between "good" and "bad," she assumed that God, too, accepted everyone, regardless of how they were viewed by society.

What God wanted and what I was willing to sacrifice for the sake of my faith had long been ongoing questions, ongoing discussions in my life. But now, as a pregnant woman, the question took on a new urgency. Not everyone was as inclusive as God and would accept my child and me as Jewish. I wanted him or her included in the community completely rather than on the outside or on the fence.

So one evening, when the conversion subject came up and Selig added that his parents wanted a Jewish grandchild and he wanted to give them that, I said I would be happy to speak to a rabbi.

And I was. I liked rabbis. Rabbis liked me. I had even dated two. I'd teased Selig that he was a good compromise—the son of a rabbi. I wasn't really joking.

Selig's younger brother, an Orthodox rabbi, recommended Rabbi Levy, a Modern Orthodox rabbi on the Upper West Side of Manhattan. I'd decided that if I were to convert, then I would do it under Orthodox auspices so there was never a question of my child's legitimacy as a Jew. In heaven, I doubted it mattered if I called myself an Orthodox or Conservative or Reform Jew, or if I ate frog legs or didn't. Here on earth, it was another story.

I owned few *frum* outfits. I had never needed modest dresses that covered my knees. And since I'd gained ten pounds, all in my abdomen, in the past two months, nothing really fit me properly. So I improvised. A loose sweater over a skirt with an elastic waistband that I'd forgotten I owned. Getting dressed reminded me a little of how I'd prepared to meet Mr. Armstrong in Israel. As if I needed to impress him, or at least not offend him, lest he judge my internal spirituality on my outerwear.

Halloween decorations festooned apartment buildings and businesses. Skeletons sat on the steps of a brownstone, and an elaborate spiderweb with huge black spiders clinging to it covered a storefront window. Everything in New York City was dramatic. And I would be raising a kid here. A country girl, who had never given a good deal of thought as to having children or how to raise them, would have a Jewish city kid.

I walked through the synagogue's somewhat imposing doors and asked the man at the entrance where Rabbi Levy's office was, then followed the corridor around past the sanctuary to another hallway and knocked on the door where his name was affixed. I wasn't nervous about meeting him, but it felt momentous. Thus far, I'd merely been flirting with Judaism. This felt like an engagement.

Rabbi Levy's bookshelves were filled with bound leather books on weighty subjects bearing Hebrew titles. They were a far cry from the church's literature, which asked, *Are We in the Last Days?*

A bearded man in his fifties, Rabbi Levy graciously invited me to sit and, after a few preliminary niceties, he asked me why I wanted to be Jewish. I didn't reveal that I wasn't quite sure I did yet. I worried that any doubt on my part would be used against me. He listened attentively when I told him straight up that I was pregnant, which was not totally obvious under my loose sweater. I said that I had considered converting previously, but it hadn't seemed necessary. I told him I'd lived in Israel for two years and studied Judaism. This, I thought, would command his respect. I almost expected him to say, "Oh, great. You're in!"

"At yeshiva?" he asked, referring to a religious Jewish education.

"No, university."

He nodded. This did not count, I realized, because studying Judaism intellectually or secularly was not the same as studying it in a place of belief.

I was waiting for him to ask me, "And so you don't believe in Jesus anymore, right?" As if becoming Jewish was defined only in its relationship to Christianity. I didn't realize until later how arrogant it was, thinking that Jesus was at the forefront for Jews, or that converting to Judaism was akin to becoming a Christian—profess your faith in Jesus, get baptized, and that was it. But neither my faith nor Jesus was discussed. It was almost as if Jesus was an embarrassing old uncle we'd rather not discuss in polite company. Given the trouble Christianity had caused the Jews in the past 2,000 years, that was understandable.

When I'd first studied Judaism in Israel, I'd found it disconcerting that Jews not only asked very different questions—the rabbis of the Talmud discussed and debated everything from pigeon ownership to what constituted work on the Sabbath—but they didn't always arrive at answers. Rather, there were a lot of questions, a lot of discussion, followed by even more questions.

This had bothered me. I wanted answers. And answers to the big questions, like "What Kind of FAITH Is Required for Salvation?" not to questions like why the Bible begins with the letter *bet*, the second letter of the Hebrew alphabet, instead of *aleph*, the first letter.

I asked Rabbi Levy how soon I would be able to convert. To my astonishment, he said I would need to take a class on keeping kosher as well as a Family Law class, and he would put me in touch with an Orthodox woman to be my study partner and teach me one-on-one. Then I would meet with a panel of rabbis, a *bet din*, and they would decide.

I hadn't seen that coming. It could be a year before I would complete those tasks, and then I still needed their permission to convert, should I decide to make that final decision. The baby would be born in seven months. I was tempted to blurt out, "Wait, wait, let me tell you everything I already know about Judaism!"

I could hold forth about how the Bible had been canonized and why the book of Esther, which doesn't mention God's name, managed to make it into the canon; and we could have a wonderful exchange about the enigmatic red heifer whose blood rendered the impure pure.

Alas, the everyday practice of Judaism had nothing to do with red heifers. Instead, rabbinical Judaism, which mainstream Jews had begun to practice after the destruction of the second temple in Jerusalem in the first century, provided the interpretation of the laws of the Torah, and answers to questions like "Can you eat legumes on Passover?" Ritual and the law were critical parts of Judaism. But I wasn't so interested in the law. I was interested in discovering how the world came into being, why we were created, and how God wanted us to live our lives. The Bible, as I had come to understand it, offered answers that made sense. We were supposed to live our lives showing love to the strangers among us.

I left Rabbi Levy's office with the names of classes at the synagogue that I should register for. They started in January, six weeks away. I felt dispirited and overwhelmed. I was pregnant, had to move in completely with Selig, find a Lamaze instructor and, oh yes, tell my parents all of this. And now I had to take a class about keeping kosher as well as one about family law.

When Selig's mother called to speak to him the next evening, he put me on the phone. She asked me how the meeting with the rabbi went. "Good," I said. "I'm going to take a few classes, and then we'll see."

"But he doesn't think you can complete it by the time the baby is born?" she asked.

"I don't think so," I said, and tried not to sound abrupt. I wasn't used to other people being involved in what, for me, was very personal business—my relationship with God. This wasn't like decorating a nursery. This was potentially converting to a faith and a people. Changing my destiny and that of my child.

Thus far, Selig's parents could not have been warmer or more welcoming. His mother was the consummate rabbi's wife. The congregants confided in her, and she sympathized and empathized with everyone. When she spoke to me, it was always "Oh, hello, dear, how are you feeling?" Privately, she told me that she'd been praying that Selig would have a baby, and this was a miracle.

"My mom is a lot like your mom," Selig once said, and that was true. Both were friends to everyone. Both believed in the essential goodness of mankind and didn't think it was for them to judge others.

Selig's ultra-Orthodox brother, the rabbi, lived in New Jersey; his sister and her family, in Boston. Since I'd gotten pregnant, they had come to the city and we'd all had dinner at a kosher restaurant in midtown. Out of respect for his brother's modesty, no one mentioned my pregnancy. The elephant in the room—my stomach—was studiously avoided. But I knew that behind closed doors there were likely whispers. Would I convert or not? Would I take being Jewish seriously or just do it in name only and later insist on retaining some kind of Christian practice?

They didn't know me well enough to know not to view me as a traditional Catholic or a Lutheran, for whom giving up a Christmas tree was a big deal. I never had a Christmas, let alone a Christmas tree, so the conventional Christian traditions were no loss.

The loss I faced was salvation.

There were moments when I couldn't even remember what I was being saved from, what I was holding on to. Whatever it was, my fists were loosening, almost ready to let go and be betrothed to another faith.

CHAPTER 40

Just after Thanksgiving, when I was three months pregnant, my sister Mary's forty-five-year-old husband, Ray, was diagnosed with stage IV brain cancer. They had three children under the age of seven. Mary was thirty-one, four years older than me.

I flew back to Indiana to stay with my nephew and nieces for a week while Ray received treatment in the hospital. It was impossible to imagine that these sweet, cute, clueless kids were going to be fatherless within six months.

I helped pack the kids' backpacks in the morning before school, hung up their coats when they came home, gave them piggyback rides and snacks, kneeled on the floor and crawled around while they sat on my back like a cowboy on a bucking bronco.

New York City and converting and all of that could wait.

———

Then at Christmas, even though we didn't celebrate, Selig and I went to Indiana. My family knew we'd been dating but had never met him. In my as-needed world, it hadn't felt necessary to make the trip because we were never really and truly committed.

But it was time to prepare them for the new reality—that I was seriously involved with a Jewish man. Announcing my pregnancy

ANGELA HIMSEL

could come later. Even though I'd gained at least ten pounds, I was
tall and it was winter. Thick sweaters hid a multitude of secrets.

My father picked us up from the Louisville airport in the white
Cadillac with the red leather interior. Selig sat in the front with him,
and I loved listening in on their conversation. At one point during the
drive, my father said to Selig, "You know, when God cursed Cain, he
placed a mark on him so that everyone would know that they should
not harm him. I've thought about this for a long time. I think that
God must have made Cain black. Then people would see from afar
that he was black, and they should not hurt him."

"Or maybe white," Selig countered in his well-trained, son-of-
a-rabbi voice.

I smiled. It took my father a few seconds to register what Selig
was suggesting. That maybe Abel was black and Cain was white, as
opposed to vice versa, and the Bible was saying that the first recorded
murderer, Cain, was white.

After about thirty seconds, my father said, "No. I think black."

Selig turned around to look at me. I rolled my eyes.

We were in this together.

———

One morning, when we were sitting at the kitchen table, my father
asked Selig what he thought about George Bush ("H. W.") becoming
president, and Selig, who was a Democrat, offered a very noncommittal,
"Let's see." My father, who didn't vote, said, "Well, whatever God
decides, that's what's going to happen anyway. It all goes according to
the One Upstairs."

"Yes, that's right," Selig agreed, and I loved him for being so kind.

Then my father asked Selig what he thought about Yasser. I whispered, "Arafat."

My father acted as if he were on a first-name basis with the leaders
of the world.

"Well, Yasser said he wasn't going to put up with terrorism anymore," my father said.

Just a few weeks before in Stockholm, Arafat had announced that he accepted the state of Israel's existence and rejected terrorism in all forms.

Selig made a general comment, neither positive nor negative, but said that it was unclear if Arafat actually meant it or if it was a public relations move, which was what both America and Israel seemed to think it was.

My father pressed harder. He seemed to think that Selig, as a Jew, had a special inside take on it, or that all Jews had the same mono-lithic view of Israel, Judaism, and God. That one Jew could speak for an entire people.

My mother gave me a look over my father's head, as she often did. We both smiled faintly and shook our heads.

Scattered throughout the cluttered house in stacks and on top of end tables was the ever-present church's reading material—the magazines, newsletters, coworker letters, and various booklets like *Did God Create a DEVIL?* All of the reading material shared two qualities: the world was coming to an end, and the literature was free.

I hardly noticed it anymore, but when I saw Selig glancing at *How to Win the War with Satan*, I smiled. He lifted his brows, and I shrugged.

My parents continued to attend the Worldwide Church of God, even though Herbert Armstrong had recently died. Apparently, he wouldn't be one of the two witnesses to Jesus's resurrection. In his obituary in 1986, *The New York Times* wrote about Herbert Arm-strong's, as well as the church's, wrongdoings:

> *The church has been embroiled in controversy, ranging from the estrange-ment of Mr. Armstrong and his son, Garner Ted Armstrong, to lawsuits by former church members and an investigation by the state Attorney General of reports of mismanagement of church funds.*

I hadn't seen this obituary, but had instead learned of Mr. Arm-strong's death through my parents. Immediately following, there had been big shake-ups in the church. There was talk that the church would observe Sunday as the Sabbath. And celebrate Christmas and Easter. And women could wear makeup. The church was basically going mainstream.

Both of my parents felt that this was watering down the Truth. That, flawed though Mr. Armstrong may have been, God often used flawed people for His message. Look at King David.

Many other members in the church felt the same way as my parents. They clung to the past, to the right/wrong, black/white, saint/sinner message that was the Worldwide Church of God.

The church would ultimately splinter, and my parents and my sister Liz would go with the group that was more closely aligned with the former Worldwide Church of God. They would still observe the holy days, still go to church on Saturday, still avoid pork and unclean fish and meat.

I didn't blame my parents. How else could they justify all of their sacrifices? Why had they avoided Christmas presents, birthday presents, and the many other trappings of conventional Christianity for so many years, if not for a higher cause? How could they justify relying on prayer cloths for Abby instead of medical care? Perhaps it would have been the same result, but they'd chosen not to search out other doctors because they'd believed. And they could not and would not consider the possibility that they'd been wrong and that their daughter might have lived with proper care.

Saturday night, we all went out to dinner at the Schnitzelbank, the nice German restaurant in Jasper that had been around forever and that I'd been to a handful of times for special occasions. The waitresses wore dirndls, the apron-like dresses that were common in Bavaria. The Deutsche Spezialitaten, the German specialties, included sauerbraten, wiener schnitzel, wurst platter, schweine schnitzel. Neither Selig nor I was worried back then about eating nonkosher meat, so we ordered hearty meat and potato meals, like everyone else.

We took up several tables in the back room, as most of my siblings, their spouses, and their children were with us. I whispered people's names to Selig as discreetly as possible. "My brother Jim, my sister Liz, her son Justin . . ."

Selig and I went over to where Ray was sitting and chatted. There was a gash across his head that revealed the stitches where he'd been sewn up post-surgery. His hair had been shaved off. He was tired. Ever polite, gentle, and quiet, his words came slowly. *Nice to meet you. This must be very different than what you're used to,* he said to Selig. I was struck by his graciousness, acknowledging how surreal this must be to Selig, even as Ray's entire life had become surreal.

His youngest daughter, my two-year-old niece Sarah, climbed up on his lap, a little afraid of this new father.

He held her close.

CHAPTER 41

I vaguely assumed that the Family Law class that Rabbi Levy had asked me to take was about raising a family in accordance with Jewish law. Maybe there would be something about the importance of Friday night dinners, prayers, going to synagogue, that kind of thing. I was kind of right but not at all how I imagined. Family Law was mostly a premarriage class, and the syllabus revealed a surprising list of topics. *Tumah* and *niddah*, Hebrew for states of purity and impurity. Breaking the hymen. Going to the *mikvah*, or ritual bath. This wasn't exactly covered at The Hebrew University. No wonder Rabbi Levy thought I had much to learn.

Just as the class seemed odd to me, I was also the odd one out. I was learning alongside fifty or so modestly dressed Rachels and Sarahs and Ronits and Deenas in their early to mid-twenties. These women had long been on a *derech*, a path, and that path entailed getting married young to the appropriate person. They had come to the class to learn when they could and couldn't have sex, based on their menstrual cycle. At four months pregnant, I now looked it. I was clearly off the *derech*. My classmates avoided looking at my belly, as if it might rub off on them.

Our teacher, Rivkie, was about my age and had shoulder-length brown hair (which I later realized was a wig, in accordance with the

Orthodox tradition that requires women to cover their hair out of modesty). She had a master's degree in social work and four children under the age of six. I could hardly fathom having accomplished all of that before the age of thirty, but she felt she was truly blessed. I grew to admire and respect her for many things, but most of all, for her sense of gratitude. It reminded me of my parents, both of whom often said, "I count my blessings every day."

Rivkie was clear and methodical in her explanations. "During your menstrual period, when you are *t'meah,* you are forbidden to have any physical contact with your husband. *T'meah* doesn't literally translate from the Hebrew as 'unclean.' When you menstruate, potential life is lost, resulting in death of a sort, and death is a spiritual impurity."

The other women sat hunched over their desks, scribbling down the finer points of menstrual blood and marital relations. I took few notes. Neither Selig nor I had any intention of following these laws. Despite the fact that his bloodline was populated with revered and respected rabbis, Selig popped shrimp into his mouth at cocktail parties and traveled on the Sabbath. Like many Jews, or observers of any religion really, Selig picked and chose which laws and traditions he would practice. He was a secular Jew, but fancied himself Orthodox since he'd grown up that way. I didn't have the heart to say that, in reality, he was far from an Orthodox Jew.

"When your period ends," Rivkie taught, "every day you do a check, a *b'dikah,* to check for blood." She held up a small, square white cloth and wrapped it around her middle finger. "It's very important, when you put it up your vagina, that you are thorough. On one hand, we don't want to encourage blood to come down. But on the other hand, you can't just swipe at it, either."

I looked up from my notebook to see if any of the other women were equally disturbed at the requirement to stick a piece of white cloth up their hoo-hahs each month when their period ended. No. They didn't appear the least bit flummoxed.

"When the *b'dikah* cloth comes out white for seven days . . ."

You stick that thing up you for seven days?

" . . . you go to the *mikvah*," Rivkie's explanation continued. "There will be a checklist there, and the *mikvah* lady will inspect you to make sure there's nothing on you. Earrings, for example, can be considered a barrier between you and the water."

A woman would inspect my body before I got dipped in the *mikvah*? These many petty rules made me tired. But everything made me tired, cranky, and teary.

It was impossible not to mentally substitute "baptism" for *mikvah*, the ritual bath. In Christianity, baptism was used to expiate either the original sin that you were born with, or the sins that you'd accrued. Either way, it was related to sin. I'd never been baptized in the World-wide Church of God. It was not something you did until you were an adult and could make an informed decision. And since I had continued to grapple with doctrine, and because the Holy Spirit never opened my mind to the Truth, I had never been spiritually ready to be baptized.

"What do you do if you find blood in your underwear *after* you've gone to the *mikvah*?" one of my classmates asked, with the same kind of seriousness that a physicist might ponder the theory of relativity.

Rivkie answered, "If it is bigger than a dime and if its color is suspicious, then you should put your underwear in a bag with your phone number on it. If you don't feel comfortable, have your husband drop it off at the rabbi, and he'll give you an answer that night as to whether you have to start over or if you're okay."

Again, no one else seemed upset at dropping her panties off at a rabbi so he could tell her when she could have sex. I felt my body tense. This contained echoes of the church: *Woman was made for man, not man for woman; women's lib is one of Satan's sly ways of getting at the American family*. So a male rabbi could inspect a woman's panties under the guise of religion. Judaism and Christianity, after all, shared a text in common, and like half-siblings, were more alike than not.

I was fanning my overheated, pregnant body while Rivkie offered a lovely soliloquy on the spiritual meaning of the laws of family purity. "During your period, and then counting seven clean days after, your husband isn't allowed to touch you, so you're forced to talk things out and not to rely on physical contact to communicate. It's not easy, but many things in life that are worthwhile are not easy. In today's world, where you think that you are entitled to anything you want, it's important to be reminded that there are limits. The Torah was thinking of women when it constructed these laws. We need a break, too. We aren't sex machines who have to perform on demand. Some men think that if you are married to them, they own your bodies, anytime, anywhere. Well, these laws mean 'I belong to myself.' There are boundaries, and men must respect your boundaries."

Finally, I thought. Some underlying philosophy that made sense and that still, thousands of years later, resonated. Boundaries. Growing up in a big family with one bathroom and where I slept with as many as two sisters, boundaries were unheard of and, as a result, were something I struggled with.

Rivkie passed around photocopies of a text in Hebrew and English. It was the "Woman of Valor" passage from the book of Proverbs, one of the Worldwide Church of God's favorite passages to quote in an effort to prove that the Bible didn't marginalize women:

What a rare find is a capable wife! Her worth is far beyond that of rubies. Her husband puts his confidence in her and lacks no good thing... She is like a merchant fleet, bringing her food from afar . . . She plants a vineyard by her own labors. She girds herself with strength and performs her tasks with vigor . . .

Rivkie said, "I wanted to share this beautiful passage about a woman who not only attends to her husband's and children's needs, but buys a field, plants a vineyard, and gives to the poor. But why is she really to be praised? Because *'grace is deceptive, beauty is illusory, it is for her fear of the Lord that a woman is to be praised.'*"

I liked that Rivkie was open about her belief in God. She had a relationship with God, and she made certain to reiterate that the laws had a higher, spiritual purpose. Yet there were times, and this was one of them, when I couldn't believe that 3,000 years after the Bible was written, so many of us, Christians and Jews, were still trying to live our lives based on this hoary, Iron Age document that upheld slavery and sexism and condemned to death people who worked on the Sabbath. Not to mention homosexuals and adulterers.

Still, I remained connected to the stories, and so, like Selig, I was picking and choosing what to accept and what to reject. I was also trying to be more open-minded about the choices of others.

After class, Rivkie gave each of us a supply of *b'dikah* cloths to check for blood during the seven days following our periods. I imagined Jesus's blood mingling with my blood, the past merging with the present. One supposedly saved, while the other defiled; one was offered as a sacrifice for your spiritual life; the other indicated that potential physical life had been lost. Sinners were made clean by metaphorically bathing in Jesus's blood. A woman was made clean by bathing in water.

On the way out the door, each woman quickly, automatically, swiped her hand across the cylindrical *mezuzah* affixed to the side of the door, then kissed her fingers. The *mezuzah* contained the central statement of Judaism, the *Sh'ma*, "Hear, O Israel, the Lord is our God, the Lord is one." I hesitated, then tapped and kissed.

I was captivated by the propensity Jews had to kiss holy objects. In the synagogue, when the Torah was taken out of the ark and carried around, the men lifted their black and white prayer shawls draped around their shoulders, touched the Torah with the fringe, and then kissed the fringe. The women touched their prayer books to the Torah and then kissed the prayer book. I wondered if these rituals were the source of the effusive kissing I'd observed among many of my Jewish friends. My family and community were enthusiastic back-slappers.

In the other class I was taking on the laws of *kashrut*, keeping kosher, I was downright queasy. I wasn't sure if it was the rabbi's manner of speaking, his voice rising up, then down, up, then down, like a ship that didn't know if it wanted to sail forth or remain in the harbor, or if it was the way he swayed to and fro. Or the subject matter itself: If you accidentally dropped a spoon that was designated for meat into a pot designated for milk, did it render both the spoon and the pot nonkosher, and what if there was liquid in the pot, and if there was liquid, how much liquid, and if the liquid was hot or cold, did that matter? Questions that were asked in a singsong voice while swaying. I brought kosher crackers with me to class to nibble on unobtrusively when I felt a wave of nausea.

Later, when everyone had cleared out, I told Rivkie how much I was enjoying her class. I'd initially viewed it as a chore, but she'd taken a weird subject and actually made it reasonable and interesting.

Rivkie said, "Thank you. I'm glad you're enjoying it."

We walked out of the classroom together. "How are you feeling?" she asked.

"Fine," I said. I always said I was fine, whether I was or not.

"The first pregnancy is the hardest, I think, but then they get easier."

"I'm sure," I said, suddenly on the verge of tears, flipping from fine to not-so-fine, which horrified me. Out of nowhere, I found myself feeling deeply sad and overwhelmed. Hormones. My brother-in-law. The almost impossible feat of merging my two worlds, or finding a bridge between them—the demons of my 1970s childhood and my adult life in 1980s New York City. Not to mention the idea of raising a child with someone I loved but who had been an inconsistent boyfriend. Although, Selig had learned to offer me the entire breadbasket over dinner. So there was hope.

"How did you come to Judaism? I know you're pregnant, of course, but . . ."

I appreciated her not assuming that it was because of a man. But she, of all people, knew that there were often several motives for doing something: the external, physical reason, and the internal, spiritual one.

"I grew up Christian, but then I went to Israel on a junior-year-abroad program, and I stayed for two years. I really loved learning about Judaism, and I felt more connected to God in some sense."

Rivkie and I walked down the dark, winter street. In front of a bank, a homeless man sat alongside his shopping cart of possessions. "What about Christianity?" she asked to my surprise, willing to address the elephant, unlike the rabbi, who'd elegantly ignored it.

"I started to question Jesus as the Messiah. How could a dead man be a deity, a savior, and pay the price for my sins? So how could I remain a Christian when I had doubts about the foundation of Christianity itself?"

There was a lot more that I could say but didn't. It was time to move past a childhood that had held me hostage and made me fear bringing a child into a world. A world that I was taught was perpetually on the brink of destruction, where Satan and his demons cavorted and, with one misstep, could lock you out of God's Kingdom. For eternity.

CHAPTER 42

At five months pregnant, I was ready to tell my parents. I called home, and when my father answered, we spoke a little about the weather. The caterpillars were black, which indicated it would be a hard winter. "Well, I wanted to let you know that I'm pregnant," I said casually, as if I was talking about an ingrown toenail. "And I'm converting to Judaism."

"I see. Well, you're an adult now, and you got to make your own decisions. Your mama and me, we done our best, and when I meet my Maker, I can honestly say that I done my best."

"Yes, you did," I agreed. Pretty much exactly what I'd expected him to say.

"Oh, by the way, if you see a rabbi, I sure as heck would like to know how they figure the date of creation. According to the Jewish calendar, Adam was here right 'round 3760 BC, but the way we've always reckoned it . . . "

"Daddy," I broke in, "did you hear me?" Perhaps I'd been too casual.

"Yeah, I heard you," he said impatiently.

"I'm pregnant."

"You can talk to your mama about that kind of stuff. But back to Adam . . . "

My mother got on the phone, and when I told her, she said, "Oh, my goodness! That's so nice!" As if this were a normal circumstance. "Are you feeling okay?"

"Pretty good," I said.

"That's good. I had morning sickness with all my pregnancies, and I can tell you, that's no fun, throwing up from the time you get up in the morning."

Now that I was older, I was newly appreciating the difficulties my mother had faced in her life, and not just the big things, like losing a child and never feeling financially secure. We still joked about how many times we'd had bean soup and cornbread for Thanksgiving. Yet, she'd never seemed bitter or angry. And one of her mottos was, "You got to make the best of things."

My mother caught me up on Rachael, who was almost thirteen and had inherited our grandma's voice and sang in the choir. Grandma Himsel was getting forgetful, she said, but Robert was taking care of her. "But you never know if she and Daddy are talking or not!" We both laughed. Their legendary fights had not abated.

When Selig and I had visited Grandma and Robert on the farm in December, she'd known who I was and that I lived in New York. She sat in her big easy chair turned toward the television. She liked to watch soap operas, and when the kissing scenes came on, my white-haired, eighty-eight-year-old grandmother had audibly sighed.

Grandma apologized that she hadn't cooked anything for us. I asked her if she'd heard from Aunt Margaret, and she said yes, they spoke every Sunday, and Aunt Margaret had sent her the Asbach Uralt chocolates for Christmas that she loved. Gretel had recently passed away, and Aunt Margaret had taken it very hard, Grandma said. "They were very good friends," Grandma said. "For many years."

Grandma reminded me that "some nasssty men live in New York City, und zey push ze women out ze vindows, ja, ze push zem out ze vindow!"

Selig and I nodded, and I said that I stayed away from all the bad areas. At one point Grandma said that Hitler had been a very bad man and, "I vould like to kick him in ze behind, ja, I vould!" For

Grandma, kicking someone in the behind was harsh stuff, tantamount to shooting him in the head. It was also a way for her to let Selig know that she was not anti-Semitic, not a Nazi sympathizer, though she was German.

On the phone with my mother, I asked how Ray was, even though I already knew. I spoke with Mary often, and his chemotherapy treatment might give him another month. When he was diagnosed, the doctor had said three to six months. "It's hard," my mother said. "But Mary's strong, and she'll get through this. I feel bad for the kids, that's who I feel bad for."

CHAPTER 43

Selig and I were having brunch in an upscale deli with friends of his, two couples I'd never met. They were clearly curious about us. We were living together, and I was pregnant. I was pretty sure that they'd decided I was a bimbo in some sense, given that I was fourteen years younger than Selig, from the Midwest, and wasn't a doctor, lawyer, accountant, or other professional. We were eating bagels with lox and cream cheese, or at least I was. Selig was having scrambled egg whites.

We were talking about the mayoral race between David Dinkins and Rudy Giuliani, and Selig was excited to see the Andy Warhol retrospective at the Museum of Modern Art. George H. W. Bush, Reagan's former vice president, had just been sworn in as president, and because our friends were liberals like us, we were lamenting another (at least) four years of Reagan conservatism—pro-gun, anti-abortion, and pro–death penalty.

It was a nice enough brunch, and I was making every attempt to be on good behavior. But I was so preoccupied.

I was pregnant.

My sister's husband was dying.

Selig and his family wanted me to convert. I wanted to do the right thing. For God—whom I was increasingly angry with and often questioned the very existence of. I'd had my crisis of faith before, a crisis that had lasted years, but it had centered on the church, not on God.

CHAPTER 44

It was difficult, almost impossible, to show up at my kosher class or my Family Law class given what was happening with Ray. I wanted to rage, "Who gives a crap about your dairy dishes? Do you think it really matters that I take off my earrings and inspect every crevice of my body to make sure nothing is an impediment to the *mikvah* waters? A wonderful man is *dying*, for Christ's sake!"

I went back again to Indiana. Ray's health had declined. He lay on the couch. Could barely lift his head. The kids clamored around him. I wanted to cry.

I was pissed off at God. Whoever God was. If God existed. Maybe there was a big void out there. No one was watching over us, no one cared. If there were no God to care about laws, why should I? Even when I hadn't agreed with the church, and even when I had ferociously disagreed, I'd always liked everything about worship. I liked the passion and the commitment. I liked how unreasonable and inexplicable and mysterious it was to worship one thing or idea or person.

Not now.

God was lost. And I couldn't find God. Couldn't even come close. Jesus wasn't the answer. Getting saved made no sense. Nobody was saved. You lived. You died. That was it. And so, why bother with religion or with any attempt to explain or justify? People died, I knew that firsthand, and it wasn't fair. They didn't deserve to die, to not be allowed to live out their lives. Children died. If there were a God, He (definitely a He in this case) was out of touch. So why worship this kind of a God?

I'd had enough training in the Bible to know that I was in good company. All of my complaints and concerns and doubts and questions had long been discussed and dissected. But I didn't care about the book of Job and how he thought he'd suffered unjustly when his wife and children died and yet, despite everything, didn't turn his back on God.

I couldn't reconcile anything. I couldn't reconcile belief with reality. And I was angry. So goddamned angry. Louise would tell me I wasn't just angry about my brother-in-law dying and my sister being a widow and her children being fatherless, but that this represented something else that I was angry about, probably my sister dying. I vacillated between feeling truly blessed that I had this baby inside me and feeling mad at whoever was nearby (usually Selig).

None of which meant that God was off the hook. I was so mad at God, it was hard to go to the classes, hard to show up to study with Malkah, the Orthodox woman the rabbi had asked me to meet with once a week for one-on-one instruction. Malkah covered her hair with a scarf, and when she offered me a cookie then took one herself, she mouthed the appropriate blessing before eating it. Malkah repeatedly thanked HaShem (God) for everything from her children to the fact that there was no traffic in the Lincoln Tunnel.

I couldn't thank God for anything. No matter what, I'd always believed in God.

Now, I wondered.

Ray died in March. I was seven months pregnant.

Death is awful in so many ways that you can't even fathom it until it hits you. You are reminded irrefutably of your own mortality. You wonder where you go next, if anywhere. An unknowable quest.

Most of all, I was hit with anger. Irrational though it was, I was angry with Ray for leaving his family and children behind. Angry that God allowed this. The funeral seemed all too familiar. Walk past the casket, look at the deceased, marvel at how he is not moving. Is completely still. That's it? Gone? And contain your tears because that's what we did in our community.

The priest, in the way of most clergy, had a reassuring voice and a message of hope. I was surprised to find myself a little comforted by his words. Ray was in the ground in the Catholic cemetery behind St. Joseph's Church, not far from where my grandparents lay. At peace, I hoped, having left behind my sister and their three young children. That left-behind-ness was a hard row to hoe.

CHAPTER 45

"I've finished the classes," I said to Rabbi Levy when we met in April, two weeks before Passover. His eyes lingered just a second on my ginormous belly, or so I thought.

"Very good, very good," he said.

The words filled awkward spaces until he decided what he really wanted to say. In my mind, his "very good" was probably anything but.

"I think you need to study a little more with Malkah. She said she felt there were things you hadn't covered yet. And then, as I said, you'll need to meet with the *bet din*, the rabbinical court."

I was right. Not very good. This was not going to happen in the next month, before I gave birth.

"For a test?" I asked.

"Yes, a test of sorts."

I was good at tests. At least, I always had been. But I was awfully tempted to say, "You know what? Forget it. I'm not in the mood to be tested." I'd been tested plenty.

And what more did Malkah have to teach me? I liked Malkah, but oh Lord, the rules! The blessings over snacks—a fruit required one prayer, nuts another. Observant Jews recited a whole host of blessings: one when they woke up, giving thanks to God for returning their soul; one after seeing a rainbow, a reminder of the covenant God made with

Noah after the flood; one after going to the bathroom, thanking God for their plumbing, and countless others. It wasn't that I didn't like that there was an acknowledgment of God as both providing blessings and being a blessing. But couldn't one, all-inclusive "Thank you, God," suffice for the rainbow and the rain?

I called Malkah. "Hi, Malkah, it's Angela. How are you?" Ever polite.

"Thank God," she said, as she did when anyone inquired how she was. Ever grateful.

"Thank God," I repeated, and it was so unconscious I hardly heard myself say it. Malkah and her ways had become internalized.

We made a date to meet again.

I was going to knock it out of the park.

In all the hours I spent with Malkah, we never spoke about belief in God. Maybe it was a given. It wasn't as if all Christians were alike, but you would not profess to be a Christian if you didn't believe in God and in Jesus.

Belief in God, and in the Bible as a record of God's will, did not seem necessary to "feel" Jewish. However, for me, without the religious component, Jews were just a unique, interesting minority group with their own customs and ideas, worth preserving but proving impossible to *be*. I couldn't *be* Asian or Italian or Indian or Kurdish, even if I wanted to. It was simply not my ancestral heritage, not in my blood.

In Israel, I'd attended a talk about Jewish identity. Two things had stood out: the speaker passionately shouted that Jews shouldn't be ashamed to say, "I'm a Jew," as opposed to "I'm Jewish." The word "Jewish" as opposed to "a Jew" was a cop-out. It was minimizing one's identity, making it a modifier, not the actual thing.

Privately, I'd agreed with the speaker. A Christian would say, "I'm a Christian," not "I'm Christian-ish." So what was with this reluctance some Jews had to announce loud and proud, "I am a Jew," rather than "I'm Jewish"?

This was a bagel thing. A *Bridget Loves Bernie* thing. How to be Jewish, and how others recognize you as Jewish.

CHAPTER 46

Patty invited Selig and me to her apartment in Queens for dinner. It was sweet of her to want to include us in her dinner party, but the last thing I wanted to do on a Sunday afternoon was drive over an hour wedged into the front seat of the car. Before we left, Selig said, "Do you want to wear something, you know, maybe a little nicer?" I was wearing maternity jeans and a big white shirt that covered my eight-month baby belly.

"No," I said. "It's Patty. She doesn't care."

"Well, maybe just wear something, you know, like black pants," Selig said. I decided it wasn't worth a fight, and I put on my black maternity pants. But I glared at him. I knew that Selig didn't really care about going to this dinner, so why was he acting like it mattered? I sat on the passenger side, brooding. Usually, I was the quintessential Midwestern girl: "I'm fine, great, sure, whatever you want, of course, no problem." My pregnancy had changed all that.

Now, I was thinking deep, dark thoughts. "Why do I have to change pants? Who cares about my pants? What's the matter with him? This relationship will never work. Maybe I'll have the kid and in a few months, I'll ever so casually say, 'You know, I think I'm going to move back to Indiana.'" The thought of that made me sad, and I wiped away a tear that had slipped down my cheek. Selig was driving and seemed oblivious to the fact that we were soon breaking up. Men.

We arrived at Patty's apartment. We got out of the car, and I pretended that everything was okay. Smile, smile. Rang Patty's doorbell, and she came out and kissed us both hello and said, "Oh, can you come downstairs for a sec, Angie?"

"Sure."

I made my way down in near darkness, then the lights went on and a loud "SURPRISE!" went up. I looked around. There were friends from my various jobs, old apartment mates, other friends, and in the corner were my sisters Mary and Sarah and my sister-in-law Kathy. They'd come to New York for my surprise baby shower, hosted by my best friend, Patty. Shocked would be an understatement. I went from person to person and said, "Oh my God! You've known this all along, and you didn't say anything to me?"

I hugged Sarah, Mary, and Kathy. "You guys are so sneaky," I said.

"Selig, you knew?" I cornered him.

"Of course," he said.

"Oh. And you didn't tell me?"

He threw up his hands. He was in trouble again. I laughed. "No, I know you couldn't tell me. But I can't believe you didn't tell me!" I really couldn't believe that Selig had been plotting and scheming with Patty on my behalf. I'd been so preoccupied with the baby.

After Selig and I kissed everyone hello, we ate tea sandwiches and opened gifts. My mother had sent along a bib she'd embroidered. On it, two birds were perched on a green branch, and above them in Hebrew it was written "Asoor Lenashek." Don't kiss. She had no idea what she was embroidering, but it was Hebrew, and that was good enough. Midwesterners liked their birds. Selig's mother sent a layette as well as a big blue bib on which was written in Hebrew "Chai!" Life!

CHAPTER 47

At the end of May, Selig and I were packing up our apartment to move to a bigger one. I was pulling boxes out of the closet and sorting through them. Chipped mugs, out. Old notes from my classes at The Hebrew University, in:

Biblical authors struggled with same questions humans struggle with: Why is there evil? Why are we mortal, not immortal? The story of the flood about more than God saving Noah and family from flood. A sophisticated tale suggesting world forever coming to end, only to re-invent itself. Speaks to individual fears that our world, our lives, will come to an end, because we are mortal. We will die.

Mary called and asked how I was feeling. "I'm fine, but this pregnancy has made me incontinent. I can't stop peeing."

"Ang, are you sure you're peeing? Maybe your water broke!"

"Oh my God!"

I thought when your water broke it was a huge gush, not a constant dribble.

She laughed and asked me if I was having any pain.

"Nope."

"Well, call your doctor anyway."

I left a message with the doctor, then called Selig.

"Should you go to the doctor now?" he asked. "I can meet you there?"

"I'll wait to hear from the doctor, okay?" And I went back to cleaning the closet.

Almost immediately, my mother and father called. Mary had called to tell them I was in labor. Then, word got out to half of Jasper, and my sisters called. Wanda loved to joke about enemas (for some reason it was just her thing) and she asked if I wanted a hot or a cold enema. Sarah said I should let her know when I went to the hospital, and she would come after work. Coincidentally, my friend Burt from my grad school days called to say hello, and I told him I was in labor. He said he would come the next day, so he could meet him or her. I called Patty, of course. She was, in many respects, responsible for everything.

I felt as if my cheering squad—composed of people from the various worlds I'd touched on and inhabited—was surrounding me.

By early afternoon, the contractions were getting stronger, and my doctor advised me to come in. Selig met me at the hospital. The labor went on and on and on. No drugs. All those years of the church and my mother eschewing modern medicine in favor of brewer's yeast and blackstrap molasses had made an impact, and I felt that going natural was the right choice.

Finally, and after much pain—*so much pain*—and screaming that frightened patients on the opposite hall, a healthy baby boy lay in my arms. The blood and gook had been wiped from our newborn's chubby-cheeked face. Now this was a miracle.

Hours later, Selig informed me we would have the *bris,* or circumcision, in our new apartment in eight days.

"Let me know who you want me to call."

"Call them for what?" I thought he meant that the circumcision would take place in our apartment as opposed to the hospital.

"To come. To the *bris,*" he said.

"Wait. This is a public event?"

The pain had barely abated, and I didn't quite know what anyone was talking about.

"Yes. Of course," Selig said.

In all the months preparing for the baby's birth, Selig and I had discussed what to name the baby, what to bring to the hospital, and did I want him to rub a tennis ball on my back when I was in labor like our Lamaze instructor suggested (the answer to that was a resounding no). Public circumcision had never *once* been mentioned. Not by Selig, not by Malkah, not by any of my Jewish friends.

I'd never been to a *bris*. I assumed that the baby was circumcised on the eighth day in the hospital. *Bris* was *brit*, covenant, and this was a covenant in the flesh. Nowhere in its etymology was the word "public."

Selig undoubtedly presumed that since I could recite the obscure Hebrew blessing over a *lulav* (the frond from a date palm tree waved during Sukkot), I would know about a *bris*. But this was not a *lulav*. And apparently, a *bris* was a big deal. People would gather in our apartment as if they were attending a birthday party and gawk while the baby's foreskin was snipped.

I could offer an intelligent discourse on the bizarre scene when Moses's wife Tzipporah circumcised her son then threw the bloody foreskin at Moses's feet (or at his genitals, depending on your reading of the Hebrew) and said to him, somewhat challengingly and very ambiguously, "You are a bloody bridegroom to me!"

Yet again, it was evident that culturally, there were big gaps in my knowledge of Judaism.

"We'll have bagels and lox and whitefish and sable. We have to have sable." Selig obsessed over the menu. Despite countless Sunday brunches with bagels and whitefish salad, I didn't recall seeing a sable. Between fish and fowl, I would hazard fish. Perhaps it was in the lox family.

"That's fine," I agreed. For the first time in nine months, I wasn't actually so interested in food, especially not after hours of intense labor. I was immersed in gazing at the tightly swaddled baby sleeping in the crook of my arm. He had fine, blonde hair like me, blue eyes like both Selig and me, and a chubby face and full lips like Selig's father. He looked peacefully Buddha-like and somewhat concerned at the same time. My me-focused universe had shifted.

This newborn who had just met the twenty-seven-year-old me and who was an as-yet-unnamed, forty-five-minutes-old stranger was now my everything.

I called my parents. When my mother answered the phone, I told her I hadn't had an episiotomy, I felt fine, and the baby was eight pounds twelve ounces. Midwesterners were fond of numbers. They were safe and concrete, far more comprehensible than emotions. Then I said, "And the circumcision will be in a week."

"O-kay," my mother responded in her usual even-toned voice. There was a pause. She clearly found it peculiar that I was informing her of this private detail.

"And I want you and Daddy to come in for it."

Another pause. "Okay, if you want us to come." That's my mom, I thought. If one of her ten kids wanted her to show up at a bullfight wearing a red blouse, she would, no questions asked.

———————

Eight days after I'd given birth, at least fifty people crowded into our apartment. The dining room table was laden with baskets of bagels, an assortment of every kind of salty fish the kosher caterer had in stock, rugelach and babka and various other pastries, and trays of fruit. An enormous flower arrangement decorated the mantel over the fireplace, lending a fragrant and festive quality to the *bris*. Far more aesthetically inclined than me, Selig had not only moved us into the new apartment, but also made all the arrangements for the food and décor. The painting of the red heifer proved to be a conversation piece.

The evening before, Selig and I ate dinner at a kosher Middle Eastern restaurant with my parents, Selig's parents, and my sisters Sarah and Rachael. I was a little concerned about how our parents would relate to one another, given the vast differences in their backgrounds and religious beliefs. My mother and Selig's mother hugged as if they'd been best friends.

Selig's father was reserved but warm, and in his years as a pulpit rabbi, had dealt with all sorts of people. So, when over dinner my father asked him how the Jewish calendar had arrived at the exact date of the creation of Adam and Eve—a subject my father had never let go of, because he liked to quantify everything from the rainfall to the exact year of the flood—Selig's father was able to offer a simple explanation.

Former roommates and people I'd worked with in various jobs in the six years I'd lived in New York City, our families, as well as Selig's friends and colleagues filled the combined living and dining room.

My father was given the honor of holding the baby, who he passed on to Selig's father. The baby's resemblance to Selig's father was remarkable, and everyone commented on it. That fact alone had gone a long way to ensure the baby's acceptance within Selig's family.

Somehow, I'd ended up at the back of our living room, so I pressed forward to have a look at the circumcision in progress. This was my first *bris*, after all, and it was my son. The wife of one of Selig's law partners tried to push me back to protect me from the procedure, which she incorrectly assumed would bother me. Luckily, I was taller than most of the people, and on tiptoes, even from the middle of the room, I could see. And what a sight it was! My father wore a white, silk *kippa* on his head. My mother stood just a few feet from the card table where the *mohel* had laid out his silver tools. My mother had remained unruffled when our hunting dog Duke bit off part of my brother Ed's ear. Blood spurting from the side of his face, she said calmly, "You'll be fine," then stanched the blood with her apron.

Both of my parents were fascinated by the spectacle. They couldn't look away.

The *mohel* made a blessing with an added phrase, "with the *intention* of becoming" a member of Israel. Not everyone understood, but that was a way to acknowledge that I was not yet Jewish, but had the intention of becoming so. Then I saw the *mohel* clamp and snip, heard the baby cry, and the milk in my breasts released into the nursing pads. I peeked down at my chest to make certain nothing had seeped onto my dress. All clear. Motherhood had rendered me one huge leak: I was bleeding, lactating, and crying, sometimes all three at once, but trying to avoid public evidence of any of them. Though it had become inevitable that I would convert, and soon join the Jewish tribe, I didn't foresee letting go of my ancestral German stoicism that ran deep in my blood. Some things you couldn't change.

The *mohel* poured some wine into a cup, put a few drops into the baby's mouth, and passed it to Selig and me to drink. Cries of "Mazal tov! Mazal tov!" erupted around me. This was the first time I'd been "mazal tov'd" for a Jewish event—my son's circumcision. It was strange but thrilling. Having a baby had granted me entrée and legitimacy in the Jewish world in a way that my years of academically studying Judaism and living in Israel had not.

In keeping with tradition, David was named for a deceased relative, in this case Selig's maternal grandfather, who'd been beloved by everyone. Selig's father offered a few words, concluding with, "My blessing for David is that he will be the best David he can be."

And then we ate. The sable turned out to be fish. It felt celebratory and fun and meaningful and tribal and right.

CHAPTER 48

On a December afternoon in New York City, holding my six-month-old son in my arms, I climbed naked out of the *mikvah*, where I'd submerged myself four times—three for me and one for David—to convert both of us to Judaism. Mentioned in the book of Genesis, "to the gathering [*mikvah*] of waters, He called seas," the *mikvah* was nothing less than the womb of the world, a place of rebirth.

Rabbi Levy, along with two other rabbis, garbed in the usual Orthodox attire—black suit and white shirt—stood respectfully with their backs turned while the *mikvah* lady enveloped me in a big robe. Then the rabbis faced me and asked, "What is your Hebrew name?"

I went blank.

It was *Bridget Loves Bernie* and the *bris* all over again. Assumptions were made about my knowledge, and so no one thought to inform me that *I* was responsible for choosing my Hebrew name when I converted.

I'd assumed that *they*, the rabbis on behalf of God, would bestow upon me an appropriate Hebrew name. In the Bible, God had changed Abram's name to Abraham, Sarai's to Sarah, and Jacob's to Israel. The name change indicated a change in their spiritual status. As parents, Selig and I had chosen our son's English and Hebrew names. Nobody named him- or herself. They were named by God or by their parents.

David was slippery and squirming, and the rabbis were waiting. I wanted to chastise them. I thought I had it covered, now this curveball?

Miriam? Sarah? Batsheva? No, no, and no. I didn't know why it was so hard to just give the rabbis a name, any Hebrew name, and get it over with. The name was only used during Jewish ritual events, like a bar or bat mitzvah or wedding. Who cared what I called myself? One's identity couldn't be reduced to a Hebrew name. But it felt important because finally I was being asked—*required*—to choose my own identity. Just as David's name linked him to his ancestors, the name I chose for myself would connect me to a Jewish woman with whom I identified in some way.

Then it became obvious.

"Ruth," I said.

A Moabite woman who'd worshipped foreign gods, Ruth had married Boaz, an Israelite man. Considered the first Jewish convert, Ruth had converted to a people, to a country, and to a religion. Her bloodline was linked to King David's and thus to the Messiah. Having studied the four chapters of the book of Ruth for an entire semester in Israel, I was deeply familiar with the themes of famine/plenty, seed/soil, the barrenness of the land and the barrenness of the womb. God had ordered Abraham to leave his country of origin and to worship Him, but Ruth had chosen her own destiny, with no outside influence from God.

And, amazingly, Ruth was my middle name.

From now on, the rabbis pronounced, "You will be called in Israel *Ruth bat Viola,* Ruth, daughter of Viola."

I went back into the *mikvah* preparation area, dressed David, put on my street clothes, nursed him for a few minutes, and then went out into the streets of New York City to live as a Jew and raise a Jewish family.

When you emerge from the waters of the womb, your parents assign your identity and choose your name. When I surfaced from the waters of the *mikvah,* baby in my arms, I became who I'd chosen to be: Ruth, Jewish mother in New York City who had forsaken Jesus, Satan, and the demons of my childhood to join the Jewish faith and the Jewish people.

CHAPTER 49

Dear reader, I married him.

While I was perfectly happy to live together with our child indefinitely, Selig's words, "I love you, will you marry me?" seduced me down the aisle in Louisville, Kentucky, the closest place to Jasper where we could have a kosher-catered wedding. My father-in-law performed the outdoor ceremony under the chuppah on a May afternoon in front of our extended families and friends.

No ambivalence, no internal turmoil. Maybe it had always been simpler than I'd thought, and settling into a more traditional home life was as appealing as what might lie beyond the horizon—whether that horizon was out the window of an airplane, a train in Germany, or the Boone Township School.

Home with Selig was first an apartment and then it was a brownstone on the Upper West Side of Manhattan. I was a "stay-at-home" mom, a phrase that irritated me because it conjured up a mother who was stuck in the house with her kid.

Twenty-two months after David was born, we had a baby girl. Rivkie was right—the second was easier. This time I was prepared for the blood and gook. The nurse took her away to clean her up and then returned her to me swaddled in a blanket. It seemed they hadn't done a great job wiping off all the blood. I rubbed against the red on her scalp, but it didn't budge. "It looks like there's still some blood here," I politely and apologetically said to the nurse.

"That's her hair," the nurse said.

It took me a few seconds to compute. Her hair was—blood? No. Her hair was blood red? No. Her hair was red.

Selig and I looked at each other. A redheaded baby. We hadn't seen that coming. My hair was blonde, his brown, and David was, thus far, a towhead. But then I remembered that both my father's paternal aunt Almeda and uncle Elmer had bright red hair, as had Grandma Himsel's brother Franz. My maternal grandfather in his youth had been nicknamed "the red man" because of his sunburned skin and strawberry blonde hair. Selig's grandmother Hannah had had red hair, as well as his great-uncle Avrum and his aunt Naomi.

It felt like our ancestors held a family meeting and determined that our daughter would inherit the recessive genes from Germany and Russia. Their DNA spiraled through time and space, a visual testament to those who came before and were with us still, in our cells, their blood coursing through our veins.

I was relieved not to have to worry about a *bris,* but we agreed we would have a baby-naming in our synagogue. Why should David be the only one to be formally introduced into the covenant, the *brit?* And then there was always sable.

But first, we needed to name this baby. For two weeks, we called her "baby." Finally, the only name we both liked was Anna, an obvious choice in retrospect. Her Hebrew name would be Hannah, after Selig's beloved grandmother.

Both Anna and Hannah, in English, were palindromes, and I adored all that this implied. Our daughter would be a palindrome, embodying balance, and she would be the same every which way you looked at her. She would reciprocate—give and take, forward and back, where the beginning meets the end and returns again, a human helix.

So on a Saturday a month after Anna's birth, the rabbi announced from the pulpit that in Israel her name would be . . . He looked over to me in the women's section of the Orthodox synagogue we attended. I took the cue and stood. This time I was prepared to provide a name. "Hannah bat Ruth." Hannah, daughter of Ruth.

Afterward, at home, we had a private celebration, and my father-in-law offered his customary: "My blessing for Hannah is that she will be the best Hannah she can be."

———

You would think that three years later, when I gave birth to another son, I would have been prepared both for the red hair and for naming the baby. I was not.

In the week leading up to the *bris*, Selig and I tossed names back and forth. In my family, there was Oscar and Edward, my deceased grandfathers. There was Christian, my great-grandfather. Nope. Selig's great-grandfathers were Zvi Pesach, or Dov Baer. No again. None of the family names seemed to fit this red-haired, fair-skinned, blue-eyed baby boy whose full lips mimicked my father-in-law's. Strong genes, those lips.

I liked biblical names with their millennia of meaning behind them. And so I mentally sifted through Abraham, Isaac, Jacob, Hezekiah, testing the sound of the name itself. Adam seemed too obvious a choice. Jacob was a tricky bastard. Joseph was kind of schizophrenic, a self-aggrandizing, favored child who at one point dreamed of his siblings bowing down to him. There were any number of Israelite kings to choose from—Jeroboam, Omri, Ahab, Zachariah, Shallum. But no. This was not the seventh century BCE, and some names don't transcend time and place.

Since the baby was born just before Hanukkah, David suggested he be named Antiochus, the second-century-BCE villain of Hanukkah who'd persecuted Jews and defiled the holy temple in Jerusalem by sacrificing a pig on the altar, thus sparking the Maccabean revolt. The benefit of a Jewish education—my five-year-old could jest about a little-known, despised figure from antiquity becoming a part of our family.

I called my parents, and, as expected, they came in for the *bris*, along with my sister Rachael, my brother Jim, and his family. This strange Jewish custom—watching a baby's circumcision followed by a festive meal—was curious enough to warrant a trip to New York.

Again, my father held the baby, then passed him over to my father-in-law. My mother made certain she had a good seat to watch. When the *mohel* prepared to announce "And his name shall be," Selig and I were still whispering, "What should we name him?"

Daniel—God will judge—was the only name we both liked, and so Daniel he became.

Again, my father-in-law said, "My blessing for Daniel is that he should be the best Daniel that he can be." I never tired of hearing him express that sentiment. That each person should be his or her personal best, be him- or herself, and not someone else. It was a cornerstone of my father-in-law's worldview, and I hoped and believed that my children would absorb it and keep it within their bodies and souls, a piece of him within them, after he was gone.

CHAPTER 50

One day I was having coffee on the Upper West Side with my friend Lili, whose kids also attended Heschel, the Jewish day school named for Rabbi Abraham Joshua Heschel, whose books on the prophets I'd studied in Israel. It was Hanukkah, which, with its focus on miracles and lights and gifts, Lili assumed served as a substitute for Christmas. "I never had Christmas," I explained, "so no."

"But you were Christian?"

"Yeah. But Christmas was a pagan holiday, so we didn't celebrate it."

My religious background in the Worldwide Church of God was incomprehensible to both Jews and mainstream Christians. I told Lili that we'd observed the Jewish holidays and also admitted that it had been hard to let go of the church teachings, even if intellectually I no longer believed them.

"If you don't believe in this church, then what happens?"

"Then you don't get saved. While everyone else is raptured to Petra, you are left behind and you have to go through the Tribulation. And during the Tribulation, all sorts of awful things happen. Parents will eat their children."

"Parents will eat their children?" Lili asked in quasi-disbelief.

For years, I had not given the cannibalism thing much thought. But now, I was once again wondering: Who *would* our parents have eaten?

I called Sarah on the phone. Over the years we had joked about prayer cloths, and I once sent her a piece of white cloth for her broken-down car. "Sarah," I posited, "which of us kids do you think Mama and Daddy would have eaten?"

"Not me," she said, without missing a beat. "Until Rachael came along, I was the youngest."

"Then who?" I prompted.

"I think they would have eaten Jim."

"Why him?"

"Oh, you know, he's the oldest son, the Oedipal thing."

"Yeah, and the firstborn son is always sacrificed."

"I think we should make them tell us which one they would have eaten," Sarah insisted.

We decided to first poll our siblings. Liz reminded me that several passages in Ezekiel and Micah refer to parents eating their children. But, upon giving it thought, Liz concluded, "I think they would have eaten Jim. He was physically much bigger."

Mary, too, felt that Jim would have been the main entrée, while Rachael suggested either Wanda or Jim. Wanda chose Ed, but when she heard that Rachael had nominated her as first course, she was insulted and flung back, "Rachael might not taste bad if they tenderized her first." Jim did not hesitate with his answer. "Well, I guess as the biggest, I would be the likely target."

It was time to get the answer that had been haunting me since 1968. This ever-so-childish and competitive part of me believed that our parents should provide us with their top ten list, ranking us according to how tasty we would be. I called Indiana. I did not think my father would find my query amusing, so I addressed the question to my mother. I explained that we'd taken a poll, and we wanted to know which of us they would have eaten. "Oh, my goodness!" my mother gasped. "I would have starved first!"

Then, after a bit more prodding, she pointed out that, after eating one child, she would be hungry in a few more days anyway and would eventually have to eat all of us. I'd like to believe that she was joking.

I raised my kids on the Upper West Side of Manhattan, which had a large Jewish population. Within blocks, there were several Jewish nursery schools and day schools, a Jewish Community Center, kosher grocery stores and bakeries, kosher restaurants, many synagogues and *shteibels* (little rooms that offer less formal synagogue services), and a lot of yenta doodling, as my friend Leslie would say. Gossip. At times it felt like I was living in a modern-day *shtetl*. I was aware of the irony of leaving a small town and re-creating it in Manhattan.

Daniel went to nursery school at Chabad, a school run by Lubavitch Jews, who were known for their nurturing manner and belief in HaShem (God) as the source of all blessings. One day, when Daniel was four years old, we were riding in a car service whose windows were tinted. Daniel asked me why the windows were dark, and I explained to him that it was so we could see out but no one could see in. "No, Mom, that's not it," he said, real disappointment lacing his words. "It's because HaShem made it that way!"

I related this anecdote to another mother from Chabad, who said, "That's nothing. Max and Dori were pushing HaShem on the swings the other day."

For Daniel, this world was not the devil's playground, but one in which God dwelled happily and safely here on earth.

All three of my kids attended Heschel through eighth grade. It was not exactly the "yeshiva in Brooklyn" I'd claimed I attended, but it was similar. In addition to math and science and social studies, the curriculum also included Hebrew, Tanakh (the Bible), and the Oral Torah. During recess, they played on the roof of the building, looking out over the other buildings in the neighborhood. The parents and the student body included secular Jews, nonaffiliated Jews, bagel Jews, Reform, Conservative, and Orthodox Jews. I had brought my children a long way from Jasper and the bookmobile.

I read *The Five Little Peppers and How They Grew* to David when he was young, and he, too, was transfixed by the tale of human strength and endurance and familial bonds. But when I tried to interest him in the *Little House in the Big Woods* series, he looked at me one evening and said, in a combination of dismay and horror, "Mom, all they do is kill pigs."

———————

Sixth, seventh, and eighth grades were a never-ending cycle of bar and bat mitzvahs, including my own kids, who were bar and bat mitzvahed in the Modern Orthodox synagogue that we attended on the high holy days and maybe a few other times during the year. My parents and many of my siblings and nieces and nephews came in for the occasions. Even though I told them they didn't have to get to synagogue at 9 a.m., they were accustomed to church services starting at the assigned time, so they arrived and went to the front and took up the first two rows of the men's section and the first two rows of the women's section—an innocent faux pas that left the synagogue regulars scrambling to find a place to sit.

There they were, these big, blondish guys with moustaches and beards wearing yarmulkes. Selig and my sons sat behind them, because there was no room in the first two rows. So the Indiana contingent couldn't look to them to know when they should stand and when to sit. Instead, they furtively glanced over to me in the women's section to copy when I sat, when I stood. They never turned around, didn't talk to their neighbors, didn't get up and have a little walkabout. They were clearly not Jewish.

———————

My daughter chose to chant the book of Ruth for her bat mitzvah, but on Friday night, not on Saturday from the pulpit, which was not allowed according to Orthodox law because she was a girl. Instead, Anna, the daughter of Ruth, chanted the entire book of Ruth in front of our guests in the synagogue.

———————

In the eighth grade there was a class trip to Israel, the culmination of their study of both the Bible and the land in which it took place, and the land that was the homeland for Jews everywhere. As a family, we had been to Israel many times. My kids had met much of Selig's father's family, who'd remained in Israel. When his family first met me, they looked at me curiously but were unfailingly warm and hospitable in the Middle Eastern manner that I had always appreciated.

One autumn Sukkot in Jerusalem, we sat on Selig's great-aunt and -uncle's balcony that had been fashioned into a small *sukkah*. It seated about six people comfortably, so we squished together. I went in and out of the kitchen with Aunt Miriam to help her bring out the food, the dessert, and the hot tea. Miriam had survived the Holocaust by coming to Israel as a teenager. Most of her family had perished in Germany. Miriam had the same German accent as my grandma Himsel. But in the 1940s, while my grandma was raising three kids in southern Indiana and longing for the comforts of her childhood home in Hamburg, Miriam was a sixteen-year-old girl separated from her German-Jewish family and headed to Israel to re-create her life. Obviously, Germany brought up horrific memories for her, and I appreciated her acceptance more than I could express.

Three of Miriam's grandkids were close to my kids' ages, and they, too, had red hair. The five redheads walking on King George Street were quite the spectacle.

One Thanksgiving, we were visiting my family in Indiana as we usually did. After my grandparents' deaths, my mother's sister Lindy had taken over the tradition of hosting dinner. Lindy and my uncle Denny raised their nine kids out on a country road a few miles from my grandparents' farmhouse. On their land, there was a pond where I took my kids when they were little to swim with their cousins. There were several hunting dogs tethered to a tree and a shed where the men drank beer and played cards. A bunch of mouser cats ran wild. Lindy also called them little shitasses.

And just like I had asked Grandma to slop the pigs on Sunday afternoons, my kids, too, asked Lindy, "Can we feed the pigs?" My city kids didn't know the words "to slop."

"Of course." Lindy gave them all some ears of corn, and I walked with them to the pigpen. The pigs were snorting and squealing. Daniel, who was about five years old, gazed up at the roof of the pigpen where, because of the gaps between the wooden slats, one could see the sky, and he exclaimed, "Look, Mom, it's a *sukkah!*"

His finding a *sukkah* in a pigpen was, I thought, truly indicative that he looked at the world through Jewish eyes.

––––––––––––

Anna once told me that I was different in Indiana when I was around my family than I was in New York, and that made sense. I dropped the "g" at the end of my words, and I took great delight in jumping out from behind the door and scaring one of my siblings or anyone else who happened to be walking by. It wasn't that I made an effort to quell my Indiana side when I was in New York, but it was a little like Talya not getting the joke about the zoo built around Kentucky. Some things just weren't translatable.

One summer when we were visiting Indiana, I decided to go to Jasper's new mega-church on Sunday with Wanda and Liz, and Anna said she wanted to come with me. It was the last of a three-part sermon series entitled "Sex by the Book," the Book meaning the Bible. The previous two had been: "What the Playboy Wants You to Think" and "What God Wants You to Know." This sermon, "What Your Spouse Wants You to Figure Out," was conducted as a dialogue between the two young, clean-cut ministers who sat on stools at the front of the large, modern, nondenominational church, which drew Catholics, Lutherans, and unaffiliated Christians from the county.

The minister joked that there were three topics guaranteed to draw a big crowd to church: sex, the End Times, and "Is There Sex in the End Times?" The ministers displayed passion and belief and prefaced almost every statement with "God wants you … God created … God's plan is . . . God forgives you . . ." I felt comforted by the familiar feeling that God is ever-present in my life and has a plan for me, individually. Yet, conversely, their certainty that they knew what God thought and felt made me emotionally back off. Certainty made me nervous. I was far more at ease with ambiguity. This was a complete reversal of how I used to be. It was much more Jewish to be ambiguous and uncertain.

Anna, at seventeen, was intently focused on the ministers' discussion about how Satan was out there tempting us to go outside the proper boundaries. The ministers warned us not to buy into the lies that Satan, that ancient serpent that led Adam and Eve astray, fed us. "We've all taken fruit from the tree. We're all sinners who fall short of the glory of God," they said.

At times it was odd for me that my children were so far removed from this kind of language. As three of the world's fourteen million Jews, they were decidedly in the minority, though it might not have felt that way in New York City. My kids could tell you the date of the destruction of the second temple but would be hard put to identify one of the apostles. I doubted they knew what an "apostle" was. Their Christian illiteracy was sometimes shocking to me, and I worried that as non-Christians, they didn't understand "inside" Christian references in popular culture.

But they didn't need to know that "go the extra mile" or "reap what you sow" were Christian phrases or that the title of Shakespeare's *Measure for Measure* was lifted from a line in the book of Matthew. And they could certainly appreciate U2's music without being aware of the many allusions to the New Testament that suffused the lyrics. Yet, some basic knowledge of Christianity would deepen their understanding of the world they lived in, which was largely a Christian one. Not to mention, a better understanding of their mother.

On another visit to Jasper, I had finished having lunch with Mary, Sarah, and Rachael at a Chinese restaurant when Mary went off to the bathroom. "Guys," I whispered, "let's leave her a note and tell her we went to Petra, the Place of Safety." Giggling like children, we wrote on a piece of scrap paper, "Went to the Place of Safety. Sorry you weren't chosen." We placed it on the table, then ran outside and hid. We watched as Mary returned to the table, read the note, then started laughing and shaking her head.

Whenever I didn't pick up the phone in my apartment, Mary would leave me a message on my machine. "Where are you? Did you go to the Place of Safety without me?"

For so long I'd been trying to find safety in Satan's world, imagining that the caves of Petra would provide me with protection, or that a church or a faith would save me. Instead, I'd found safety in unexpected places: under the makeshift canopy of Alise's bed; in the pages of books that transported me, as Polly Pepper would have said, to a perfectly splendid place; and around the kitchen table with friends in Jerusalem.

For so long I'd been seeking the bridge between earth and heaven, trying to figure out how I could get to God. I thought the answer was encoded within our DNA. In spiraling fashion, it went on and on, two strands that led to our Creator. We were as close to God as we were to ourselves.

There may be frog legs in heaven. That's God's choice. But I realized that instead of blood, my words and my behavior served as a *korban*, a sacrifice, to bring me close, not to salvation, but to God. At a nice, steady, measured pace.

EPILOGUE

December 2017

The El Al security agent at Kennedy airport looked down at my passport, then up at me and, in an Israeli accent, asked me the purpose of my trip to Israel.

"We're burying my mother-in-law," I replied.

"I see. Where?"

"Har HaMenuchot. In Jerusalem," I said.

"Have you been to Israel before?"

"Yes."

"When?"

"Many times, and I lived there for two years in college."

"You are Jewish?"

"Yes."

"I see. You speak Hebrew?"

"A little."

In rapid Hebrew he asked me my name. I responded in Hebrew. His eyebrows lifted.

"You belong to a synagogue?"

"I do."

"When is the last time you were there?"

"A month ago."

"Why?"

"A friend was the Torah Chatan."

"I see. And what about the holidays? Where do you spend them?"

"In New York City."

"Have you spent holidays in Israel?"

"Yes."

"Which is your favorite?"

"Sukkot."

"How many days do you celebrate it?"

"Eight," I answered, and I didn't have the patience or energy to say, "Except if I'm in Israel, then it's seven."

For half of my fifty-six years, I'd been Jewish. Nonetheless, what people saw on the outside would always be what they saw. In my case, they never saw a Jewish woman.

"You understand why we have to ask these questions? Because maybe someone has a bomb . . ."

Finally, he put the security tape around my suitcase to indicate I'd been screened, and I got my ticket then boarded the plane for Israel, along with Selig's brother Jonathan, his sister Debbie, and their spouses. Selig was in London and would join us in Tel Aviv.

As the plane took off, I thought about when I had last seen my mother-in-law. She was ninety-seven, and her health had been failing. She'd remained her essential self—sweet and loving. She kissed our hands when we sat next to her. When Selig, David, or Daniel wore shorts, she told them they had nice legs. They liked hearing it.

I often said I was lucky to have had such a wonderful mother-in-law, but more importantly a devoted grandmother who thought the sun and the moon shone in the faces of her seventeen grandchildren and nineteen great-grandchildren.

It was dusk in Israel when we arrived the following day, my mother-in-law's body in cargo in a cardboard box labeled "human remains."

Arrangements had been made in the hours after her death for the burial society to meet us at the airport and transport her to Jerusalem in a hearse. We followed in taxis.

Har HaMenuchot, literally, "Mountain of Those Resting," is the largest cemetery in Jerusalem, with dramatic views of the Judean Hills. I had probably passed it thirty-six years before when I first came to Israel.

My father-in-law had been buried there twenty-one years prior. Whenever we went to Israel, we placed a stone on his grave and said psalms in his honor. I hadn't attended my father-in-law's funeral in Jerusalem. The kids were little then, and I was still nursing Daniel. So this time, the religious, Israeli funeral for Selig's mother was not just meaningful but also exceedingly interesting to me.

Before we went to the grave for burial, we convened in a small building nearby. The men, most of them wearing black hats, black suits, and white shirts, sat on a long bench on one side, while the women sat on a matching bench on the other side.

Selig, his sister Debbie, and his brother Jonathan were beckoned to go into a small room. Selig and his brother came out, both with their shirts ripped and the pockets on their jackets torn, the traditional signs of mourning. Their hearts, likewise, had been rent.

Debbie remained inside, and then a sharp scream followed by convulsing sobs pierced the somber quiet. I rushed to open the door but wasn't allowed in.

Debbie finally emerged, still crying hysterically. I assumed it had all been too much for her. Debbie had handled her mother's care for several years in Florida. It wasn't until two days later that Debbie told us that the man in charge of the burial society had, without warning and without explaining what he was doing, pulled the covering and then the shroud off my mother-in-law's body and asked Debbie to identify it.

Then slowly and with some ceremony they brought the body out on a stretcher-like apparatus and placed her in the middle of the floor. She was covered in a thick blue and white fabric with Hebrew lettering on it.

There were eulogies—none by women—and then the men gathered around the stretcher and carried her to the grave, big flashlights lighting the way in the December dark.

More Hebrew prayers, and then the outer covering was removed and her body, wrapped in its shroud, was lowered into the cold winter dirt. Her body was a garment, too; the soul wore it on its journey in this life, and it was torn.

The burial crew made fairly quick work of placing planks atop her body then shoveling the earth on top, offering the shovel to the men to bury their dead.

And the dust returns to the earth as it was, and the spirit returns to God who gave it.

Ecclesiastes 12:7

I buried three of my own dead in the space of eleven months. First was my eighty-three-year-old mother. A week before her death from congestive heart failure, both of my parents were in their respective hospital beds in the living room, and my brother Ed had pushed them close enough to allow my father to hold my mother's hand. She wasn't too pleased about this arrangement. Daddy said, "Well, Mama, I don't know if you'll be here when Jesus returns."

It was unclear if he meant that she would be dead or that she wouldn't be worthy. My father had clung to the Worldwide Church of God, which later morphed into the United Church of God. At ninety-one, my father was holding on, still hoping to be in the world of the living at Jesus's return, which he believed was coming very soon. Because of his health, he hadn't been able to attend church for several years, but every night until he'd broken his hip, he leaned back in his recliner late at night and prayed. I overheard him many times when I visited. Like my mother-in-law, he prayed for each of us individually. They both had God's ear.

My mother's funeral was held at the local mega-church in Jasper that Wanda attended. My older brother Paul had fallen into a diabetic coma weeks before and was still recovering in the hospital. He'd been able to FaceTime my mother, and she had seen that he was on his way to recovery. Oldest to youngest we sat in nine chairs, much as we had when we'd attended church together as children, or when we took photographs as a family. We accepted condolences from our extended family and friends.

She had a closed casket. "I don't want half the county gawking at me when I'm dead!" she had often said. One of her quilts was draped over it, and several hung on racks nearby. At the end of the service, when everyone except family had cleared out, we opened the casket to let my father see my mother, his wife of sixty-three years.

She looked beautiful. Just like in old photos. They'd fixed her hair, closed her mouth, put makeup on her. She looked like herself. But dead.

Daddy sat in the wheelchair and held her hand. He cried. He talked to her. "Mama, why did you have to do this?" he wailed. My sister Liz said, after an interminable ten minutes, "Daddy, you have to let go now. It's time. We have to close the casket."

Something I would never have been able to do. Close the casket.

"Her hand was so cold," he repeated. "It was so cold. And then I took it again. I don't know why I done that."

My three children, along with most of my mother's other twenty-five grandchildren and fifteen great-grandchildren, accompanied the coffin out to the hearse. Three of my cousins drove their police and sheriff cars at the head of the mourners' caravan as we slowly made our way to the cemetery.

My mother was buried next to Abby.

———

In New York City, I sat *shiva* for my mother for a day. I covered the entry mirror with one of the many quilts my mother had painstakingly and lovingly embroidered. I draped others across the couches, along with pillowcases and the bib she'd crocheted for David for my baby shower, "Asoor Lenashek" in Hebrew. "Don't kiss." I placed photographs of my family on the table and accepted the condolences of the close Jewish community I'd become a part of twenty-eight years before.

The rabbi and a quorum of men recited *kaddish*, the mourner's prayer, and my friend Sandee, without asking, understood that she should stand at my side and recite it along with me.

Meanwhile, in Indiana, my father was in terrible shape.

The day after the *shiva*, I flew back with my daughter, Anna, who had just left her farming fellowship in Connecticut. Like my mother, Anna loved going to thrift stores and yard sales, composting everything from tea bags to leftover vegetables, and working with the land.

Daddy was worried about the windshield wipers. "We have to change the windshield wipers!" He was clearly not present.

"Mary did it," I lied.

Saturday night my father stayed up late with Rachael, Anna, and my great-niece Rayley—four generations gathered together. He spoke lucidly for a long time. A patriarch of old. He said, "You don't have any idea how good you make me feel. This is better than anything I've ever had." The three of them stayed and stayed, and scratched his back and hugged him and held his hands.

In the early morning, he was in horrible pain. His body was shutting down. We stood with him and gave him morphine. In the afternoon, he awoke and looked in the distance and said, "Mama? Mama? Heavenly Father . . . Great God."

I leaned close to him. "Daddy," I said. "What did you see?"

He turned to me. "Oh, Tater. What? Nothin'."

It was a cold January evening. He died that night surrounded by much of his family. Eleven days after my mother.

At my father's funeral, we sat on the same nine chairs. Paul remained in the hospital, stronger but not strong enough. My younger brother John's forehead had an angry red welt. "What did you do?" I asked. In answer, he rubbed his fist against his forehead.

For the service, my cousin Cindy sang the Brahms's Lullaby first in German, "Guten abend, gute nacht," good evening, goodnight, and then in English, "Close your eyes, now and rest . . . " Her voice soared and rose, just like my grandma's had when she was picking peppers in the garden or cooking potatoes on the old, wood-burning stove.

Daniel, a pianist, played Chopin on the keyboard. My father had always loved hearing him play, and when we went to Jasper, Daniel would practice on the piano in the parish center building at St. Joseph's Church, and my father would sit quietly and listen as he went through his repertoire. My grandmother's musical gene had made its way through the generations.

This time the line of mourners drove past the family farm in Haysville where my father had been born, where we'd spent so many Sundays visiting Grandma and Robert, and where Jim lived now.

At the cemetery, after the minister spoke, the row of uniformed members of the military called out, then lifted their rifles up and shot into the air three times, a final salute to their fallen comrade. A bugler played "Taps," and the music was sorrowful and plaintive. Then they ceremoniously removed the American flag that covered my father's coffin, carefully folded it, and gave it to Jim.

After the funeral, we returned to the social hall at the church. John sat with Selig, my three kids, David's girlfriend, and Debbie and Alan, who had flown from Florida for both my mother's and father's funerals. John said to me, out of nowhere, "Thanks for everything, Ang."

"I didn't do anything."

"No, you done a lot for me. And I appreciate it."

John had been troubled for some time, but it had gotten much worse since his partner, Lucy, died ten years before. He'd avoided seeing my parents, but just weeks before they passed away, Ed had insisted he visit. Ed had outgrown his prayer cloth ways.

I hugged John and said, "Come to New York and visit me. But wait until spring. The weather is so terrible now."

Looking at John, I thought, he won't make it another twenty years. Not even fifteen or ten. Maybe five. He chain-smoked and rarely showered or shaved. He slept on a lumpy mattress on the floor of his apartment, which to my knowledge had never been cleaned. We brought him my parents' Meals on Wheels. John was so negligent of his health, I was worried that he was going to die of something stupid.

I sat *shiva* for my father in New York City for a day. Again I covered the mirrors and slowly recited the mourner's prayer, *kaddish*, again with Sandee at my side.

Two weeks later, I called John to wish him a happy birthday. He didn't answer. I didn't expect him to.

A few weeks after that, I had a dream. Someone was racing down a runway. He was free, and I was happy for him. But then I saw that there was a cliff at the end, and he was jumping into an abyss, and in my dream I screamed, "Nooooooo!" At the bottom of the cliff was my mother, smiling with her arms lifted, ready to catch whoever or whatever came to her.

Three days later, Wanda texted to say that John was gone. I thought she meant he had left, disappeared. But he was dead. He'd hanged himself.

My mother died December 28, my father January 8, and John in the middle of February. Three in the space of seven weeks during the darkest months of the year. My spiritual friend Susan said, "Seven. That's the number of completion."

I went back home. This time for John. No casket. No body. Paul was there, still with a feeding tube in him, but alive. In a line we sat, oldest to youngest, our parents not there, and now our brother gone. We were a different family.

I'd delivered eulogies first for my mother, then for my father, and now for John. Though inadequate, words were all I had to try to summarize three people's lives and their unique personalities and legacies. I spoke about the family they grew up in, the choices they had made, the choices that had been made for them, and how they had been shaped by all they had experienced that made them who they were. Their identity.

The mortician dug on top of my mother's fresh grave and placed John's ashes on her casket where her arms would be, ready to receive him.

In all the years I'd been Jewish, I had been a high-holiday Jew, and a mother-of-the-bar/bat-mitzvah Jew; I'd been a "march-for-Israel"

Jew. I'd been a latke-and-Hanukkah-gifts Jew. I'd been a debate-Israeli-settlements-and-anti-Semitism-at-Shabbat-dinner Jew. I'd been a committed, but not always consistently observant, Jew. Basically, I'd been myself. Then I was a mourning Jew. And that meant bringing my entire Jewish self to the community. To my family. To myself.

And by Jewish self, I mean all of the complicated ways of being Jewish: being religious or not; believing in God or not; being a Zionist or not. Because no matter the answer to these questions, if you identified as a Jew, you were a Jew.

In New York City, it was largely the Jewish community I'd become a part of that supported me and held me up and brought me food and comfort and prayed with me. People I hadn't seen in years showed up at *shiva*. People from synagogue with whom I had shared pleasant "Good Shabbos" greetings showed up. The head of my kids' day school showed up. It was what you did, as a Jew.

When I converted, I felt it was a personal, individual decision between God and me. I could never claim being a part of the Jewish tribe by blood or by history. Even the El Al agent at the airport knew that. As a mourner, I was a part of two tribes: my birth tribe who giggled with me when I told inane Kentucky jokes; and my adopted one, with whom I could discuss Josephus and King David's tomb and the Canaanites with earnest pleasure.

When I look at my children, I see how the branches of our families' trees reach toward the past and sway into the future, *l'dor v'dor*, from generation to generation. Their roots are nourished by the Patoka River and the Jordan River, the Hudson River and the East River. My children are a future I was petrified would never come.

ACKNOWLEDGMENTS

Thank you to my indefatigable agent, Deborah Harris, and to George Eltman, whose enthusiasm and tenacity rivals only my own. Fredric Price, Founder and Publisher and Amy Oringel, Editor of Fig Tree Books toiled and cheered in equal parts. I deeply appreciate your belief in this book, and your efforts to make it the best it could be.

To my ten siblings, eight in this world and two in the other, you are my rock. And to my extended family, blood or not, present on this earth or in the ether, I could thank you till the cows come home but it would never suffice.

Thank you Alise Hadley for sharing your dreams and for holding my purse.

In Israel, I met a number of people who influenced how I came to view the world, which in turn informed so much of who I became. I hold them in my heart today for all they have been and are to me. Amy Brody, Louise Garfield Blumenthal, Deena Grossman (of blessed memory), Patty Johnston, Professor Shalom Paul, Annie Papernick, Talya Saadia Candi, James Young and my beloved advisor, Golda Werman. Ruth and Yasmin, thank you for sharing your road with me.

In New York City, an inordinate number of fellow writers have read and re-read this book. They now know more about me than me. Scary. I am enormously grateful to:

Judy Jordan (of blessed memory), Mary McGrail, Rebecca Packer, Lauren Sanders

Jennifer Birmingham, Anne Newgarden, Ida Picker, Barbara Schneider

Hettie Jones, David Robinson, Sanjna Singh, Alison Stateman Mort Zachter

Tajlei Levis, Adelaide Mestre, Gabrielle Selz, Sara Selz, Victoria Rowan, Elise Zealand

Tena Cohen, Jacqueline Johnson, Aimee Lutkin, Peter Vilbig, Anne Yoder

It is impossible to individually acknowledge the many friends who listened when I read a new prologue over the phone or who suggested, "I think you should write this as a play." Please know I cherish each of you, and the advice has been duly noted.

In part because of Selig, our three children, I'm delighted to say, turned out to be compassionate, funny, and fairly bright. Thanks for working that out.

ABOUT THE AUTHOR

Angela Himsel is a freelance writer in New York City. Her work has appeared in *The New York Times*, *The Jewish Week*, the *Forward*, and *Lilith*, and she received an American Jewish Press Association Award for her column "Angetevka" on Zeek.net. Angela holds a BA from Indiana University, which included two years at The Hebrew University in Jerusalem, and an MFA from The City College of New York.